CRITICAL QUESTIONS

Invention, Creativity, and the Criticism of Discourse and Media

Edited by

WILLIAM L. NOTHSTINE

CAROLE BLAIR
University of California, Davis

GARY A. COPELAND
University of Alabama

 **Custom Publishing**

Boston   Burr Ridge, IL   Dubuque, IA   Madison, WI   New York
San Francisco   St. Louis   Bangkok   Bogotá   Caracas   Kuala Lumpur
Lisbon   London   Madrid   Mexico City   Milan   Montreal   New Delhi
Santiago   Seoul   Singapore   Sydney   Taipei   Toronto

Critical Issues: Invention, Creativity, and the Criticism of Discourse and Media

McGraw-Hill's Custom Publishing consists of products that are produced from camera-ready copy. Peer review, class testing, and accuracy are primarily the responsibility of the author(s).

10 11 12 13 14 15 QDB QDB 12 11

ISBN 0-07-287523-2

Custom Editor: Jody Campbell
Production Editor: Nina Meyer
Printer/Binder: Quebecor World

PREFACE TO THE McGRAW-HILL PRIMIS EDITION OF <u>CRITICAL QUESTIONS</u>

We undertook the project that led to the 1994 publication of <u>Critical Questions</u> with two goals in mind: First, we wanted to introduce the student critic to the rewards of media and rhetorical criticism by a route other than those disciplinary standbys, theory and method. We believed there was value in approaching the topic through the study of critical invention--how critics select the questions they want to ask of a text as critics, and how those questions can evolve over the writing of a critical essay.

Second, and more broadly, we wanted to raise the awareness within our several disciplines of the problem of critical invention itself. We believed, and in Chapter 2 we marshaled a good deal of evidence to support that belief, that disciplinary neglect of this question was warping the relationship between critics' interests and commitments and the criticism they write.

Over a dozen of our colleagues generously shared their own experiences in commentaries contributed for the book, tracking the path that their ideas traveled from first notion to finished essay. Those commentaries were and are the heart and soul of <u>Critical Questions</u>.

For our students--as both readers and practitioners--we hoped to make critical research more accessible. For our disciplinary colleagues, and indeed for ourselves, we hoped "to make the easy gesture difficult"--to force our critical practice to take into account the important but invisible question of where our critical questions come from. It's gratifying that, almost a decade later, colleagues continue to assign readings from <u>Critical Questions</u> for their students, even though its out-of-print status made it more difficult every year to secure copies. For our colleagues, and to help keep alive a set of issues whose importance has not decreased in the intervening years, we have worked with McGraw-Hill Primis Custom Publishing to bring out this re-issue in a convenient and affordable form.

iv

All of the original essays by the contributors to <u>Critical Question</u> are in this edition. The book you are reading is unchanged from the original 1994 edition with one exception: The twelve reprinted chapters and journal articles, to which our contributors' commentaries refer, have not been included in this edition. Those chapters and articles are listed in the Bibliography of Supplemental Readings in this edition, and we encourage our readers to study them in tandem with our contributors' accounts of the process that led to their finished form.

We extend our thanks to Jody Campbell, Custom Publishing Representative for McGraw-Hill Primis Custom Publishing, for his help and guidance on this project.

William L. Nothstine
Carole Blair
Gary A. Copeland

CONTENTS

Part II

CRITICAL INVENTION: MAXIMS, COMMENTARIES, AND CASES

MAXIM 1

MAXIM 2

CRITICAL QUESTIONS: BIBLIOGRAPHY OF SUPPLEMENTAL READINGS

Thomas W. Benson, "The Rhetorical Structure of Frederick Wiseman's *Primate*." *Quarterly Journal of Speech* 71 (1985): 204-17.

Carole Blair, Marsha S. Jeppeson, and Enrico Pucci, Jr. "Public Memorializing in Postmodernity: The Vietnam Memorial as Prototype." *Quarterly Journal of Speech* 77 (1991): 263-288.

Barry Brummett. "Premillennial Apocalyptic as a Rhetorical Genre." Central States Speech Journal 35 (1984): 84-93.

Maurice Charland, "Constitutive Rhetoric: The Case of the *Peuple Québécois*." *Quarterly Journal of Speech* 73 (1987): 133-50.

Bonnie J. Dow. "Hegemony, Feminist Criticism, and *The Mary Tyler Moore Show*." *Critical Studies in Mass Communication* 7 (1990): 261-274.

Robert L. Ivie. "The Metaphor of Force in Prowar Discourse: The Case of 1812." *Quarterly Journal of Speech* 68 (1982): 240-53.

Michael C. Leff. "Redemptive Identification: Cicero's Catilinarian Orations." *Explorations in Rhetorical Criticism*. Ed. G. P. Mohrmann, Charles J. Stewart, and Donovan J. Ochs (University Park: The Pennsylvania SUP, 1973): 158-77.

Elizabeth Walker Mechling and Jay Mechling. "The Campaign for Civil Defense and the Struggle to Naturalize the Bomb." *Western Journal of Speech Communication* 55 (1991): 105-133.

Janice Hocker Rushing and Thomas S. Frentz. "The Frankenstein Myth in Contemporary Cinema." *Critical Studies in Mass Communication* 6 (March 1989): 61-80.

Martha Solomon, "The Rhetoric of Dehumanization: An Analysis of Medical Reports of the Tuskegee Syphilis Project." *Western Journal of Speech Communication* 49 (1985): 233-47.

Bryan C. Taylor. "*Reminiscences of Los Alamos:* Narrative, Critical Theory, and the Organizational Subject." *Western Journal of Speech Communication* 54 (Summer 1990): 395-419.

Philip Wander. "The Rhetoric of American Foreign Policy." *Quarterly Journal of Speech* 70 (1984): 339-361.

PART I

CRITICAL INVENTION: A GENERAL ORIENTATION

CHAPTER 1

INVENTION IN MEDIA AND RHETORICAL CRITICISM: A GENERAL ORIENTATION

William L. Nothstine, Carole Blair, and Gary A. Copeland

The aim of this book is to explore the fundamental choices made by rhetorical and media critics when they choose to write or speak *as* critics. For experienced critics, we hope this will offer a productive reexamination of practices with which they are already familiar. But for the beginning critic, some background discussion of these practices and assumptions is in order. What is rhetorical or media criticism? What are its goals? And what part does invention—the fundamental choices of subject matter and approach—play in such criticism? These topics are the focus of this chapter.

This book is motivated by the conviction that rhetorical and media criticism can and should be worthwhile activities, for two reasons. First, rhetoric and its formative media are themselves important things to study, and are, at base, what rhetorical and media critics do study. The study of rhetoric considers talk and mediated discourse (including photographs, advertisements, musical compositions, paintings, situation comedies, films, novels, and so on) to be *consequential,* to have effect in the world. Not just everything that could be said or done actually is said or done, and as a result those things that *are* said and done are marks and measures of the culture, the speaker, and the language that generates them. Moreover, what is said or done has effect—sometimes easily seen, large and notable consequence, and sometimes fleeting, even negligible, perhaps almost undetectable effect. In any case, instances of language use *do* things. And rhetorical and media criticism, at least in our view, ought to be concerned with what rhetorical and mediated texts do and can do.

Second, when people act as rhetorical and media critics, they engage in rhetoric themselves. To act as a critic is to speak or to write, and that action is itself, like other instances of rhetoric, consequential. It is an investment in studying and writing (or speaking) about something that has already been said or done by someone else. It takes up a text and re-circulates it, that is, "says" or "does" that text differently, and asks the listener or reader to re-understand and re-evaluate the text, to see and judge it in new ways suggested by the critic. Criticism of media and rhetoric, conceived in this way, is a profoundly worthwhile activity, for it commits the critic to reflect upon important choices: whether to speak, what to speak about, how to speak, and to whom to speak. And it commits the critic to reflect upon the consequences of these choices for the critic and a community.

To act as a rhetorical or media critic is to act in relation to a text of the past (one already said or done), in the present, with or to an audience. It is therefore a *social* act in every sense. It is invested in living in a particular community, in a culture, and in the world. Moreover, to act as a critic is to act from a particular stance that is constructed socially, since who we are at any given moment is a matter of our *being with* others—our families, friends, acquaintances, genders, races, nationalities—both now and in our pasts. All of those connections affect what we will speak about, how we will speak, and what we have to say. Not only does criticism address events that occur within these arenas, but it also uses the principal resource—language—belonging to and defining those settings. Because language is a socially shared phenomenon, belonging not to one individual but to many, when one uses it, one always is in social territory.

In addition, the critic speaks or writes *to address others,* for the primary purpose of having an effect on the thinking or acting of an audience. Even the critic who speaks or writes as a beginning critic, perhaps for the purpose of fulfilling an obligatory course assignment, is still addressing someone else (an instructor), and asking that individual to accept or accord with the critic's choice of text and way of speaking about it.

One might assume, thus, that because all attempts at criticism have consequences or because they are all connected to one community or another, they are all equally important or worthwhile. But this would ignore the thoroughly social character of criticism: Just as our various communities and cultures value particular events differentially, the community of rhetorical and media critics must select what it values most. What kind of criticism should be most highly valued? Our view is one we believe at least some other critics share: that rhetorical or media criticism should be considered most valuable and worthwhile when it provokes its audience to think or act differently and in socially responsible ways.

How can rhetorical and media criticism manage such provocation? We think that criticism should be most highly valued when it acknowledges, acts upon, and is reflective of its own character as social. That is, we believe that criticism can provoke most effectively when it takes account of these three themes: criticism's investedness in community, its residence in language, and its commitment to an audience.

▓ Criticism Is Invested in Community

When critics set out to do criticism, they make socially directed and motivated choices. First, critics decide what to write about. Every critic is different, of course, and the choice of texts to study is a critic's personal decision. However, suggesting that the choice is personal is simply another way of saying that it is socially situated. That is, a critic occupies a particular location within and among various social-cultural networks, simply by virtue of being human. It is the case, also, because the alternatives a critic has available—the plethora of texts from among which the critic may choose— are socially generated. They too are located within communities and other, larger social collectives.

Furthermore, the critic chooses to single out an event from an enormous constellation of such events. All critics must attend to this implication: Every time a critic chooses a text to study, that choice already implies that a community the critic occupies or addresses should pay special attention to that text because that text was chosen at the expense of countless others. Thus the critic implies, by the choice of texts, that the chosen text is more significant than others for some reason. This does *not* mean that critics always must choose the most recent, obvious, newsworthy, prominent, historically influential, artful, famous, or infamous text to study. It does mean, however, that the choice of a text should be made on the belief that a critical analysis of that particular text has something to offer—a different way of understanding or acting—to the community the critic addresses.

The relationship of criticism to community (or communities) suggests that critics might pose questions like the following to help clarify their choices of texts for study: With what communities do I identify myself? What might critical study of this text have to say about what is worth doing or worth knowing, in the values of these communities? Whose interests does this text appear to serve? To whom does it speak? To whom does it not speak? What are the consequences for individuals and/or the community if they embrace this text?

Questions such as these do not have to be posed exclusively in an isolated self-dialogue. In fact, the critic can learn a great deal by discussing a text with others, perhaps many others. In this way the critical essay becomes an extension of conversations the critic has already begun with others of similar (or perhaps very different) interests.

▨ Criticism Resides in Language

To act critically is to have a voice, and to speak or write about an event. Acting critically, thus, is to use language. However, critics, just like all other speakers, are caught between *using* language and being *used by* it. Because language is social, each of us speaks the language of our communities or cultures. How well we speak it may determine how effectual our criticism will be. This means, in part, that good criticism should fulfill the demands of all language use—it should be clear, interesting, appropriate, and forceful. It also means that the practices of criticism involve rewriting, editing, amending what one has set out to say as a critic. This process is never neutral or "right," like correcting the multiplication in an algebraic proof. Criticism grows and transforms as it is revised and changed. Criticism, even in the earliest stages of thinking through questions, involves unexpected turns, changes of mind, and reversals. This is not a flaw in the process or a sign of error. Such moments simply are part of the critical act. They arguably are even a positive aspect of criticism, for while they may appear to slow the process, a critic's "mistakes" and turns are part of learning what is worth doing and worth understanding, and perhaps will indicate how better to proceed the next time.

The demands on criticism go further than writing or speaking well, however. To speak well *as a critic* is to use not just one's native tongue but the language of criticism as well. To speak as a critic about a text is to single oneself out as capable of talking about a text in interesting and worthwhile ways. Rhetorical and media criticism demand some experience with and understanding of rhetorical and media texts at large as well as of the particular text the critic has chosen to study. One source—one of several—for this experience and understanding is the extensive body of scholarship already accumulated by critics of media and rhetoric. Study of this scholarship is one way to gain familiarity with the ways in which other critics speak, including the theoretical metaphors they employ, and the ways they support their assertions, qualify their findings, and display their reasoning. But this does not mean that a critic should merely emulate or model other critics' talk or ways of thinking about texts—it means that one should become sufficiently competent and familiar with the language of criticism, as with any language, so that one may effectively express *one's own* ideas and judgments.

The language of criticism is extraordinarily nuanced and complex, so much so that few critics ever master all of its many "theoretical dialects." But this nuance and complexity allow a critic a broad variety of ways to interpret or judge a text, according to the interests of the critic and the possibilities of the text itself. The language of criticism allows and often encourages certain kinds of questions on a critic's part, of which these are only some of the most general: What about this text makes it similar to or different from others? What is the significance, if any, of those similarities or differences? What are the components or constituent aspects of the text? How do they relate to one another or to the whole text? Is there a part or aspect of the text that stands out, and if so, why? What makes it convincing or unconvincing to a given audience? What do others see in this text that I do not, and how can they see it this way? What can I say about it that it does not say already? What do I see in the text that might not be so obvious to someone else? How can I make my case for what I see to someone who does not understand the text the way I do?

Such exploratory questions can be asked by critics as they begin to investigate texts. Most of these exploratory questions are derived from some general, theoretical view of rhetoric or media, and competent pursuit of such questions will require some familiarity with these theoretical bases. However, questions like these frequently lead to other, more specific, more interesting, or more arresting issues that the critic may wish to pursue— often, but by no means always, articulating them in the special language of rhetorical or media theory.

The questions we have suggested here are by no means intended to be used as a procedural checklist. They are simply suggestions, guides to ways in which critics can consider what sorts of texts are worth studying, and what approaches seem most likely to be profitable in this study. And although frustrating, it is also true that no text immediately reveals itself to the critic as a satisfactory one for that person to study and write about, and no question will be equally productive when asked of every possible text. Even a critic who has found satisfying answers to the sorts of questions we suggest may still decide that some other text, or some other question about that text, might be more worthy of her/his and the reader's time and energy.

Criticism Is Committed to an Audience

The moments of choosing, studying, and speaking or writing about texts most certainly provide critics themselves with opportunities for learning and deliberation. But criticism is a public act, not a private one; it addresses an audience, making a case for re-understanding or re-valuing, and making that case *to* someone. Considerations of who that audience is should have an important constructive influence on critical speaking or writing. This is, in one respect, no more than a reiteration of the two previous points: that criticism is invested in community and that it resides in language. However, it does demand one further consideration. Because criticism itself is rhetorical, critics must be willing to place their speaking or writing into a public arena, where it may be judged and responded to like any other text.

We have suggested that rhetorical and media criticism should provoke socially responsible thinking and acting. "Responsible," in this context, frequently does *not* mean "orthodox." It means instead that criticism should be responsive to the concerns and well being of the communities in which it resides and to which it is addressed. It means that critics should be willing to speak to and within those communities in informed and thoughtful ways. And it means that critics should be prepared for both disagreement with and criticism of their work. Criticism is judged, we argue, by the degree to which it is provocative and worthwhile. This judgment will be rendered in the communities it enters.

Critics acknowledge their commitment to an audience when they ask questions such as the following: What benefit, beyond satisfying my own curiosity, will be gained by critical discussion of this text? What can be said about this text that should be said in the context of my community? What should my understanding or evaluation of it suggest in terms of the ways in which others in my community think or act? Is it worthy of the time and attention I will have to give it in speaking and writing about it? Will it be worth my reader's time and attention to grasp my understanding or evaluation of it?

Such questions, of course, will not all be equally useful in finding initial direction for a critical essay. Nor are they the only questions with which a critic may begin. Criticism that is provocative, that convinces an audience to think or act differently and in socially responsible ways, may arise from unusual or even idiosyncratic questions. "Speaking the language" of rhetorical and media criticism, therefore, does not mean repeating a few orthodox phrases. It means finding a way of understanding or judging a text, and building a case for it in the most thorough, compelling, and convincing way possible using the resources of the language of criticism.

▓ Reclaiming the Question of Critical Invention

This book is somewhat unusual among texts on media and rhetorical criticism because it focuses discussion on critical invention, rather than critical method or critical object. For reasons that we discuss in detail in Chapter 2, the available scholarly literature provides innumerable examples of the final *product* of criticism, the finished essay, but very few illustrations of the *process* of criticism—the practices of constructing, refining, and exploring one's critical question or thesis, which are the domain of invention. In Chapter 2, we shall examine trends in media and rhetorical criticism that have led critics often to be insensitive to and unaware of their own inventional practices. Specifically, we argue that attention has been drawn away from critical invention by the culture of "professionalism," which has (among other consequences) caused critics to be preoccupied with generating or contributing to theory rather than participating in civic life, and to adopt as a goal an image of the objectivity of science and technology that even scientists themselves would reject. Reclaiming inventional practices, we firmly believe, is crucial for the critic, whether beginning or experienced, and for the communities in which the critic resides.

Critical invention, we believe, is highly resistant to formalized, methodological prescriptions. Rather than some monolithic system imposed upon critics from above or outside, critical invention instead exists as a diversity of practices, as varied as the kinds of individuals who become critics and as disparate as the situations and communities in which they practice.

Since these inventional practices are rarely discussed explicitly, if at all, we have chosen to return to critical invention by the most direct route: by *asking* critics to describe their own inventional practices. The last two chapters of Part I are original position pieces by Roderick P. Hart and Michael M. Osborn, addressing the general themes of critical invention with regard to these critics' own body of work. Hart identifies his own critical concerns with matters of policy, and describes the political and procedural framework from which his writing emerges. Osborn reflects on his greater concern for the artistic dimension of discourse, rather than the policy dimension.

Following these, in Part II of this book, the inventional moments behind individual critical essays are recounted in thirteen original commentaries contributed by practicing critics. We have invited these critics to reflect upon the following moments in the inventional process, with respect to the critical essay that accompanies their commentary:

1. the selection of text or object and critical approach
2. the source of the initial critical question
3. the changing scope of the project
4. obstacles, blind alleys, and detours in writing, and their consequences
5. possible ethical issues in the questioning or writing
6. the influence of manuscript readers
7. the resemblance of the finished essay to the original idea

Each commentary describing critical invention, from the individual critic's point of view, is paired with the finished essay so that the reader can compare the product of criticism to the author's description of the inventional practices. To be sure, these commentaries detail markedly different approaches to doing criticism, but they also describe practices that are admirably motivated by the urge to write provocative and worthwhile criticism.

The choices these authors describe make up the operations by which critics truly and originally *show themselves to be critics*. While these choices are always, finally, individual in nature, they do display the themes we have associated in this chapter with provocative and worthwhile criticism.

▓ Four Maxims to Guide Critical Invention

We dislike universal, abstract, methodological strictures and formulae for critics. We are interested instead in the specific and varied practices and motivations that guide critics' work. So we have organized our collection of commentaries on critical invention in Part II around four maxims—practical and moral advice on critical invention. Like all maxims, these express "truths" grounded in what is general rather than what is universal, and they are derived more from practical experience than from abstract principle. The four maxims we offer have a mixed lineage: They are shaped partly by truisms of rhetorical practice, partly by themes emerging from our examination of the commentaries by our contributors, and partly by our own convictions about the role of invention in criticism. In Part II we have grouped together the commentaries we felt threw the practical implications of each maxim into sharpest relief, either by directly addressing those implications, or by indirectly addressing them through contrast with the other commentaries in the same section.

Maxim 1: Criticism Requires Understanding and Pursuing One's Own Interests

Critics should begin the search for things worth writing about as critic by reflecting on their own experiences, curiosity, and commitments—with what they care about, and think would be worth understanding. Critics should judge finished criticism, in part, by the extent to which its conclusions are useful or insightful for them, and relevant to their own experiences, curiosity, and commitments.

The commentaries in this section of Part II recount how critical projects get started when critics begin to examine important aspects of their experience: Bonnie J. Dow explores the connection of her study of hegemony and feminism to her enjoyment of the adventures of an early television role model of the feminist woman, the character Mary Richards. Similarly, Elizabeth Walker Mechling and Jay Mechling found that their study of the 1950s civil defense campaign was fueled by powerful images and memories of growing up during the early years of the Cold War. And Thomas S. Frentz and Janice Hocker Rushing report that their own study of images of technology in popular media began with their own apprehension about the role technology was beginning to play in their own lives.

Maxim 2: Criticism Is Written to and for an Audience

Careful consideration of the audience(s) should offer critics direction in many important initial choices, from choices of subject and critical questions to determining the value of the conclusion(s) they expect to draw. Critics should remember that the value of their finished criticism will be judged, in part, by the extent to which it "speaks the language" of their readers and to which its conclusions are useful or insightful for them.

The commentaries in this section of Part II show different ways that consideration of audience can shape criticism: Thomas W. Benson describes how commitment to his professional audience shaped his decision to write for that audience about the documentaries of Fredrick Wiseman. Maurice Charland describes his choice to study Quebec nationalism as that of a critic who wants to write for a professional audience to which he is something of a newcomer, and who must therefore rethink his approach in terms of the context in which his desired audience will likely read the criticism. In the third commentary in this section, William L. Nothstine traces the changes in a manuscript on the PTL Ministry scandal as it was rewritten for three audiences: readers of a weekly magazine of political opinion, participants at a professional conference, and readers of a scholarly journal.

Maxim 3: Criticism Is Both Served and Confined by Theory and Method

Theoretical abstractions and methodological dictates can function to limit and direct the critic's formative choices about what texts to examine and what to say about or ask of them. This limiting and directing function can help focus the critic's concentration on potentially interesting things to write about, but it can also make it more difficult for the critic to exercise individual imagination, judgment, and intuition in making those same choices.

The four commentaries in this section of Part II describe different ways that critics have relied on theory and method to serve their critical purposes: Robert L. Ivie explains how the rigors of his approach to criticism gave him the distance he felt he needed to study American war rhetoric. Barry Brummett, by comparison, describes theory as balanced and kept in check by his own curiosity about the rhetoric of apocalyptic fundamentalists. Martha Solomon describes the circular movement, between her reading of the Tuskegee Syphilis Reports and her reexamination of theoretical texts on rhetoric, that shaped the questions she asked of those reports. In the last commentary of this section, Michael C. Leff recounts the methodological choices he made in one of his early essays, and speculates on the ways his study of Ciceronian orations might have been improved if he had viewed the role of theory and method differently.

Maxim 4: Criticism Rarely Travels a Straight Line to Its End

A variety of factors and forces can intervene to redirect the path criticism takes while the critic is still writing it. As a result critics often have to search for new ways to reach their original goals in writing, or for ways to redefine the goals themselves. Remember that the early formulations of critical questions or goals must be regarded as provisional.

The commentaries in this section of Part II all reflect upon the capacity of criticism to take unexpected turns as it is being written: Carole Blair describes how she and her coauthors felt obstructed by the seeming complexity of responses to the Vietnam Veterans Memorial, until they considered the possibility that this complexity itself offered the key to understanding the Memorial. Philip Wander traces the transformation of his essay about American foreign policy from a partisan cry against the Vietnam War to "historical scholarship" published some years after the end of that war. In the final essay of this section, Bryan C. Taylor compares his own attempts to reconstruct his inventional practices in his commentary for this book with the various attempts to tell the "story" of Los Alamos, and concludes that all such self-understanding will be partial at best.

▓ Conclusion

Critical invention is a region the boundaries of which are marked off by the distance between a critic's first entanglement with an issue or text and the culmination of that involvement in a provocative and worthwhile critical essay. We have dedicated this chapter, and indeed this book, to the exploration of that region after a long period of professional neglect.

Although this book is a first step toward retrieving the question of critical invention and its place in criticism, we have by no means resolved the matter here. Were critics required to postpone raising the question of invention until they had discovered a "solution," the question would never be raised, to the loss of all concerned. But the vigor, imagination, and commitment contained in the following essays reaffirm for us the value of beginning, and the importance of asking questions, even—and perhaps especially—when the answers are not yet obvious.

▓ Additional Readings

The following essays address various aspects of the processes and practices of invention in media and rhetorical criticism. They do not always agree with one another, nor are they always in complete harmony with our own position in this chapter. But this is in part why we recommend them, especially to the beginning critic, as further investigations of the varied practices by which critics begin their criticism. Other commentaries on critical invention are discussed in the text and notes of Chapter 2, "Professionalization and the Eclipse of Critical Invention."

Benson, Thomas W. "The Senses of Rhetoric: A Topical System for Critics." *Central States Speech Journal* 29 (1978): 237–50.

Benson discusses nine broad standpoints from which critics may examine texts, whether oratorical or non-oratorical, including: the investigation of the author's intentions to the persuasive possibilities of the text; the examination of a text's capacity to have unintended social consequences; and the evaluation of the extent to which a text displays ethical commitment, as well as artistic merit or pragmatic consequences.

Campbell, Karlyn Kohrs. "Criticism: Ephemeral and Enduring." *Speech Teacher* 23 (1974): 9–14.

Campbell identifies two important issues: *what* should be studied by the critic, and *to what purpose?* Her answer divides criticism into two broad types: social criticism, concerned with understanding the practical consequences of discourse for the formulation of issues and the justification of policy in particular cases; and academic or professional criticism, directed toward general theoretical understanding rather than response to individual situations.

Crowley, Sharon. "Reflections on an Argument That Won't Go Away: Or, A Turn of the Ideological Screw." *Quarterly Journal of Speech* 78 (1992): 450–65.

The "argument that won't go away," which Crowley examines, is the debate among critics about the connection of ideology and criticism: Do all critics write from some ideological position, however clearly articulated, and hence have responsibilities to clarify and account for their own interests? Or is "ideological criticism" a way for critics of a particular political bias to "find" in a text only what they already expected to see there?

Foss, Sonja K. "Rhetorical Criticism as the Asking of Questions." *Communication Education* 38 (1989): 191–96.

Foss describes the benefits for the beginning critic of focusing on general questions that characterize "thinking rhetorically." She describes three broad categories of such questions: questions about the relationship of a text to its context; questions about the ability of a text to construct a particular reality for its author and audience; and questions about the text as an expression of its creator.

Gronbeck, Bruce E. "Rhetorical Criticism in the Liberal Arts Curriculum." *Communication Education* 38 (1989): 184–90.

Gronbeck describes three talents the beginning critic should acquire and develop: facility with the language of rhetorical criticism; proper understanding of the various contexts within which texts may be examined and interpreted; and preparation for the making of aesthetic, moral, and pragmatic judgments about the uses and abuses of texts. He shows how these talents are directly related to the goals of liberal arts education, "the development of the mental facilities necessary for leading a mature life in society."

Hart, Roderick P. "Contemporary Scholarship in Public Address: A Research Editorial." *Western Journal of Speech Communication* 50 (1986): 283–95.

Hart argues that criticism of public address should be directed toward the conceptual or theoretical implications of individual cases, rather than preoccupied with the case itself. Given this starting point, he identifies several patterns of criticism that undermine movement in this direction, including: fixation on details of occasion or personality; and allowing the jargon of technical criticism to substitute for clear critical insight.

Hillbruner, Anthony. "The Moral Imperative of Criticism." *Southern States Communication Journal* 40 (1975): 228–47.

Hillbruner argues that, while criticism should attend to the aesthetic judgment of the "means" (that is, to the theoretical explanation of how a text functions), critics cannot ignore their responsibility to assess the "ends" of rhetoric as well—to judge and respond to the social and moral consequences of texts. To this end, Hillbruner identifies the moral imperatives for the critic: to seek the truth, to tell the truth, and to expose lies.

Klumpp, James F., and Thomas A. Hollihan. "Rhetorical Criticism as Moral Action." *Quarterly Journal of Speech* 75 (1989): 84–97.

Klumpp and Hollihan identify the role of the critic as part interpreter of events, part teacher, part social actor. They explore the possibilities and demands of this role by offering their own examination of an instance of popular discourse. They conclude that the basis of the critic's link to matters of social consequence is "the creative energy of criticism—the inventional power."

Nilson, Thomas R. "Criticism and Social Consequences." *Quarterly Journal of Speech* 42 (1956): 173–78.

Nilson begins with a point of disagreement among critics: Should criticism concern itself with rendering ethical, practical, or artistic judgments on discourse? Or are such judgments practically impossible and theoretically irrelevant? He lists several grounds for judgment of effects, all consistent with the general principle that such judgments should encompass the influences a text has on the society upon which it has impact, not simply its influence on an immediate audience.

Rosenfield, Lawrence W. "The Anatomy of Critical Discourse." *Speech Monographs* 35 (1968): 50–69.

Rosenfield identifies the role of critic as that of the expert commentator who offers reasoned judgments about texts. He further explores a variety of critical foci, starting points for criticism defined by differing degrees of emphasis laid upon author, text, context, and the critic's own interests within that criticism.

Scott, Robert L. "Focusing Rhetorical Criticism." *Communication Education* 33 (1984): 89–96.

Scott suggests questions that critics may find useful in selecting texts and critical approach: Does the text being considered fit comfortably into conventional rhetorical categories, or it a comparatively unconventional instance? Is the preliminary intention of the critic to focus on the message itself, or its underlying value premises, or the strategies it seems to evidence? He argues that criticism will often be more productive and useful when it recognizes that the answers to these two questions interact to shape the value of the conclusions the critic may draw.

Wander, Philip, and Steven Jenkins. "Rhetoric, Society, and the Critical Response." *Quarterly Journal of Speech* 58 (1972): 441–50.

Wander and Jenkins consider criticism to be "coming to terms with an object in terms of one's values." These values show themselves in what one chooses to study as a critic, how one forms an interpretation of it, and how one attempts to communicate this interpretive response to others. They argue against approaches to criticism that construe the ideal of "objectivity" so as to resist or deny the association of criticism with the critic's commitments and values.

CHAPTER 2 ⬚

PROFESSIONALIZATION AND THE ECLIPSE OF CRITICAL INVENTION

William L. Nothstine, Carole Blair, and Gary A. Copeland

How are the fundamental questions that guide critical research developed, refined, and justified? The implications of this question, sometimes misunderstood but more often flatly ignored by modern critical researchers, provide the focus for this anthology. In this chapter we investigate the background of the question, tracing how political, historical, and ideological considerations have shaped discussion of critical invention. This investigation will require examination of the grounds for a number of interrelated critical practices and assumptions and a reexamination of contemporary criticism's relationships to philosophy, science, pedagogy, and politics. Our particular focus will be upon professional rhetorical and media criticism, but the concerns raised here are relevant to literary criticism as well as to historical and interpretive research.[1]

Although we believe that the question—how are critical questions developed, refined, and justified?—has been systematically slighted, our goal in this chapter is not to provide a systematic answer to it.[2] Instead, the principal goal for this essay is to explore how the question of critical invention has come to be slighted, why, and at what cost.[3]

By "critical invention," we mean the formative acts preceding and prefiguring the completed critical essay. Critical invention, in this sense, is approximately equivalent to inquiry, "the creation of what is new in any discipline or endeavor" (LeFevre 2). Invention is an active process involving discovery and production. In criticism, it includes the choices animating the decision to write about a particular text, the constructing and choosing of things to say about that text, and decisions about how to say them. It is not just a process of individual reflection; it is, as Karen Burke LeFevre points out, a social process:

> Invention may first of all be seen as social in that the self that invents is, according to many modern theorists, not merely socially influenced but even socially constituted. Furthermore, one invents largely by means of language and

other symbol systems, which are socially created and shared. Invention often occurs through the socially learned process of an internal dialogue with an imagined other, and the invention process is enabled by an internal social construct of audience, which supplies premises and structures of belief that guide the writer. Invention becomes explicitly social when writers involve other people as collaborators, or as reviewers whose comments aid invention, or as "resonators" who nourish the development of ideas. . . . Finally, invention is powerfully influenced by social collectives, such as institutions, bureaucracies, and governments, which transmit expectations and prohibitions, encouraging certain ideas and discouraging others. (2)

We are interested in making critics' inventional practices explicit for two reasons. First, we believe that the far-reaching consequences of the culture and ideology of "professionalism," as it has been construed in academia, have included profoundly negative repercussions for criticism, including blinding critics to their own inventional practices. To acknowledge the problems and issues of critical invention may be a first step in loosening the hold of the institutional ideology of professionalism on criticism. Second, and equally important, students who are called upon to produce critical essays are all too often left with nowhere to begin, because the formative practices of thinking and writing critically are almost never articulated or specified in textbooks or in published professional criticism. We believe that neither practicing critics nor students of criticism can afford to leave these practices unarticulated or unacknowledged.

We acknowledge willingly that the issues regarding critical invention, such as those raised in this anthology, are not usually considered worthy of discussion; that is precisely our point in raising them. The most "trivial" or "obvious" assumptions frequently become more important and less apparent when discussed openly and evaluated carefully. The very fact that critics' inventional acts are taken for granted is what entices us to examine them. We believe that our own scholarship, and that of our colleagues in rhetorical and media criticism, is itself rhetorical and thus subject to questioning and critique at the level of its own rhetorical assumptions and practices.

The initial encounter of a critic with a text is an essential and formative constituent of the critical act.[4] Equally significant are the critic's grounds for the decision to write about that text, as well as decisions made in probing its possibilities, making interpretive and evaluative choices, and finding the words to re-present the text to readers of a critical essay. These are the inventional moments of criticism, the practical acts that constitute it and that lead to its culmination as a "finished" critical essay. Their significance to the critical act is undeniable. Yet, critics who work within the confines of a *professional* critical role generally treat their own inventional acts as the unspeakable, or at least as the unspoken.[5] Readers of critical essays witness the product of these actions but are rarely granted access to practices behind the process.[6]

It would be unusual, for instance, to read a critical essay in which any of the author's personal or political reasons for initial interest in the critical text addressed in that essay were revealed. More typically, the author would argue that the text is (or should be) interesting because of its capacity to illustrate a theoretical point. Also unusual would be a critic's acknowledgment or discussion of having had a change of mind or heart while grappling with the text. Such a change and the thoughtful reflections that engendered it would be considered dubious inclusions in a critical essay. So too would any real focus on the critic's enthusiasm or distaste for a text or any mention of attempts to account for the critic's own reactions. Likewise, critics are unlikely to discuss the obstacles they have encountered, the points at which they "got stuck" in the process, the aspects of the text that resisted their interpretive focus, or the ways in which editorially demanded revision may have pulled their essay in directions they felt were inconsistent with their original interests. Such content is considered irrelevant, trivial, idiosyncratic, or—heaven forbid—subjective, and therefore "inappropriate" to critical writing. These absences in scholarly critical discourse are symptomatic of the larger issue we intend to pursue in this chapter.

The "cover-up" of these issues of critical invention is not the result of individual or conspiratorial directive. The problem, instead, arises from community norms and historical practices. Practicing critics form a professional community that maintains and is maintained by particular, regularized norms. One of these norms is the concealment of the critic's inventional acts. Beginning critics, observing that no one else reports these acts, and having been taught that such material is inappropriate material for inclusion in a critical essay, will understandably be inclined to pass over such matters themselves. As critics gain more experience, these acts are taken for granted more and more, receiving little, if any, reflection, and considered not worth discussing in the precious space they would occupy in a journal article. Since, presumably, an even more experienced critic serves as a gatekeeper (a journal editor or referee) for other critics, any attempts to incorporate reports of the inventional process would commonly be turned back at the gate. It is unlikely that gatekeepers have to do much blocking of this sort, though, because the pedagogical arm of criticism commonly censors these "obvious or trivial" aspects of a critical work prior to a manuscript's submission for publication.

Thus critics refuse discussion of their inventional practices, because they have learned to, because they have imitated the practices of others who do so, or because the gatekeeping function has forced them to do so. But the teachers, role models, and gatekeepers are not the *causes* of the problem. They too are its *symptoms*, having themselves been caught up in the same historical, normative practices as all other critics. We all speak the discourse of our community. Professional critics speak the discourse unique to their critical community, a discourse of product at the expense of process; of theory at the cost of practice; and of knowledge, gallantly if unsuccessfully guarded from the intrusion of interest.[7]

The norms of the contemporary critical community are the product of academic professionalism. By "professionalism" we mean a culture in which individuals practice socially valued skills in exchange for the exclusive right to practice those skills, the right to impart the knowledge necessary to the skills, and prestige. Professionalism in academia is also a historically identifiable ideological edifice held together by three interlocking supports: disciplinarity, the creation and enforcement of academic disciplines, which divide knowledge into separate territories, each with its own proper methods of investigation; scientism, the reduction of all "knowledge" to a somewhat limited interpretation of the assumptions and techniques of modern science; and pressures toward civic and experiential disengagement on the part of the academic professional. (Each of these central terms—*professionalism, disciplinarity, scientism,* and *civic disengagement*—will receive further discussion later in this chapter.) Professionalism, as it is currently practiced in academia, causes criticism to be transformed—or, more precisely, reduced—from a process to a product. Since invention and creativity are aspects of the process of criticism, rather than of the final written product, our understanding of them has become a casualty of this reductive movement. In the next section of this essay we shall present an investigation of professionalism and its institutional supports as a general ideology within which virtually all scholarship, including criticism, operates. Following that, this chapter will trace the implications of this analysis of professionalism for media and rhetorical criticism in the speech communication field.

▓ Professionalism and Its Institutional Supports

An adequate discussion of the eclipse of critical invention cannot go far without acknowledging the tremendous shaping influence of professionalism on academic institutions and workers. The ideology of professionalism is founded upon the demarcation of a body of expert knowledge to which the professional is heir and guardian, based on extended formal study and often formal or informal apprenticeship (Wilshire 48).

Professionalism has been a fundamental part of the American middle-class experience of the past 150 years. The emergence of professionalism, with its social influence and mystique, has been a potent force toward upward mobility for its practitioners in the many fields influenced by it,[8] but it has had a broader social function as well. The professions took on the role of an aristocracy in a putatively classless society and offered authority in a putatively democratic society. As Gerald Graff suggests, "Faith in professional expertise gave a measure of reassurance to Americans who had always lacked traditional authorities and now, after the Civil War, found themselves confronted by bewildering industrial and social changes. But in exchange for this reassurance, these Americans were obliged to surrender their independence of judgment to experts" (*Professing Literature* 64).

The rise of professionalism in American education is typically linked to the ascendancy of the German university model in the late nineteenth century.[9] The professionalization of the American university, marking a replacement of the old college ideal of reinforcing liberal culture, involved the establishment of disciplinary departments and majors as well as graduate programs for in-depth study. Like their German forerunners, American universities took as their directive the advancement of knowledge rather than the transmission of culture. Thus, research became the keystone of the institution. Professional researchers, that is, professors, would be judged by their accomplishments in "discovering" and publishing original contributions to knowledge. Because advancement of knowledge, not culture, was the aim, these researchers would be "freed" to pursue their research with the detachment and neutrality becoming a professional.[10] The universities would serve society principally by supporting the development and publication of new areas of knowledge, and secondarily by instructing students in these areas of knowledge and by advising decision makers in the public realm. The new ideology supported, and in turn was supported by, the disciplinizing of higher education, disengagement of professionals from civic and cultural experience, and a stance of scientism.

Disciplinarity

The knowledge and unified research practices that generate knowledge in a field constitute a discipline, the *sine qua non* of professionalism.[11] The founding canons of a discipline not only define the intellectual area proper to it, but they also serve as a powerful, authoritative force for screening out claims and claimants not of the discipline.[12] The functions of the divisions and norms created by disciplinarity are thus profoundly self-interested and conservative. As Edward Said writes:

> It is patently true that, even within the atomized order of disciplines and fields, methodological investigations can and indeed do occur. But the prevailing mode of intellectual discourse is militantly antimethodological, if by methodological we mean a questioning of the structure of fields and discourses themselves. A principle of silent exclusion operates within and at the boundaries of discourse; this has now become so internalized that fields, disciplines, and their discourses have taken on the status of immutable durability. Licensed members of the field, which has all the trappings of a social institution, are identifiable as belonging to a guild, and for them words like "expert" and "objective" have an important resonance. To acquire a position of authority within the field is, however, to be involved internally in the formation of a canon, which usually

turns out to be a blocking device for methodological and disciplinary self-questioning. (22)

Disciplines create both the accepted categories of knowledge and a mystique to separate these categories from one another. In doing so, they also segregate the professionals of one discipline from the professionals of another. In academia, of course, this is accomplished primarily through the bureaucratic logic of the department structure. The existence and legitimation of disciplines largely eliminate the need as well as the opportunity to discuss the possible network of relationships between and among disciplines, the rationale for disciplines, or even what constitutes a discipline.

Disciplines are, by definition, autonomous, self-contained, and self-regulating (Weber x). That is, they are restrictive in character. But as Michel Foucault has suggested, they are also productive. They "have their own discourse," and they "engender . . . apparatuses of knowledge (*savoir*) and a multiplicity of new domains of understanding. They are extraordinarily inventive. . . ." ("Two Lectures" 106). Even these productive characteristics of disciplines, their discourses and apparatuses, work to differentiate and exclude, however. Even "colleagues" at the same university frequently are unable to communicate across their disciplinary divisions, for their discourses and apparatuses allow for no common language in which to converse.[13] Members of a discipline, thus, serve as the almost exclusive audience of another member's discourse. Scholarly discourses address primarily other professionals of the same field.

This restriction of audience also means that the nature of the relationship scholars have to their students has had to be redefined. A few generations ago, the justification of a university education—and of public support for it—was that it prepared students to participate fully and actively in civic and cultural life. But as Bruce Wilshire notes, contemporary undergraduates, through the disciplinary major designed by their professionalized faculty, "are treated as if they were preparing to become graduate students, specialists, young professional academics" (79). In some disciplines, such as accountancy or advertising, the basis for this assumption is evident and plausible; yet this assumption is held with equal firmness in areas such as history, anthropology, literature, or sociology, where far less support exists for such an expectation. By indoctrinating these students in disciplinary discourses and practices, however diluted for ease of learning, their major courses prepare them for careers that the overwhelming majority of them do not seek and even more will not attain. Terry Eagleton's ironic description of students in literary criticism probably is not atypical: the "content of their education was almost wholly beside the point; few of them were likely to find an acquaintance with Baudelaire indispensable for personnel management" (91). The point is that disciplinary discourse *seeks* to confine its audience only to specialists and to students it holds hostage against the grant of a degree.

Civic and Experiential Disengagement

One of the clearest marks of professionalization is the impulse to unify a discipline. This is an obvious corollary to professionalization, because it is unity that presumably gives a discipline its identity. But if it is to demarcate its boundaries, a discipline must actively separate itself from other realms of knowledge and experience, chiefly through a clearly differentiated subject matter and set of practices. Its population, the professionals who comprise the discipline, must respect and guard those boundaries. A discipline also appears, thus, to require organization of those who belong to it in a guild or professional society, the group that names, contains, and legitimizes the existence and maintenance of the professional.[14] Disciplines thus quarantine academic experience from contamination by knowledge, practice, and experience from outside the discipline and the university.

The professional association tends to usurp from the university the primary loyalties of academic workers as well as the power to set standards for judging their work, particularly at "graduate institutions."[15] In return, the association and its members offer the service of judging the quality of individual faculty members' research. The university (and any culture at large beyond the edge of campus) is excused from much of the responsibility of evaluating the results of a faculty member's scholarly work by the availability of "outside reviewers," who are members of the profession, and who serve as gatekeepers for professional publications and/or evaluators in tenure and promotion cases.[16]

The power of the professional association, to offer judgments or to provide a reservoir of other professionals who may offer judgments, can be maintained only under two conditions. First, the association must represent a specific—that is, unified—expertise. It cannot, after all, offer judgments of scholarly work falling outside a narrow specialty. So its domain must be relatively narrow, explicit, and unified. Second, the judgment by professionals of other professionals must be made at a distance. In other words, the "local" activities of a professional—such as teaching or service to a community—cannot be invoked as criteria for professional evaluation. Such "local" concerns therefore remain functionally outside the domain of professional activity. A scholar's "research product" is, by the profession's light, the only reasonable standard of professional judgment, for it alone is public and accessible. Thus, the power of the profession remains its ability to display unity, and its unity continues to be focused in research.

Because research entitles the academic worker to the role of "expert" or "professional," academic practice becomes oriented toward achievement principally in that arena. Such focus has an isolating effect on the individual. The image of the research scholar has consequently become one of "self-denial," with "the individual forsaking discernible comforts and social graces in order to follow his calling" (Haber 284–85).

Thus, "expertise" seems to depend upon the scholar's removal (to the extent possible) from experiences of everyday life. Comforts and social graces are the least of the losses; as Wilshire suggests, "individual advancement within professions [tends] to supplant civic duty" (64). Since service, and other civil activities, hold little discernible place in contributing to or judging an individual's professional expertise, they become less important than research and are segregated more and more from it. Even teaching is typically regarded as in opposition to the pursuit of expertise. As Jacoby puts it, "professionalization leads to privatization or depoliticization, a withdrawal of intellectual energy from a larger domain to a narrower discipline" (147). Drawn away from the civic life in favor of the professional identity, one is increasingly enjoined, in Wilshire's phrase, "to clap oneself in the nutshell of one's theory, to line it with mirrors, and to count oneself king of infinite space" (72).

Under such pressures, addressing a community beyond one's own discipline quickly becomes suspect, as Russell Jacoby notes in his observation that academics are not considered "serious" professionals if they write for general audiences (153). Moreover, and more specifically in the humanities and social sciences, even those research emphases that might hold direct relevance for a nonacademic community find little or no application or inspiration in that community. The judgments rendered by scholars on the moral world at large, writes Wilshire, thus "tend to be construed in ever more technical senses, imperiling the sense of their broadly human significance, and of how they might be *true* of human life" (49). As a result, while unified professional groups demand and receive the loyalty and adherence of the academic worker, professionalism disengages the worker from public experience and involvement, thus augmenting the isolation already imposed by disciplinarity.

Scientism

The image of knowledge and power that has emerged from the modern culture of professionalism, and that in turn supports that culture, is overwhelmingly a technological one. "Knowledge" has come to refer to the methods and instrumentations by which professionals study things as much as to the results of those studies. Those possible objects of study not amenable to a discipline's theories, as operationalized in its methods and instrumentations, might as well not exist (Wilshire 72).[17] The sum total of this reduction of knowledge to technology we call "scientism." A more complete description of scientism is provided by Tom Sorrell:

> Scientism is the belief that science, especially natural science, is much the most valuable part of human learning—much the most valuable part because it is much the most authoritative, or serious, or beneficial. Other beliefs related to this one may also be regarded as scientistic, e.g., the belief that science is the

only valuable part of human learning, or the view that it is always good for subjects that do not belong to science to be placed on a scientific footing. (1)

The ideology of professionalism hallows the discovery of knowledge and thus encourages scientism. It particularly encourages attempts by the social sciences and humanities to gain scientific status—and thereby strengthen their disciplinary status—by appropriating or emulating the practices of the so-called "hard" sciences. Scientism shows itself as a set of practices guided by a worldview. This worldview is not always complete, explicit, or entirely coherent, but it does display several recurring and identifiable features.

According to this adopted worldview, the modern natural sciences enjoy a consensus regarding the fundamental matters of method, stance, and theory. The social sciences and humanities can and should emulate this consensus in their own domains. The fundamental questions guiding scientific research should be ideologically neutral, detached from historical and pragmatic considerations, and directed toward the eventual construction of unified theory. Four general themes animate this worldview: the cult of objectivity, the goal of theory building, the elevation of method as the means of theory testing and construction, and faith in consistent scientific progress.

The primary element in this set of assumptions is well known: the proper stance for the researcher is one of objectivity—practical, ethical, and intellectual distance from the object of study. Objectivity is taken to be necessary for theory building and guaranteed by method. "Objectivity" here is an umbrella term for a collection of philosophical principles, a hodgepodge held together more by tradition than by any logical or philosophical coherence it might possess. The objectivist cant features the presumption that the questions worth asking, and the answers worth having, are generally empirical in nature and positivist in temperament.[18] As Wilshire correctly observes:

> To say, as many do, that positivism no longer exercises strong influence in the university is a self-deceiving fiction. Positivism was—and is to a great extent—"in the air," not just confined to philosophy departments, and practically no department in the university goes uninfluenced. In some cases it is gross and inescapable to any attentive eye. The constricted attention to "testable facts," and the cognitive as opposed to the emotive, cripples the imagination and unnecessarily restricts the scope of study. This occurs in many departments of history and economics, for example—also in "the better" departments of art history and music history, or musicology. (207)

To be sure, professionalism has produced some of its greatest cultural effects (although not without a price) in those disciplines whose "knowledge base" has been most directly tied to empirical methods and empirical outcomes: medicine, engineering, and so on. Small wonder that other emerging disciplines found that route tempting.[19]

But it has been more than just a temptation. As Stanley Aronowitz suggests, "modern science demarcates itself, not by reconstituting the object, but by defining rationality in a specific way" (8). To the extent that its definition took hold and was generalized beyond natural science, other areas of inquiry had to pursue scientific goals and practices or risk being labeled "irrational," that is, unfit to produce knowledge and therefore not deserving of professional status. That the equation of science and rationality *has been* widely accepted seems clear, both within academic institutions and society at large.[20] Thus, the onus on disciplines is obvious. Aronowitz expresses it clearly: "All inquiry is obliged to direct itself to science, or, by inference, to distinguish itself from science" (viii).

Perhaps no practical consequence of this pressure is more ironic than the modernist scholarly horror of the rhetorical. Professional scholarship generally strives to prevent as much as possible the open recognition of the rhetorical character of its own writing. In history, for example, as Hayden White points out, disciplinary and professional status could not go forward until it was settled that the coherence of history was derived from the evidence itself, not from the rhetorical inventiveness of the historian:

> As long as history was subordinated to rhetoric, the historical *field* itself (i.e., the past or the historical process) had to be viewed as a *chaos* that made no sense at all or one that could be made to bear as many senses as wit and rhetorical talent could impose upon it. Accordingly, the disciplining of historical thinking that had to be undertaken, if history considered as a kind of *knowledge* was to be established as arbitrator of the realism of contending political programs, each attended by its own philosophy of history, had to consist first of all in its de-rhetoricization. (128)

Hence producing methodically rigorous, but impersonal, reports substitutes for engaging an audience and their world, ethically and intellectually, as a persuader. The claim of such reports to our assent is based on the rigor and objectivity of their methods, rather than the ability of writers to adduce *good reasons* for an interpretation—with emphasis on both the moral and rational implications of that term "good reasons" (Toulmin 110–15; Said 15).

Second, traditional science set for itself the task of theory generation. Sorrell explains the view of scientific empiricism:

> Science is a conjunction of well-confirmed scientific theories, and scientific theories, however disparate their subject matter, may be viewed as partially interpreted logical calculi. The calculi contain axioms and postulates from which observational truths are supposed to be derived. Taken together, the calculi of the different sciences add up to the body of truths of science. (4–5)

On this view, scientific theories are unified. Such theories serve one or both of two functions: prediction and explanation. Prediction is the identification of causal mechanisms for the purpose of making inferences about future events; explanation is the invocation of causal principles to account for an already-given state of affairs. Both explanation and prediction are to be distinguished, in modern science, from the rendering of a judgment (Kerlinger 9–10; 459–62). Scientific theories are at their best when their explanatory and predictive functions are most generalizable (Feigl 10–11; Kerlinger 11). The best theory thus accounts for or predicts the broadest range of phenomena in the simplest formulation (Holton 205–6).

The reliance upon scientific method for confirmation or falsification, the third characteristic of scientism, vouchsafes objectivity. "Testability" in principle is considered one of the most basic requirements of theory.[21] The methods required for testing are held to be observer-neutral, available to anyone properly trained to verify or falsify the results of another's test (Feigl 11). Michael McGee and John Lyne summarize this "story of scientism":

> Science is universal in the sense that the logic of its inquiry is the same in any domain where knowledge is possible. The universal objective of inquiry is explanation and prediction. An event is explained by showing that it occurred as the result of laws, rules, or principles of nature and society; and knowledge of laws, rules, conditions, and so on makes prediction possible. . . . No claim will be acknowledged as fact until it has been verified by observation, and no proposition will be treated seriously even in theory unless it is possible to envision the conditions of its verification. (383)

Scientific methods allow for empirical generalization, the "raw material" of theory generation and testing.

Finally, the attitude of scientism is an optimistic one; the theme of scientific "progress" animates and supports it. Gerald Feinberg expresses this attitude as well as anyone: "As time goes on, we can expect to see each link in the chain between simple and complex phenomena grow gradually stronger. This will reinforce the view held by most physicists and many other scientists that we are dealing with a single subject matter and that a single set of fundamental laws ultimately governs all natural phenomena" (181). Scientism exaggerates this position to suggest that "the advance of science will ultimately provide definitive solutions for the problems of society" (Davis 193). Even when the optimism is not so far-reaching, science is set up within the culture of professionalism as the means of knowledge production, claiming "exclusive access to truth" (Wilshire 153).

One problem with this characterization of the process and practice of science is that, since the early part of the twentieth century, natural scientists themselves have largely abandoned it. "It is a pity, then," writes Stephen Toulmin with understated irony, "for scholars working in the humanities to continue shaping their critical attitudes and theories by relying on a contrast with modern science that—among scientists themselves—no longer even *seems* to exist" (101). Of course, the image of science as formulating its questions for research based on "the facts," rather than on the prior interests of the scientist, was never very accurate (Toulmin 101; Pirsig 97–100). Instead, this naive image of the project of science has been far more important to the social sciences and humanities in their quest for institutional clout. Page Smith points out the irony implicit in this state of affairs: "Whereas the would-be scientists talk about detachment, objectivity, neutrality, the dispassionate treatment of data, the 'hard' scientists and their biographers talk of passion and obsession, of hunches and of inspiration, of insight, excitement, and profound emotion" (282). In the age of post-Heisenberg science, when the "uncertainty principle" has become a cornerstone of research in that most fundamental of sciences, researchers in physics and the rest of the natural sciences have abandoned the objectivist view to the social scientists and humanists—if they will have it.[22]

The other problem, of course, is that the canons of traditional science, even if they *were* accepted in the physical sciences today, would not *therefore* be appropriate or useful to other areas of inquiry. It does not follow from success in one arena that the same means will produce an important or useful outcome in another. But such is the *non sequitur* on which scientism has proceeded.

▤ Professionalism and Research in Speech Communication

The effects of professionalization have been felt in every field, but perhaps most profoundly in those that deal in interpretive or critical research. Eagleton, Said, and Graff all discuss professionalism's effect on literary studies, for example. White does likewise for history, Wilshire for philosophy, and Jacoby for political science. Our focus is upon rhetorical and media criticism, typically resident in departments of speech communication. The thorough professionalization of this particular research community, of course, has implications of internal consequence for its practitioners and students.

But the ramifications of a professionalized rhetorical and media criticism may reverberate more broadly, for two reasons. First, critics of media and rhetoric typically study events of *public* culture, with clear pragmatic consequences, practical contexts, and frequently even pragmatic intent. Critics of rhetoric and media justify their researches in large measure on the grounds that the texts they study—from classic orations, government pamphlets, feature and documentary films, and television comedies to televangelism, medical reports, and public memorials—have obvious and consequential socio-cultural effects. Thus, we could argue that criticism's separation from public voice and public idiom and its scientistic impulse to evacuate scholarship of political or ethical considerations are even more troubling in media and rhetorical criticism than in other areas of research. Second, other fields of scholarship recently have demonstrated an intensified interest in rhetoric as a possible means to alleviate the effects of more traditional and rigid conceptions of their discourses of inquiry. The fact that a largely professionalized rhetorical criticism is even possible should sound a warning to those who would turn to rhetoric as a clear way out of the morass of professionalization that threatens to choke off their own research pursuits.

Speech, the early twentieth-century forerunner of the speech communication discipline, was formed largely as a result of interests in practical pedagogy rather than research. Departments of speech and the National Association of Academic Teachers of Public Speaking (NAATPS), now the Speech Communication Association, had as their central concern the teaching of "oral English" (Wichelns 3). But very early in the new discipline's history, the pressure to professionalize made its entrance explicitly and with rather more candor than might be considered decorous. For example, one of the NAATPS's founding members, James A. Winans, wrote in 1915 that "by the scholarship which is the product of research the standing of our work in the academic world will be improved. It will make us orthodox. Research is the standard way into the sheepfold" ("Need" 17). Winans continued, suggesting that teaching as well as reputations would be enhanced "when we have the better understanding of fundamentals and training in the methods which test and determine truth. . . . And in the process of investigation many new truths, before unsuspected, will be discovered. . . . We talk of standardization of our work; but there can be no standardization until we have standardized truth" ("Need" 18–19). He suggested that the "difficulty" would be "getting into a sufficiently scientific frame of mind" ("Need" 22). Later that year he predicted confidently, if inaccurately: "The very practical nature of our work will save us from the excesses of research" ("Should We Worry?" 199).

Although a strong tradition of liberal rhetorical research in the emerging speech field maintained itself throughout the early twentieth century in a rather uneasy relationship with a tradition of social scientific research in the discipline (Pearce 260–64), the will to professionalize continued unabated if largely unrealized. Lester Thonssen and A. Craig Baird's resistant statement in 1948 suggests the strength of that will to professionalize:

> Rhetoric, as the intermediary between the will to action and the achievement of the result, must accordingly be conceived as both a political and ethical instrument. This is another way of saying, perhaps, that there must be a *moral principle* supporting and guiding the liberal tradition. While there has been some disposition to resist the inclusion of such a principle in the scheme of learning—a circumstance resulting from our virtual deification of the so-called scientific

spirit and method—its return as an active force in the field of knowledge is necessary. A sustained faith in democracy itself depends upon it. (467)

However, as mass communication and communication research emerged in their own right in the decades following World War II, such resistance to professionalization finally all but collapsed. "Mass communication" eventually became the research venue of researchers once based in sociology, psychology, and political science, but by the late 1950s most of these pioneers were returning to studies more closely allied with their respective former disciplines. Mass communication research was largely relinquished to members of departments of speech, journalism, or radio-TV, who found in this new field the theoretical and methodological rationale by which broadcasting and journalism programs would justify their academic positions.

Both journalism and speech were once specialized areas of English department curricula—journalism being a specialized form of written English analogous to speech's focus on oral English. In addition to their common origins, departments of speech and journalism also shared the common problem of seeking academic legitimation while being viewed as skills programs (Carey 283). And, as Raymond Carroll notes, departments of radio-TV also "evolved largely from Speech departments, when a few schools established curricula during the early 1930s" (3). The courses such as "radio speaking" were natural additions to speech departments' curricula in times when most speech departments were still geared toward the practical training of teachers, clergy, and others who could use the arts of practical speaking.

Just as speech, following Winan's urging, "began getting a sufficiently scientific frame of mind," journalism attempted to further its own professionalization by staking out areas of knowledge and research. As James Carey describes it, "practical training in journalism was given the intellectual gloss by joining it to studies in ethics, history, and later in law" (284). Journalism, like speech, felt pressure to establish for itself what Carey called "a new scientific legitimacy" (286). The boom in the study of mass communication process and effects during the 1940s, primarily by sociologists and psychologists, offered journalism departments a chance to acquire "scientific legitimacy" by appropriating a field of professional knowledge and research: mass communication.

Most of the major scientific studies of mass communication, including the work of Paul Lazarsfeld, Carl I. Hovland, and others, much of which had been done immediately before or during World War II, were codified in the volumes edited by Wilbur Schramm, most notably *The Process and Effects of Mass Communication*. Schramm's books became primers on both theory and methodology in journalism departments, speech departments, and the newly emerging communication departments.

The 1949 publication of *The Mathematics of Communication* by Claude Shannon and Warren Weaver also contributed to the increasingly professional, scientific character of mass communication research, as well as contributing to its shortened name—communication (or communications) research. The mathematical model of information and communication, developed by Shannon and extrapolated by Weaver, seemed strongly to suggest that a general theory of communication was indeed possible. As Carey summarized the situation, "cybernetics and information theory had a legitimating and shaping effect for they suggested that the study of mass communications might be established on a fully scientific basis, that they contributed a core imagery and vocabulary to the field in the form of [Shannon's and Weaver's] graphic model" (285). Even more tantalizing, the general theory of communication might be reducible to mathematical form.

Everett Rogers noted the disciplinary implications of this new field of knowledge, mass communication: "We see that 1959 was really a time of transition, as communication research moved from departments of sociology, psychology, political science, and specialized institutes like Lazarsfeld's and into departments of its own" (21). These departments of communication were usually constructed from faculty, or even whole departments, originally called journalism, radio-TV, and speech.

Communication research brought with it new "options to studying journalism or the newspaper or the magazine—one could study mass communications. There were now options to studying speech, or rhetoric, or drama—one could study communications" (Carey 285). It further embraced scholarship in areas later to be termed interpersonal communication, organizational communication, and so on, areas also drawing heavily from research traditions begun in sociology and psychology.[23] The introduction of the study of communication to traditional rhetorical studies within the domain of the speech field promoted a heavy influx of scholars principally interested in methods borrowed from the behavioral sciences, and whose theorizing was often oriented primarily toward electronic and print communication rather than oral communication. Thus, speech departments found themselves driven, by the ideological demand for "unity" within a discipline, to accommodate both rhetorical studies and the scientific study of communication, although frequently neither faction felt much of a common bond with its counterpart (Brown 201).[24] The challenge has been described by both Jesse Delia and W. Barnett Pearce,[25] and was nowhere better summarized than in John Bowers's memorable epithet: "The critic thinks he knows; the scientist knows he knows" (171).

The social scientists' determination to unify the discipline around a theoretical core was loudly voiced and frequently repeated—usually by the communication researchers themselves but sometimes also by convinced rhetoricians.[26] Henry McGuckin, for example, urged communication researchers and rhetoricians to "heed with real conviction one another's contribution to what is ultimately a single purpose" (172). Carroll Arnold elaborated, suggesting that "the tendency to say that rhetorical scholars and communication scholars live in separate worlds is the consequence of simply paying too much attention to methodologies and too little attention to how we are conceptualizing the ultimate stuff being studied and how we are building toward ultimate theories about that stuff we partly share" ("Rhetorical and Communication Studies" 80). Karlyn Kohrs Campbell clearly concurred: "What all of us in this discipline seek to discover—whatever our special interests and competencies—are the processes that characterize human communication" ("Criticism" 12).[27]

By 1975, Gerald Miller—himself a dominant voice among communication researchers—had concluded confidently that "there seems to be no serious problem in achieving rapprochement between the humanistic and scientific approaches to speech communication" (239). Miller was correct, as far as his statement goes, but the rapprochement that he and others of his persuasion sought would be at a high cost to rhetorical criticism, as we shall argue in the next section. Mainstream rhetorical criticism finally capitulated to the ideology of professionalism, a victim of the disciplinary call to unity, scientizing itself and compromising or discarding altogether its earlier defense of a pragmatic, pedagogical, public orientation.

▓ The Professionalizing of Rhetorical and Media Criticism

It is relatively easy to document that critical inquiry in speech communication has been, to a considerable degree, professionalized. The difficulties lie in choosing, from among the seemingly endless possibilities, the evidence that most clearly marks the professionalized culture and in documenting the consequences of the disciplinization, disengagement, and scientizing of criticism. For the sake of practicality and relative brevity, we shall document the pervasive influence of professionalization by referencing "metacritical" literature—scholarly and textbook materials describing, prescribing, and justifying the particular character of critical practices within rhetorical criticism.[28]

Our intention is to construct from these various materials a text that represents a culture or discourse community—the community of professional rhetorical and media critics. No individual critic has rendered this whole text as an idealized, coherent view of criticism; what we present is a composite of voices. Although it is a textual construction, we are confident that it will have at least some resonance, some intuitive familiarity, as a legitimate way of reading what still appears to be the mainstream of contemporary criticism, what Michael Leff refers to as "modernist rhetoric."[29] Individuals whose voices we have appropriated may occasionally object that our rendering of their arguments has not captured their motives or intentions with perfect fidelity—but this objection would be beside the point. We are attempting to locate the ideological structure that serves as the primary discourse of the critical community in speech communication. It is precisely our point that we and our colleagues, as professionals, are *all* implicated at this level in norms and practices we might be unaware of or even struggling against in our own teaching and writing. Indeed, as the next section of this book shows with sometimes painful clarity, even we, the authors of this chapter denouncing the influences of professionalism, are complicitous in the very practices we are resisting here, whether we like it or not.

We shall focus primarily on the scientizing of criticism, for here is where this discourse of professionalism emerges most clearly. Scientism reproduces and sustains disengagement and disciplinization, just as it is sustained by them. We shall discuss those mutual supports and some of their consequences following our discussion of the scientization of criticism. The implications of this professionalized criticism are legion; many of them will go unremarked here, in the interest of focusing attention especially on the consequences for inventional practices in criticism.

The Scientizing of Criticism

A review of the literature of rhetorical criticism localizes the themes of scientism we identified earlier in this chapter: preoccupation with theory building, the cult of objectivity, reliance upon method for confirmation and falsification of claims, and even the ideal of progress—although this last shows itself in some unexpected ways in critical discourse, as we shall see below.

It seems no accident that the critical community would assume the mantle of scientism in response to the calls for unification and theory building on the parts of their scientifically inclined colleagues in communication. The most obvious evidence of this tendency among those writing about criticism has been to describe science either as a model or as a different form of inquiry. Edwin Black's comparison-contrast of the scientist and the critic in 1965 certainly is the most prominent case of both of these tendencies. While acknowledging that critics and scientists pursue different ends, he concluded that science had provided "achievements to be emulated by the critic" (*Rhetorical Criticism* 9). He suggested that the influence of science on criticism had been "wholesome," in making critics "conscious of their methods," and in encouraging them "to become systematic, to objectify their modes of inquiry, and to restrict themselves to demonstrable, or at least arguable, generalizations" (2). The Committee on the Advancement and Refinement of Rhetorical Criticism, of the 1970 National Developmental Project, took a more exaggerated stance, contrasting the "critic-scientist" and the "critic-artist":

> At one extreme, we envision the critic acting much like the scientist: deriving hypotheses from systematized constructs, controlling extraneous variables, minimizing error variance, operationalizing terms, arriving at low-order inferences about classes of events with a minimum of experimenter bias. At the other extreme, we envision the critic functioning artistically: immersing himself in the particulars of his object of study, searching for the distinctive, illumining with metaphor the rhetorical transaction. (Sloan, et al. 223)

The critic-artist did not fare very well in the Committee's efforts to advance and refine rhetorical criticism.[30] In addition to the above description of the critic-artist as merely "functioning," in contrast to the critic-scientist "acting," the critic-artist consistently appeared as a role in need of defense but difficult to defend. For example, the critic-artist's "reports are hardly as unsupportable as is frequently maintained. . . . Admittedly we are hard pressed to indicate how the arguments are made convincing" (Sloan, et al. 223).[31]

That the Committee was "hard pressed" illustrates the problem of describing or justifying critical research in relation to science or in an environment wherein professional knowledge is the *desideratum* and science is respected as the only, or at least the superior, route to knowledge. Even when criticism is simply contrasted with science, the virtually inevitable result is that criticism will be viewed as inferior or, at the very least, less "advanced" in its development. Bernard Brock, Robert Scott, and James Chesebro, for example, suggest that current critical work in rhetoric is "pre-paradigmatic" (20). By this designation, they treat criticism as if it might or even should move toward a paradigmatic state as science ostensibly does in Thomas Kuhn's description of succession in scientific knowledge. The implication, of course, is that criticism remains in a primitive state by contrast to the more advanced position of science. Such comparisons and contrasts are by no means unusual.[32] But as critics continue to model their goals, stance, language, and writing practices on this image of science, only the *comparisons* between criticism and science retain much enthusiasm; the *contrasts* drawn between criticism and science have begun to seem a bit disingenuous.

Critics have embraced the goals of science perhaps from political necessity, given the prestige science has enjoyed and its installation as the premier, if not the sole, epistemology of modernity. "Theory" has become virtually the singular objective of criticism; even "judgment," which might seem a definitional end of anything called "criticism," has become a secondary and often quite expendable goal. For example, the Committee on the Advancement and Refinement of Rhetorical Criticism took criticism's principal function virtually for granted: "Whether rhetorical criticism *ought* to contribute to theory seems to us to be beyond question" (Sloan, et al. 222). Foss suggests variously that "any essay of rhetorical criticism cannot not contribute to theory" ("Criteria" 287), that "rhetorical criticism must begin with the asking of a research question so that the critic is able to contribute to rhetorical theory as a result of the study" (*Rhetorical Criticism* xi), and that "the purpose of rhetorical criticism is to explain how some aspect of rhetoric operates and thus to make a contribution to rhetorical theory" ("Constituted by Agency" 34–35). Richard Gregg counsels that "our best criticism ought to be both particular and summative. That is, it ought to illuminate particular situations and at the same time suggest hypotheses regarding human rhetorical behavior that, when added to the insights of other critics, provide generalizable understandings of the human rhetorical condition" (60). And Andrews claims that "development and refinement of rhetorical theory" is a function of criticism that, "in a sense, subsumes all others" (12).[33]

On this view, criticism is treated as scientific or "pre-scientific" in character. Bowers forwarded the notion of a "pre-scientific" criticism in 1968, arguing that the end of such criticism should be

> to contribute to an economical set of scientifically verifiable statements accounting for the origins and effects of *all* rhetorical discourses in *all* contexts. This point of view requires that rhetorical criticism be viewed as an early part of a process eventuating in scientific theory. Hence, the adjective "pre-scientific" is appropriate. The term implies that, in this frame of reference, the rhetorical critic's principal task is to produce testable hypotheses which, when verified, will have the status of scientific laws. (163–64)

Bowers's arguments were frequently so condescending toward criticism that it is a bit surprising to find critics who would agree with him. Bowers spelled out what critics "must learn" and what they "must" do in order to accomplish what science would "require" of them (166). After suggesting that criticism might have the most to contribute to the scientific enterprise by operationally defining terms, he labeled the task of operational definition "a relatively trivial matter" (167). Nonetheless, some critics have accepted this subordinate role for criticism. Roderick Hart does so explicitly: "It is in their roles as pre-scientists that rhetorical critics can add substantially to the development and refinement of synthetic, inclusive, and predictive theoretical statements about human persuasion" ("Theory-Building" 70). Others have accepted Bowers's prescription without the label of "pre-science." Horace M. Newcomb likewise argues that television criticism can open new areas for empirical research while also providing a test for criticism's conclusions (226). Brock, Scott, and Chesebro suggest that one of the ways in which criticism serves theory is to "give rise to insights that can then be phrased as principles for further use or hypotheses for further testing" (17). James Andrews agrees, suggesting that a critic "may generate hypotheses upon which new theories can ultimately be built" (13).[34]

Critics' treatment of rhetorical criticism as itself a scientific process is more common but typically less than explicit. Ernest Bormann is technically correct in pointing out that few rhetoricians would call rhetorical theory "scientific" (53). That is, no one seems to want to be caught uttering an explicit statement to that effect. However, if criticism's principal purpose is to contribute to rhetorical theory, and if rhetorical theory is treated as a functional equivalent to scientific theory, then it certainly would follow that rhetorical criticism is treated as fundamentally equivalent to a scientific activity. Contributing to theory *is* regarded as the fundamental goal of criticism by a number of critics, as we noted earlier. And the theory to which criticism contributes *is* described in ways suggesting similitude, if not identity, with scientific theory. Barry Brummett makes the case clearly:

> Rhetoricians often seem to regard their theories as close parallels to more conservative, hypothetical-deductive social science theories. Gronbeck sounds like a social scientist when he claims that Burkean scholars try to generate "a systematic set of covering propositions." Black argues that rhetorical theory, apart from the more insignificant theories derived from logical necessity, is grounded in "regularities" of psyche or discourse. McGee explicitly claims that "if it is to achieve the status of 'theory,' any prose must reliably describe, explain, and predict." Zarefsky agrees that rhetorical theory should be both testable and predictive. Swanson demands that a rhetorical study pass "objective tests of its accuracy." ("Rhetorical Theory" 97)[35]

Brummett's catalog is not exhaustive, but it is in every sense exemplary. Yet, even given the stature and accomplishment of those critics he names, it is possible to augment his case. Hart can be counted among those who treat rhetorical theory as scientific in character. He suggests that "theory is richest when it accounts comprehensively for multiple events rather than individual instances, for the comparatively unmonitored rather than the widely observed activity, for the regularized rather than the idiosyncratic" ("Contemporary Scholarship" 294). Andrews concurs as well: "By theory, we mean a body of plausible generalizations or principles that explain a complex set of facts or phenomena" (12).

Andrews's mention of "explanation" represents a further level of the infiltration of rhetorical criticism and theory by scientism. While one might expect criticism's principal operations to be interpretative and/or evaluative, contemporary critics align themselves with scientists in describing their work as primarily explanatory in nature. In summarizing the "specific analytical tasks" that the Wingspread conferees formulated for the profession, Arnold lists six; he introduces them as follows: "1. We need clearer explanations. . . . 2. We need clearer explanations. . . . 3. We need more precise explanations. . . . 4. We need fuller explanations. . . . 5. We need explanations. . . . 6. We need more precise explanations" ("Reflections" 195–96). Brock, Scott, and Chesebro describe "the critical impulse" as an awareness "of circumstances that seem to cry out for explanations" (10). Hart defines rhetorical criticism as "the business of identifying the complications of rhetoric and explaining them in a comprehensive and efficient manner" (*Modern Rhetorical Criticism* 32). Leah Vande Berg and Lawrence Wenner cite explanation as one of the "primary purposes of criticism" (10). Sonja Foss equates explanation and theory contribution in discussing the goal of rhetorical criticism ("Constituted by Agency" 34–35). Brockriede values only explanatory and some forms of evaluative criticism as "significant argument" ("Rhetorical Criticism"). If these critics' references to explanation are reflective ones—that is, if they understand explanation to be an account of causality—their views of criticism's goals align with the objectives espoused in traditional conceptions of science.[36] William Brown, in his discussion of critical research in mass media, certainly seems to be aware of the implications of his suggestion that one of the proper roles for criticism is to reach for the ultimate goal of behavioral science—prediction and control. He writes, "depending upon the individual critic's specific version of 'usable explication,' the yield from criticism may be knowledge . . . theoretically capable of leading to prediction or perhaps even control of mediated-communication outcomes, with a concomitant view of reality working like a machine" (207).

Explanation does not always appear in these accounts to *replace* understanding or judgment as proper goals of criticism. As in Wayne Brockriede's case, explanation and judgment are both recognized as legitimate goals. However, normative judgments of all varieties—ethical, political, and moral—are frequently devalued. Mark Klyn, for example, argued in 1968 that criticism "does not imply . . . any categorical structure of judgment, or even any judgmental necessity" (147). Bowers, elaborating his vision of the pre-scientific critic, explained that his view "ignores, though it does not prohibit, the critic's evaluative activities" (164). Hart seems little bothered by the recognition that "theorist-critics may be in positions to do little for the cause of justice-in-our-times" ("Theory-Building" 76).

Campbell goes further, distinguishing between "ephemeral" social criticism and "enduring" academic criticism:

> The social critic enters the arena of public controversy and appraises contemporary acts before all their consequences are clear and all the relevant facts are known. Such a critic is committed to participating in the free discussion of issues relevant to a particular time and place. The academic critic explores and analyzes whatever acts will aid in explicating the essential processes of human symbolization. Both functions are vital, and both forms of criticism need to be

affirmed, but the distinctive purposes of each need to be recognized. ("Criticism" 13–14)

Despite Campbell's acknowledgment of the importance of the appraisal accomplished by social critics, she argues that professional journals are not the proper outlets nor professional colleagues the proper audience for such work ("Criticism" 10). Campbell thus forecloses, albeit indirectly, the possibility of judgment as a legitimate function of academic criticism by privileging "explication" as the province of the professional critic.[37]

Brock, Scott, and Chesebro seem rather nonplussed by the apparent inevitability of the conclusion they draw: "Try as we may, the evaluative component appears to remain an enduring feature of any critical impulse" (13). Their ambivalence about judgment is explained by their recognition that "evaluation of others can often be awkward, upsetting, and difficult for both the critic and those being judged" (12). They never seem to emerge from this difficulty; their discussion is confused and confusing. At one point, they "hold criticism to be an art of evaluating with knowledge and propriety" (13). At another, they suggest that "the critic may choose to deemphasize the evaluative function of criticism" (16).[38]

These shifts toward explanation and the corresponding devaluations of judgment are funded by the currency of objectivity. We could not hope to make the case more succinctly or accurately than James Klumpp and Thomas Hollihan have:

> The dominant interpretation of the rhetorical critic's purpose over the last three decades has formed from the relationship of critical method to social science. Indeed, the perspective of the critic as morally neutral has sprung primarily from the linkage with the objective methods promoted by American social science during that period. The celebration of critical objectivity, rooted in a trend common to many disciplines in this century, reached its full flower in the 1960s among those attempting to find comfort in academic departments experiencing the growth fueled by increased interest in social science and social engineering. The oft-longed-for unity of such departments was often achieved around the central symbols of the common task of "building and testing theory." After agreement on goals, the social scientists' tolerance in method made room for the rhetorical critic. The result was a self-image for critics that valued "objectivity" defined as moral noninvolvement. (92)

Although Black, in his 1965 monograph, still admitted judgment as a function of criticism, his commitment to objectivity was explicit and unswerving.[39] He argued that, like scientists, critics have "two vitally important activities, which are to see a thing clearly and to record what they have seen precisely." The critic "tries to become, for a time, a pure perceiver, an undistorting slate on which an object or an event external to him can leave a faithful impression of itself, omitting nothing" (*Rhetorical Criticism*, 1965, 4).

Today, most critics, including Black, would be unlikely actually to lay explicit claim to objectivity, as Black himself did in 1965. However, critics remain mesmerized by the objectivist cant to whatever degree that they pretend toward moral neutrality or distance, that they insist upon method to ensure against the intrusion of interest or idiosyncracy, or even that they exalt subjectivity as a corrective to the excesses of objectivity, as Black did in the preface to the 1978 reissue of *Rhetorical Criticism.* More frequently, the issue of stance is passed over completely or treated with ambivalence. Most current commentators take their lead from the Committee on the Advancement and Refinement of Rhetorical Criticism, which suggested that criticism is best when "the critic immerses himself in particulars and at the same time stands, psychologically, at a distance from them. . . . Theory is made richer by the critic's involvement in the events he studies; theory is made clearer by his transcendence of those events" (Sloan, et al. 224). Likewise, Malcolm Sillars implies that all criticism is always already evaluative, no matter what its stance (3–4), but he classifies three critical approaches as "objectivist," and is able to distinguish value analysis from ideological critique on the grounds that the former is more "objective" (148). Karyn Rybacki and Donald Rybacki claim that "the problems posed by subjectivity" can be "overcome" (13). Hart suggests that the critic's "special discernment" is the capacity "to stand simultaneously in the midst of and apart from the events experienced," and to "point out features that the too-involved" individual would miss because of "the immediacy and excitement of the event itself" (*Modern Rhetorical Criticism* 33). Foss goes so far as to emphasize the subjectivity of the critic:

> Subjectivity is acknowledged . . . when the critic admits interest in and involvement with the artifact and explains the nature of the interest and involvement: "I became intrigued with this film because of how I responded to it" or "I worked on the campaign to elect Jesse Jackson," for example. The critic also acknowledges subjectivity by revealing to the reader experiences and values that affect the critic's perceptions and judgments—"I am a Democrat," "I am a feminist," "I grew up in the late Sixties," "I like abstract art," "I do not own a television." (*Rhetorical Criticism* 25)

One difficulty with Foss's account is that it is counterfactual; it is extremely rare for critics to reveal their own interests, personal characteristics, or habits in their professional writings.[40] The other is that to call involvement and personal characteristics "subjective" is simply to reproduce the subject-object dualism grounding traditional empiricist science, while favoring the other half of the pair. Such attempts to purge criticism of objectivism are doomed to the extent that they are partial attempts. So long as *part* of the collection of objectivist tenets is retained as grounds for rejecting *other,* perhaps more obviously objectionable parts, the overall philosophical position remains secure—incoherent, but secure.

Moreover, the critical community remains resistant to impulses that clearly culminate in judgment or action. The energetic—not to say hysterical—reaction from some to Philip Wander's 1983 essay, "The Ideological Turn in Modern Criticism," was one notorious case of such resistance.[41] Similarly, while critical approaches found under the general rubrics of feminism and poststructuralism (including deconstruction) may share little in common with one another beyond the impulse to question authority and dislodge traditional ways of thinking, those who write criticism from such stances have met with their share of resistance and antipathy as well. Foss observes that "Feminist criticism . . . is often met with hostility, defensiveness, or amusement. It strikes many students, associate editors, and editors as inappropriately political or ideological" ("Constituted by Agency" 47). And, while Hart apparently tries to give deconstruction a hearing in his textbook, his account fails to live up to any standard of fairness save equal time. It is difficult to be impressed with the evenhandedness of statements like: "Deconstructionists win few popularity contests" (386); or "Deconstructionists are often accused of being anarchists, who treat communication as an impossibility and who are, as a result, nothing more than radical debunkers" (386–87). It is significant that Hart classifies deconstruction as a form of ideological criticism, since most deconstructionists distance themselves from ideological critique.[42] But critical to our point is that Hart's scheme of classification allows him to set different so-called "ideological critics" off against each other:

> Marxists charge that postmodernists—or deconstructionists, as they are often called when operating as critics—play wasteful semantic games and that feminists are politically naive. Feminists resent the paternalism of Marxists but agree with them that deconstructionists play wasteful semantic games. For their part, deconstructionists feel that Marxists are tedious moralizers, that feminists take rhetoric too seriously, and that they, the deconstructionists, play wasteful semantic games but that that is the only game in town. (*Modern Rhetorical Criticism* 383)

Setting aside what some would view as inaccuracies in this account, note that these different groups of "ideological critics" have consumed each other before the chapter about them is three pages old.[43] Certainly, there may be other defensible reasons to resist ideological, feminist, and poststructuralist critiques. But it seems no accident that these forms of critique, all thematizing power, frequently culminating in judgment, and typically articulating the need for fundamental change, have encountered the resistance they have.

Critics' emphasis on method also signals a residual impulse toward the objectivity sustained by scientism. Even the choice of the terms, "method" and "methodology," suggests a scientistic influence. Critics' elaborations of "method" make the case even more clearly. Hart, for example, suggests a need for "methodologies for treating the message as a dependent variable" ("Theory-Building" 76). Lawrence Rosenfield proposes as a "methodological" concern the critic's need to decide "what sorts of measurements or readings" to take on the text (104); he suggests that the critic's reasons are "the product of 'measurement' " (103); and he elaborates various "permutations" of four "variables" (source, message, environment, critic) that articulate the stance of the critic (104–5). Method has been and continues to be of prime concern to most critics. Brock, Scott, and Chesebro claim that "methodological statements" function as a kind of "shorthand" for the choices a critic makes (510). Foss takes the point further, arguing that "what we know in the area of rhetorical criticism has come largely from a featuring of agency or method; our knowledge about criticism and the beliefs we hold about it are methodologically derived" ("Constituted by Agency" 35).

Even though critics do not now frequently claim, at least not explicitly, that their methods are their guarantors of objectivity, the continued significance of method suggests that some will toward objectivity remains, despite the relative scarcity of claims to it. That impulse does manifest itself, for instance, in the reassurance of "reliability" or the "replicability" of studies. Brockriede, for example, suggested that the critic attempts a "degree of intersubjective reliability" by risking argumentative confrontation ("Rhetorical Criticism" 167). He continued:

> when a critic advances a significant argument about a concrete rhetorical experience or about a general concept of rhetoric, a reader can confront it usefully. If he tries to disconfirm the critic's argument and fails to do so, the intersubjective reliability of that argument is increased. If he can disconfirm or cast doubt about the critic's argument, that argument must be abandoned or revised. (174)

Although Brockriede understood reliability to rest upon the potential for argument, and not upon method, the *desire* for reliability nevertheless signals a will toward objectivity.[44] Hart clearly places his confidence in the capacity of critical methods to enable replication: "Because theory necessarily builds upon some convergence or replication of insight, it would behoove some of us to refine our analytical tools so that others in the field can share in the 'how' as well as in the 'what' of our researches" ("Theory-Building" 73). Thomas Farrell seems to agree, advancing several standards for judging "non-scientific" approaches to communication, one of which is methodological rigor. Farrell poses the criterion as a question: "Could others employing the method find approximately the same things?" ("Beyond Science" 124).

The honest answer to Farrell's question, if it were posed of virtually any approach to rhetorical criticism, probably would be in the negative. Most of these approaches do not really qualify as "methods," in any meaningful sense, to begin with. They are more properly conceptual heuristics or vocabularies; they may invite a critic to interesting ways of reading a text, but they do not have the procedural rigor or systematicity that typically characterizes a method. In fact, it is arguable that they are at their best, critically, when they are least rigorous "methodologically." Still, many critics treat them as if they were equivalent to the analytic methods and instruments of science, and as if they provided a direct and universal-access bridge for the critic between "data" and theoretical generalizations.

Just as in the sciences, methods are taken by critics to be the tools with which one must be equipped in order to test hypotheses and build theory. Theory testing and building are thus two sides of the same coin for some critics. Brummett describes theory testing as understood by rhetorical critics:

> Many rhetoricians view rhetorical criticism as the means to test the regularities asserted by rhetorical theory; criticism is to rhetorical theory what experiment and other methods are to social science theory. . . . Although Clevenger sees criticism as primarily descriptive, he explicitly argues that it can and should *test* a rhetorical theory. Farrell's theoretical 'models' are informed and tested by criticism. ("Rhetorical Theory" 97–98)[45]

Foss completes the picture with her description of theory building:

> The findings of the analysis may be shown to confirm some tenet of rhetorical theory. . . . The critic also may discover that some principles or constructs in rhetorical theory need to be modified or qualified to make them more accurate or to provide more useful explanations of a rhetorical process. . . . Another way in which the critic may contribute to rhetorical theory is by formulating a new model or theory. The critic may discover that the theoretical model used for the comparison simply does not accommodate the discoveries made in the analysis and that a new theoretical explanation is needed for how a rhetorical process works. (23–24)

Foss's description demonstrates how theory "testing" leads to theory "building," on this view. And her language ("findings," "confirm," "discover," "constructs," "accurate," "explanation") seems to confirm the analogy Brummett draws between criticism and scientific method.

However, hypothesis testing is a questionable analog for rhetorical criticism. Black claims that "there is not a single case in the literature of our field in which a rhetorical theory has been abandoned as a result of having failed an application of criticism" ("A Note" 333). And Brummett argues that "rhetorical theory is *never* tested in the sense that social science theories are" ("Rhetorical Theory" 98). He explains: "A critic who finds that he or she cannot apply fantasy theme analysis to a piece of discourse will simply turn to Burke, Aristotle, or some other theory, and the 'failure' of the rejected theory never sees the light of published day" ("Rhetorical Theory" 99). Yet despite the apparent accuracy of Black's and Brummett's assessments, critics continue to claim for criticism the capacity to test rhetorical theories.

In all of this scientistic labyrinth, what of the text, the rhetoric, that a rhetorical critic engages? It does make an appearance in these accounts, all too often described as "data," "evidence," "case studies," or "samples."[46] The rhetoric that critics take up in their work is thus typically reduced methodologically to fodder with which to fill the theoretical silo. Campbell's position is perhaps the most blunt, claiming, "what must be specified are the factors that constitute critical excellence and critical outcomes or objectives that contribute to rhetorical *theory*. At this level, criticism and theory are indistinguishable" ("Criticism" 11). Campbell adds, "what we learn about the specific rhetorical acts is secondary; they become illustrations or means through which the reader apprehends the nature of symbolic processes themselves" ("Criticism" 12). Foss agrees: "Criticism no longer serves a useful purpose if it has been devoted exclusively to an understanding of a particular artifact" (*Rhetorical Criticism* 6). Hart goes so far as to suggest— twice—that "the rhetoric of plumbers' conventions, the proselytizing which occurs at meetings of the Catholic War Veterans, [and] the dialectic at the local city council meeting" would be more useful objects of the critic's attention than a presidential campaign. They are more typical, more ubiqui- tous, and therefore pay more "theoretical dividends" ("Theory-Building" 72; "Contemporary Scholarship" 293). The basic point appears to be that it does not matter much *what* text one chooses for criticism, because "all texts are filled with data" (Hart, *Modern Rhetorical Criticism* 45).

What remains evident, however, is the move to reduce the critical essay to a commodity or product. The Committee on the Advancement and Refinement of Rhetorical Criticism referred to this product as "findings" (Sloan, et al. 226, 227). Andrews suggests that a critic "must be able to communicate to others the results of his or her critical observation and inquiry" (5). Foss picks up the terminology of both: "The report of the findings of the analysis constitutes the bulk of the essay. . . . The critic tells what has been discovered from an application of the method to the artifact and provides support for the discoveries from the data of the artifact" (*Rhetorical Criticism* 21). Of course, the terms "findings" and "results" are not themselves problematic. The difficulty is that they are deadly accurate in describing the scope of a critical essay—it has become a product, not a representation or exploration of the critical practices behind the product.

However even if, for purposes of argument, we accepted the scientistic suggestion that it is appropriate for a critical essay to be merely a product, a report of findings, we would quickly encounter an even thornier problem: assessing the quality of this product. We may then ask, what has criticism provided us? What are its results, its findings? What theory has it built or modified—rather than merely borrowing for its purposes? Perhaps the focal irony of the scientization of criticism, and the point at which we will culminate our discussion of it, is crystalized in Gregg's astute, if offhand, observation that "whether, if at all, the explorations of rhetorical critics have contributed to our theoretical understanding of human rhetorical behavior" is a "question that has not received much attention" (42).

We regard the studied silence of media and rhetorical criticism on this point, compared to the optimism of modern science, as extremely telling. The question is a potentially embarrassing one, in two senses. On its face, it raises the possibility that criticism is not making proper progress toward what should be the goal of any professional discipline: contributing significantly to an encompassing "theoretical understanding" of its subject area. But if in fact it means—as we suspect it does—that critics should be questioning the very legitimacy of this goal, this is only slightly less uncomfortable, since it forces us to question norms that have at least served to organize our sense of ourselves as critics and professionals, and to set out instead into what must surely seem uncharted waters. The silence of criticism on its own ultimate theoretical productivity thus emphasizes the poor fit between a scientized model of professionalism and contemporary critical practice.

Disengagement of Critical Experience

As we suggested earlier, in the drive to unify a discipline, a guild is produced that comes to sanction only research activity as truly professional work. The will to knowledge that pervades this professional guild diminishes the importance of other realms of activity, such as teaching and participation in political or social groups. And it segregates such larger community involvement from the experience of professional culture. The broad professional demand for knowledge production certainly has contributed to the scientization of criticism. In addition, though, criticism's scientistic posture produces and is reproduced by the balkanization of the critic's domains of experience and knowledge.

It probably is true that whatever public or civic voice rhetorical criticism originally had came from critics who, in the early years of the discipline, took their civic duty to be teaching—preparing young men and women to be active, vocal participants in their culture. Critical pedagogy took a conservative form of which many of us might now disapprove; it frequently held up "masterpieces" of oratory or the careers of great orators as models to be studied and emulated.[47] But the connection of criticism to pragmatic, civil affairs was clear and proximate (Thonssen and Baird 22), and the classroom was the link between the two. Also clear was the recognition that the texts produced in the larger community had material effects on individuals in real situations, and that rhetorical critics, therefore, had the "responsibility of considering the ethical implications of public statements" (Thonssen and Baird 471).[48]

As the goal of knowledge production grew in importance to become the primary task of the academic professional, however, the links between the scholarly, pedagogical, and public realms were altered. By all appearances, it is the students who have fared the worst in the change. The students' role as an audience to professional criticism is frequently one of apprentice to master. Those who do become academic professionals themselves, therefore, are equipped to provide continuity to the knowledge-production industry. But those who do not—and this is the great majority of students—may well leave the university culture knowing more about how to be citizens of the academic community than they do about ways of being, thinking, and acting in a larger, public culture.

Often crucial to this academic citizenship is at least a *Jeopardy*-level familiarity with the frequently opaque language of the professionalized critic. As a test, we conducted a haphazard tour through three rhetorical criticism textbooks—not scholarly journals, but *textbooks*—and in about twenty minutes generated a partial listing of the professional critical argot academic critics inflict upon their students, an incomplete lexicon in English, Greek, Latin, and *faux*-French already numbering in the neighborhood of one hundred terms. (Germanisms had, by the time of our test, apparently come into vogue and passed back out again.)[49] Yet even if modern academic criticism were more intelligible to students, it still would only rarely speak to the hearts of such readers, "who must often wonder where the joy and appreciation is to be found in such a tedious and officious activity" (Nothstine and Copeland 22). So while students do, technically, count as an audience or market for professional criticism, they are for the most part a captive audience, whom academic critics treat with the disrespect of being frequently inaccessible and almost always disconnected from *their* interests and concerns.

The larger, general public, as a potential "audience" for professional criticism, seems to have even less of an obvious stake in listening to professional critics. Members of that group are unlikely to be much interested in the "results" of the critic's "findings," except in those cases where these readers' concrete concerns might be addressed. But to the extent that professional critics seem to value the concrete, situated event only as "data" for theoretical generalizations, as springboards for their feats of scholarly virtuosity, not as interested, consequential discourse, communities outside the academy are unlikely to find their concrete concerns noticed, much less addressed and engaged. Brock, Scott, and Chesebro observe that "if [critics] are interested in influencing society, they will almost certainly be required to convey an evaluative judgment" (506). But the scientization of criticism has rendered judgment, or any other form of engaged reaction,[50] as incidental at best to the critical work. Thus, professional critics' construal of their own professionalism alienates them from the potential public audience. But this alienation, in turn, reinforces the tendency toward scientism; if the

□ Critical Invention: A General Orientation

public at large is not an audience, then the obvious audience consists of other professionals, who do value theoretical virtuosity.

It is occasionally fashionable (and the last decade has been one of those occasions) to lament the extraordinary and unwholesome influence that academics have on American society. We have listened as a former vice president of the United States, for example, attacked the "cultural elite" of the academy, media, and performing arts. At about the same time, a former secretary of education bemoaned the pernicious agenda apparently underlying the movement toward "diversity" and "multiculturalism" on American campuses. However, with apologies to Dan Quayle, William Bennett, and the rest of academia's detractors, it seems clear that the delicate fabric of society is in no danger from radicals (or anyone else) who are members of the academic critical culture.

The lines of possible contact with society, from either the left or the right on campuses, are all but severed for rhetorical and media critics as with their colleagues in other disciplines. Jacoby explains: "This conservative nightmare lifts with any daytime inspection of universities. What happened to the swarms of academic leftists? The answer is surprising: Nothing surprising. The ordinary realities of bureaucratization and employment took over" (134). As Said writes of leftist literary critics, "Eagleton, [Frederic] Jameson, and [Frank] Lentricchia are literary Marxists who write for literary Marxists, who are in cloistral seclusion from the inhospitable world of real politics" (22). Samuel Becker notes the same trend toward political disengagement in media studies, particularly in the United States. Rhetorical critics too are engaged, with rare exceptions, only with and by others of their professional kind. Scholarly critics and their criticism today scarcely participate in a public culture; to accuse them of *undue* influence is therefore to charge them with an offense of which they are altogether innocent.

The public is thus quite safe from academic criticism. In exchange, academic critics themselves are guaranteed a large measure of safety of a very different sort. The professional culture rewards critics in several ways for remaining in the professional role of *non*participant observer. One of the rewards is the designation of "expertise," which we address in the next section. Another is material reward in the forms of hierarchical and monetary advancement in the university culture.

But the cloistering of critics and the sanctioning of the professional critical role it generates seems to guarantee critics even more. Campbell suggests that "social criticism . . . will not be enduring; its importance and its functions are immediate and ephemeral." But by contrast, " 'academic' or 'professional' criticism can make an enduring contribution to the discipline" ("Criticism" 11). Thus, the durability of professional work is what recommends it; the desire to immortalize ourselves in that work seems to be the animating force. Hart makes the reward even more explicit in his suggestion that we forsake *"anecdotal fixation,* an over-extended concern for the details of time and place," for the *"conceptual record,"* the "only record that will outlive us" ("Contemporary Scholarship" 284, 285).

This "immortality" from "enduring contribution to the discipline," however, must be weighed against the contributions critics might otherwise have made to any public culture. By that measure, "immortality" shows itself to be a Faustian bargain indeed. As Richard Cherwitz and John Theobald-Osborne observe,

> After reading highly specialized rhetorical accounts of messages, one is often left with the question: Of what value is such criticism to those in society who transmit and receive communication? Or more specifically, To what extent can the insights gleaned by scholarly criticism be used constructively to promote better politics? These questions are more than trivial; for at core, the rhetorical art is a practical one, an art that we intuitively know makes a difference for the vast majority of people not ensconced in academe. It is for this reason that critics cannot sidestep or ignore such questions. (73)

One of the reasons rhetorical and media critics cannot avoid these questions is the nature of the texts they study: "The underlying pedagogical and scholarly assumption of our discipline is that communication has the power: to arouse emotions; influence the direction, intensity, and salience of beliefs; transform and nurture the development of ideas; and instigate action" (Cherwitz and Theobald-Osborne 52). Another is the question of what some critics might actually wish to do. Philip Wander and Steven Jenkins's poignant questions are worth our serious reflection:

> Let us suppose that a critic honestly became emotionally involved with his subject—that he found it important down to the very ground of his being. Are we to tell him to write about it as though he were not so interested; are we to suggest that he write about something less involving? Are we, in other words, to request the critic, for professional purposes, either to lie about or to ignore what to him is vitally important? (446)

Unfortunately, because of the ideological forces we have been examining, the professional critic must answer, "Yes." Professional critics are not in the business of involvement and advocacy; the nature of their work, as it is currently construed, demands neutrality and seeks theoretical explanation. As a result, the possibility for critics and their criticism to serve as a genuine source of knowledge, power, or ethics in a public culture is diminished almost to zero.

Disciplining Critics and Criticism

The rise of modern departments of speech in universities took place shortly after the ideology of professionalism in American higher education began to take shape. The effects of disciplinization are not always easy to demonstrate, because disciplines are in all respects artificial abstractions, with years of accreted right and privilege, and because the very idea of a "discipline" is so familiar that it is almost invisible.[51] However, it occasionally does appear explicitly as a justification or excuse for some practice or habit, as in Hart's metaphorical warning: "Many of us in public address feel greater kinship with our colleagues in departments of history than with our cousins in speech communication studying compliance-gaining. I believe that that is a dangerous condition because it frustrates the development of holistic and analytically precise theories of human communication" ("Contemporary Scholarship" 285). Hart reminds his readers of the professional necessity of border guarding and the dangers associated with consorting with those of another disciplinary clan—our theory construction efforts will be victimized.

A more common, and telling, metaphor for the discipline is that of an economic community, within which Hart's disciplinary "kinship systems" barter goods and products. Herman Cohen, for example, observes that "the trade balance with related fields is negative. We import much more than we export. We frequently cite the work of other fields but our work is seldom cited" (287). Charles Berger virtually echoes Cohen: "The field of communication has been suffering and continues to suffer from an intellectual trade deficit with respect to related disciplines; the field imports much more than it exports" (102).

These metaphors both display and reinforce the ideology giving rise to our understanding of critical (and other) scholarship as commodity or product. They also expose disciplinarity as the restrictive and even xenophobic mechanism that it is, screening out contact with members (and ideas) of other disciplines and keeping the product "homegrown," as Berger quaintly puts it (104). For members of the profession, the product's quality often seems to be of less concern than the "Made in Speech Communication" label sewn into the lining.[52]

Supporting the research edifice and the entire professional structure, for better or worse, is the reward and punishment system explicit in disciplinarity. "Discipline," after all, is a verb as well as a noun. It is worth considering how these collective entities we call disciplines go about the work of "disciplining" individuals, rewarding decorum and good judgment, and penalizing or "correcting" inappropriate or "bad" behavior.

The grant of the title, "expert," must be counted among the principal rewards the disciplinary system can offer. In fact, it follows as a necessary entailment of the system. Because disciplines are specialized and rigidly bounded by educational and productivity requirements, they are peopled by specialists—"experts." The experts maintain their expertise to the extent that they do what the system demands, that is, contribute to "knowledge production." If scientism has created rigid and narrow criteria for what counts as knowledge, disciplinarity tends and maintains those requirements. It grants status only to those whose work meets those rigid criteria. The reward system is, as we commented earlier, inherently conservative, but it also is potentially disabling to criticism.

Critics, perhaps critics of rhetoric and media especially, are vulnerable in such a system of reward, since they study texts generated in public and popular cultures, texts that anyone who inhabits these cultures presumably already finds intelligible to some degree. Thus, when Eagleton describes the "contradiction on which criticism finally runs aground—one between an inchoate amateurism and a socially marginal professionalism" (*Function* 69), there must be some resonance for rhetorical and media critics, perhaps even more than for the literary critics with whom Eagleton is concerned. Professional critics' students and fellow citizens probably believe that they have a fair grasp of what they hear and see going on about them. Their colleagues in other academic departments probably dare to presume that they do, as well. So, how—without the professionally sanctioned title of "expert"—can an academic critic claim any more authority on such matters than any other reasonably observant, thoughtful individual?

This tension emerges rather clearly in criticism textbooks. Andrews distinguishes between critics as "serious" students of rhetoric and others who will seek to make intelligent responses to public discourse (4), and between "trained professionals" and "casual observers" (14). Similarly, Foss suggests that "we engage in the process of rhetorical criticism constantly and often unconsciously," but that adeptness and discrimination are acquired by "formal training" (*Rhetorical Criticism* 3). Hart follows suit: "Everyone is capable of doing rhetorical criticism without ever reading *Modern Rhetorical Criticism*. By having lived and talked for several decades or more, all of us have done the homework necessary to do criticism" (*Modern Rhetorical Criticism* 36). But, as he later suggests, "it is possible to become more perceptive as critics if we (1) adopt a useful set of critical attitudes and (2) ask the right sorts of questions when inspecting rhetoric" (*Modern Rhetorical Criticism* 40). Andrews also makes very clear what he considers necessary to the expert: "Becoming a critic involves the careful practice of a craft. The rhetorical critic 'practices' in the sense that any professional does, through the continuous application of specialized knowledge to situations for which he or she is trained" (61). Walter Fisher concurs, suggesting that "everyone engages in critical acts; few elevate them into an art form. The principal difference between the ordinary criticizer and the critic is knowledge" (76). He continues:

> The critic possesses special, comprehensive knowledge of the nature and functions of the objects and acts that he examines. He has at his command a wide range of models to choose from, a fine sense of the appropriateness of given models in the evaluation of particular objects of criticism, a capacity to make his

models explicit, if necessary, and he can cite attractive, convincing reasons to justify his judgments. (76)

While the tension between amateurism and expertise shows itself here, so does its approved means of resolution—professional knowledge. Small wonder that critics are highly motivated to contribute to theory and to construct elaborate technical apparatuses that enable the scientistic project. It is precisely such work, not their practical insights into public culture, that separates them from amateurs. The reward system effectively reinforces both the scientistic impulse and the civic and experiential detachment attendant upon the professional ideology. Thus, the "decorum" and "good judgment" that are rewarded by disciplinarity with the badge of "expertise" are precisely those actions that support and contribute to the ideology of professionalism.

As we suggested earlier, a discipline may also be prepared to encourage a judicious silence on the value of criticism's theoretical output. The peculiar abstractness of disciplinarity may help to explain how critics collectively have managed to avoid Gregg's important question: Have the explorations of rhetorical critics contributed to our theoretical understanding of human rhetorical behavior? Although it is the discipline that provides outlets for publications, advocacy on behalf of its members, conferences, and career placement services, it does not produce scholarship; individuals do. Individuals are rewarded (or sanctioned) for their research "production." If a research product is "good," judged by whatever measures, the discipline is enhanced, along with the individual researcher. For example, Hart notes with approval "the *field's* growing ability to produce scholarly books" ("Rhetorical Research" 2. Emphasis added). However, the same does not seem to be true in reverse. If a research product is "not good," judged by whatever measures, it is the fault of the individual. For example, Berger speculates that "it is possible that persons seeking advanced degrees in communication are, for some unknown reasons, risk averse, and therefore not particularly motivated to develop theory" (108).

Thus, it may be that we as a discipline have managed to avoid answering Gregg's question by virtue of the disciplinary truth that scholarship is not done by disciplines but by individuals.[53] That is, while the discipline is portrayed as the site of opportunity—the economy, to extend the earlier metaphor—individuals are understood as those who do or do not avail themselves of opportunities to produce. Thus, the question of what "the discipline" or a subfield has "produced" can be dismissed, for the discipline is not the producer but only the site of production. Of course, this is a naive view of material conditions and of individual autonomy, but it is a convenient naiveté. By clinging to it, disciplinarity is able to prop up an enterprise that has done little to assess the "products" of its own labor. It does so by allowing critics the luxury of never having to pose the question of what their own work, taken collectively, has produced. Unburdened by the appearance of any evidence to the contrary, the members of a discipline are thus free to assume that they are making collective progress, in the best scientistic tradition, toward the grand professional goal of increasing "our theoretical understanding of human rhetorical behavior."

Disciplinarity also contains negative mechanisms to reinforce adherence to the professional ideology. The most obvious of these are also the most materially consequential. In academia, individuals are disciplined, kept in line as it were, by the repressiveness of the tenure and promotion system. An individual is very unlikely to succeed in that system without the explicit approval of disciplinary colleagues—journal editors and referees, writers of recommendations and endorsements, and so forth. Another such repressive mechanism is the "analysis of research productivity." These are heavily quantified lists tracking, for example, the appearance of a scholar's work in the citations of fellow scholars' publications, or ranking the "most prolific scholars" in the discipline, based upon the numbers of articles published in particular journals. The justification typically offered for the compiling and publication of these bibliometric exercises is their asserted ability to provide "a yardstick by which to measure the research productivity of a faculty member" (Hickson, Stacks, and Amsbury, "An Analysis" 231). But one can certainly be forgiven for wondering whether such a "yardstick" is to be used as a measure or as a cudgel. Because of these mechanisms, the individual *must*, at least to a large degree, speak the community's discourse—and had better speak it a lot, too. To do otherwise is to risk deferrals of one's own advancement, or even unemployment. And even this serves the discipline's larger interests: after all, the fewer "experts" there are, the more precious their expertise must seem.

But other, less obvious, instruments of discipline make nonconformity "merely" uncomfortable rather than dangerous. In speaking outside the culturally cloistered, scientistic, disciplinary discourse, the academic critic runs the risk of being thought an oddball or worse. No one had to wander far at Speech Communication Association conventions in 1982 and 1989, for example, to overhear multiple, whispered conversations about Thomas Benson's "Another Shooting in Cowtown," and Michael Pacanowsky's "Slouching Toward Chicago." The reaction to such nontraditional scholarship runs the full spectrum, from *sotto voce* remarks about iconoclasm to publicly expressed complaints about those who rely upon or emulate the work of "limp-wristed, incomprehensible, beret-wearing leftists"—a characterization actually uttered publicly at a professional convention, we are both surprised and dismayed to report. This chapter, in fact, runs similar risks, for it not only speaks from at least partly outside the professional community's discourse, but also seeks explicitly to displace that way of speaking. And, of course, we are also implicating ourselves herein to the extent that our own voices have participated in the discipline's standard discourse. The three of us, along with the contributors to this volume, are consequently flirting with charges of high treason, lunacy, or both. The scientization and consequent depoliticization of criticism thus serve yet another purpose: They guard against the possibility that the critic will expose the professional system to scrutiny.

▨ Recovering Critical Invention from the Void

At the outset of this essay, we specifically exempted ourselves from having to provide answers to the problems we were going to raise. But we were careful to make no such ingenious promises about expressing hope, because in fact we do have some hope for professional critics, beginning critics, and their criticism.

If criticism were *absolutely* professionalized, following the dictates of the disciplinary voice we have reconstructed and explored in this chapter, the critic's inventional procedures would be all too clear. The critic would choose a text to study purely because of its representativeness or its unique-ness (Sillars 19). The "representative" text would help the critic in building a theory (Hart, "Theory-Building" 72); the "unique" text would aid in "testing its limits" (Rybacki and Rybacki 11). Once finished with this blood-less task of choosing a text, the critic would select the appropriate method for isolating and analyzing its "data." The method would discipline the critic's gaze toward only those features of the text that were relevant to the theoretical objective. The critic would render a theoretical conclusion and go on to locate another text to exploit in the same manner, while another critic might conduct a reliability check, by replicating the first "critical" venture.

If anyone actually believed that this was a fair and accurate rendition of what critics do, who would ever decide to be a critic? And if there were any critics still to be found, who would read their relentlessly dreary work? We believe that the answer to both questions is obvious: *no one would.* And this is what gives us cause for hope, even in the shadow of the professional edifice. As much as we believe that critical work in speech communication might sometimes be more interesting than it is—and we do think that from time to time—*none* of it, even on its worst days, is so utterly stupefying as the professional ideology would suggest that it should be. In fact, the critics whose words we have appropriated here to reconstruct the traces of the professional ideology—Andrews, Black, Brock, Scott, Chesebro, Campbell, Fisher, Foss, Gregg, Hart, and the rest—do not *ever* write colorless criticism; their work is engaging and provocative, sometimes delightfully maddening.

Thus, while we have no compelling or demonstrative proof, we must confess to several hunches about critics and their inventional practices. We think most critics probably choose to study particular texts because those texts interest them, whether or not they have any intrinsic or immediately obvious potential for theory contribution. We believe critics take up their practice in part because the experience itself of criticism—that vital energy and sense of moral and intellectual engagement—draws them forward. Most critics, we believe, *become* critics for reasons other than to build explanatory theories and generate "results," desiring to understand in some way how they and their readers can and should react to events in the world. And finally, we suspect that critics are at least as interested in affecting the public cultures of which they are a part as they are in being entombed in a desiccated "most prolific scholars" list.[54]

If our speculations are correct, it does these writers and teachers a grave injustice to call their observations about these texts either "objective" in the sense of being neutral, or "reliable" in the sense of being replicable (Nothstine 161–63). And if we are correct, we have located the starting point for our search to retrieve the question of critical invention in the gap between the dictates of professional ideology and the practices and experiences of critics.

But even believing, as we do, that critics and their work are not *absolutely* scientized, disengaged, and disciplined, professionalism remains the dominant discourse that the critical community speaks. As such, professionalism disciplines its adherents at least to *appear* to conform. One of the clearest ways in which critics keep up this appearance is by concealing or at least leaving unarticulated their inventional practices. They do so because they are too messy, involved, uncertain, and unscientific—in short, too "unprofessional," in the most pleasing sense of that word—to conform to the ideals of disciplinary discourse.

But critics' silence about their inventional practices has consequences. First, it catches critics up in the uncomfortable stance of arguing that inquiry in the sciences and human sciences is fundamentally rhetorical while not acknowledging the rhetorical character of their own inquiry.[55] Second, critics' silence helps to maintain and reproduce the professional ideology. It allows critics to mime and even parody science (Eagleton 92), actually believing somehow that the goals and practices of critical inquiry resemble those of the sciences; or it allows critics to continue with practices that they do not examine and to which they do not admit because they *pretend* subscription to the professional, scientistic creed. But perhaps the most serious consequences of this silence are in the criticism classroom.

Critical Invention in the Classroom

Faced with the first assignment in the criticism class, the first response of the student—the beginning critic—might reasonably be, "Where do I *start*? How do I know what's worth *doing?*" Fair questions—indeed, crucial questions—but as long as the norms of professional criticism are reproduced without examination in criticism courses, no consistent and practical answer is likely to be forthcoming, for these are precisely the points where professional criticism remains silent. Criticism textbooks are illustrative of this problem, but they are *not* themselves the problem; they reflect the difficulties anyone encounters in teaching criticism that is still in the thrall of the professional ideology. Andrews is certainly right to observe: "One of the rhetorical critic's first problems is deciding where to begin. If one is going to undertake to explicate and interpret the rhetorical dimensions of a particular message, be it a speech, a pamphlet, an editorial, or a proclamation, it makes obvious and good sense to begin with the message itself" (16). But *what* message? And why that message? And having begun with that message, what now?

Hart offers a position on how *not* to choose: "No message is inherently worthy of study. Just because a given text fascinates the critic does not mean that study of it will be worthwhile" (*Modern Rhetorical Criticism* 46). Foss and Sillars, as well as Brock, Scott, and Chesebro, all might soften this position to some extent, maintaining that critics may legitimately choose for criticism those texts they are interested in (Brock, Scott, and Chesebro 10; Foss, *Rhetorical Criticism* 5–6; and Sillars 18–19). But Foss cautions that, while the text might be "of interest to the critic," it should also be "capable of generating insight about rhetorical processes" (*Rhetorical Criticism* 11). Brock, Scott, and Chesebro sound a similar warning:

> Any criticism will automatically have a starting point, even though critics do not consciously make such decisions. However, if these decisions are consciously made (which in some cases will mean that critics seek to uncover their perspectives), they can be more certain that the decisions are consistent with their materials, their purposes, and the sorts of judgments they intend to make. (505)

They make their point more concisely, if more obliquely, when they advise critics to "pick products that will be fruitful to criticize" (14).

Yet this is a circular answer to the problem—for one could hardly expect to know whether criticizing "the product" will be fruitful, or capable of generating insight, after all, until one has already begun to engage it as a critic. Despite Scott, Brock, and Chesebro's good intentions, neither beginning critics nor experienced critics are very likely to *know* "the sorts of judgments they intend to make" before they begin the groping, circular process of critical invention.

Even if the problems of selecting a text for critical investigation are temporarily set aside, however, the difficulties continue, for decisions must be made regarding how to approach the text, what to ask of it or say about it. That road, too, is lined with danger signs. Andrews, for example, warns that "many questions will be irrelevant or of minor significance in certain cases" (62). Both he and Hart hold out the promise that the critic's sophistication and ability to know what kinds of questions to pose will increase with "maturity" (Andrews 62; Hart, *Modern Rhetorical Criticism* 45), which may be the case, but is unlikely to offer much help or comfort in the here-and-now to the critic who is not yet "matured."

Another way that textbook authors often handle the problem of critical invention is a logical response to this dilemma: provide beginning critics with questions to pose of texts (Andrews; Foss; and Hart). Providing the questions leads to other issues, however. For example, why these questions and not others? At least this question is easier to answer: The questions provided are ones that the discourse of the professional critical community recognizes as appropriate or important. But what if a critic wishes to pose a question that is not "approved" by that community? Surely that question should not therefore be dismissed as illegitimate. This issue may be the most troublesome, because it contains the insidious potential for automatically dismissing an individual critic's own interest in favor of the concerns of the professional community.[56]

The same effect, privileging the concerns of the professional community, results from providing beginning critics with professional critics' published essays to study, since once again it asks readers to guess at the hidden *process* by studying the completed *product.* Andrews's comments on the critical essays anthologized in his textbook are typical of this pedagogical strategy: "The samples demonstrate the results of combining imagination and scholarship to reach critical conclusions. These studies are, of course, the work of mature critics, and beginning students are unlikely to emulate them. But the studies do provide points of departure for discussion and may serve as stimulants to students' own critical work" (xii). The problems here are evident: The critical essays demonstrate the *results* of imagination and scholarship but contain not a hint about the process by which imagination and scholarship bring about the result, for the reasons we have devoted this chapter to exposing.

Brock, Scott, and Chesebro's discussion reveals the same lapse between description of the critical impulse and the final product, even as they recognize that a critic "must form his or her own discourse":

This is not intended to be a handbook on the mechanics of writing critical essays. . . . We hope this text goes behind the mechanics of writing criticism to the theory and method involved. We have sought to identify perspectives and approaches that are likely to be of value to the rhetorical critic. We hope to raise some important questions about junctures at which the critic must make decisions that will shape specific pieces of criticism. We believe that the essays included within this volume are apt to remain important to the substance of rhetorical criticism into the foreseeable future. At the same time, we have included essays that should stand as illustrations not only of each method but of critical writing. (22)

Later, they remind the reader that "we have included applications of each method because we wanted to maintain a link with the actual writing of rhetorical criticism" (502–4). But the essays, of course, can reveal nothing of the *link* to writing; that link is invention, and its presence and operation have been concealed to the greatest extent possible by the ideological mechanisms we have been tracing throughout this chapter. So again, the beginning critic is left with no choice but to *attempt* to emulate the goals and norms of these professional writings as they indirectly show themselves in published essays, and hope for the best.

Foss takes a different approach, although she also includes illustrative critical essays. She addresses the "process of producing an essay of criticism," and "provides guidelines for the critic concerning . . . (1) discovery of the rhetorical artifact and research question; (2) formulation of the critical method; (3) critical analysis of the artifact; and (4) writing the critical essay" (*Rhetorical Criticism* 11). Foss's attempt to deal with this process is a crucial effort; each of the four moments she describes constitutes at least a locus for the choices that the critic must make. However, the process of choice as she describes it soon becomes ossified as a set of regulatory, mechanistic apparatuses. In treating the eight "methods" of criticism included in the text, for example, Foss reduces each of them to a series of prescribed, businesslike techniques. Neo-Aristotelian criticism is thus routinized into the procedures of "reconstruction of context," "analysis of the rhetorical artifact," and "assessment of effects" (*Rhetorical Criticism* 75–80). Feminist criticism, likewise, becomes these procedures: "analysis of gender in the artifact," "discovery of effects on the audience," "discussion of use of artifact to improve women's lives," and "explanation of artifact's impact on rhetorical theory" (*Rhetorical Criticism* 155–60). So, while beginning critics offered these guidelines for criticism are less likely to feel completely abandoned in the inventional process, they are also less likely to find that the process recognizes or serves the interests they themselves might have in writing criticism, unless coincidentally they have the interests presupposed by the procedures themselves—not always a very likely circumstance.

Foss's text and her drift toward the mechanization of critical invention are particularly important when read together with her work assaying the limitations of criticism driven by method ("Constituted by Agency"). There she recognizes most of the limitations and difficulties we have discussed in this chapter.[57] For example:

> Our focus on method confines our criticism to a particular setting or context—in this case, an intellectual, academic one. Technical jargon, the making of minuscule distinctions among categories, and—if it shows off a method—analysis of sometimes trivial topics are made to seem relevant and appropriate by a focus on method. As a result, our criticism is likely to be of interest only to our colleagues in speech communication departments and, even then, only to those who work in our area of specialization. ("Constituted by Agency" 38)

And:

> The subjectivity of the critic is downplayed in the discourse about rhetorical
> criticism because we do not feature the agent or critic in that discourse. We may
> not do so because we are uncomfortable with subjectivity, for how can criticism
> be rigorous or legitimate or scientific or any number of good things if it is rooted
> in individual experience and bias? ("Constituted by Agency" 42)

But Foss's textbook reproduces those problems. That is neither unique to
Foss nor an indictment of her work. Her work mirrors the inexorable problem faced by any critic who also teaches rhetorical criticism. Most academic
critics no doubt recognize that many or most of their goals as critics are not
shared by most of their students and that their inventional processes probably do not match the scientistic guise with which they cover them. Yet it is
not at all clear for many critics how criticism might be taught if not on the
"professionalized model." The result is that professional critics' procedures
and goals become presented in mechanized and denatured form, misrepre-
sented in the belief that doing so will make them somehow "teachable."

Revitalizing Criticism

But despite its ambivalence toward the beginning critic and its tendency to
fixate on often-arcane theory, media and rhetorical criticism nevertheless
espouse sincerely the goal of "opening up" rhetorical works and their constituent media to the understanding of a wider audience, literate but
nonspecialist. We believe that Foss is in earnest when she writes, "One
purpose of rhetorical criticism . . . is to understand a rhetorical artifact
better and, consequently, to use that understanding to help others appreciate it or to change some aspect of the society that generated the rhetorical
artifact" (*Rhetorical Criticism* 6). Likewise, Hart's sincerity could not be
mistaken when, in the next chapter of this anthology, he explains his identity
as a critic: "I am a critic because I often do not like the language my
contemporaries speak nor the policy options they endorse. I am a critic
because I feel that rhetoric should move a society forward rather than
backward, that it should open and not close the public sphere, that it should
make people generous and not craven. I am a critic, ultimately, because I am
a citizen." Implicit in both of these statements, and the many more like them
one can find among the published declarations of our colleagues, is the
conviction that criticism can and should make provocative and worthwhile
contributions to public discussion.

    Because this conviction is genuinely held, if not yet perfectly realized,
media and rhetorical criticism ought to do whatever it can to escape the fate
of some other branches of criticism in this century. As Said (10–12) and
Jacoby (112–39) note, such movements in literary criticism as the Anglo-

American New Criticism and the French *nouvelle critique,* and much of Marxist criticism in several disciplines, once determined to be accessible and influential to the widest audience, are now all-too-seldom heard by any outside their narrowly drawn academic audiences (Said 10–12; Jacoby 112–39).

It would be naively optimistic about the institutional and cultural forces we challenge to imagine that the future of criticism will be transformed simply by our revival in this book of the question of critical invention. Yet the return to the question of critical questions is clearly a necessary precondition if criticism is to emerge from its present cloistered state in which critics are isolated from public culture, from their students, and from one another. This first step is but one of several that must contemplated. Another step will be taken as critics experiment with different forms of writing and expression *as* critics, and with breaching the boundaries currently separating disciplines. Another step will be taken as editors tolerate departures from the standard models of professional critical scholarship, rethinking which critical practices they really want to use their institutional power to encourage. Another important step will be taken when administrators demythify the significance of disciplinary turf barriers as well as the relationships among scholarly writing, professional journals, and knowledge production. A terribly important step will be taken when teachers of criticism have access to an alternative teaching model designed to promote the values and practices of media and rhetorical criticism to a new generation of critics, enabling these beginning critics to write to and from various communities, rather than exclusively the community of professional critics. When and if this moment arrives, critics will have the opportunity to write criticism that draws strength and vitality from their initial commitments to community, to ethics, and to ideology, as well as to theory and profession, rather than struggling to conceal them.

▓ Notes

[1]As later sections of this chapter will demonstrate, we intend "media and rhetorical" to refer primarily to critics and criticism connected with the disciplinary history of the speech communication field. Our purpose is thus to designate a disciplinary category, rather than a purely theoretical, methodological, or substantive one. The speech communication discipline's experience with the issues of professionalization has in many ways been similar to the experience of other fields, such as history, literature, film, journalism, or sociology, and its history can be instructive to those readers more familiar with these neighboring disciplines. But speech communication, owing to aspects of its particular disciplinary history, has also faced tensions that have not generally been experienced even by substantively similar fields. Readers from other disciplines may thus find speech communication's *atypicality* instructive as well.

[2]We assume as our general stance one defended by Foucault, who argued that we are not disqualified from raising questions or problems if we do not immediately "solve" them. To impose such a stricture would be to foreclose any acknowledgment or discussion of a problem unless or until one can solve it. Instead, he suggested that it may be of at least interim value

for critics "to bring it about that they 'no longer know what to do', so that acts, gestures, discourses which up until then had seemed to go without saying become problematic, difficult, dangerous. The effect is intentional." Rather than having an "anaesthetizing" or "sterilizing" effect, his critique was intended to mobilize "a long work of comings and goings, of exchanges, reflections, trials, different analyses" ("Questions of Method" 84). Also see "Critical Theory/ Intellectual History." We hope, instead of dictating our own "solutions," to initiate discussions and experiments aimed at solving the problem we attempt to characterize in this book.

³Here our goal is in line with, and is meant to extend, the work begun by Wander and Jenkins, and supplemented by Wander. Wander suggests that "in an academic context, for example, an ideological critique would bore in, at some point, on the connection between what scholars in a given field call 'knowledge,' even 'scientific' knowledge, and professional interest. It would confront ideals professed with what they obscure in either theory or practice in light of the possibilities for real or 'emancipatory' change" ("Ideological Turn" 2).

⁴We mean by "text," in part, what we believe others reference by terms like "artifact" or "object." That is, we mean the rhetorical or media event the critic has chosen to address through critical writing. We deliberately avoid these other terms because of our discomfort with their implications. We have chosen "text" to designate that which the critic addresses for two reasons. First, it is broad enough to encompass a variety of events; it is at least as unconfined in scope as "artifact" or "object," so as to allow for the inclusion of extra-verbal acts (music, painting, sculpture) or extra-verbal aspects of verbal forms (material action and scene in a dramatic performance). Second, "text" has come to designate a critical operation rather than a fixed material object. It or "discourse," as used in most critical circles, refers to a construction or construal by the critic of the event(s) to be analyzed. See Barthes; Bové; Brummett, "How to Propose"; Foucault, *Archaeology;* and McGee, "Text."

⁵Wander and Jenkins concur: "The play of values takes place at three points in the critical act: selection, response, and communication. One discovers that a particular object holds interest over against any number of other potential objects; one tries to understand both the object and one's interest in it; and one decides what to say about it." But, as they also observe, "These questions [of value] lie at the heart of criticism as we conceive of it, but the practice of academic criticism tends to divert us from this kind of questioning" (441). They suggest what we intend here, a consideration of "the institutional context of scholarship and how it encourages and discourages certain modes of thought, research, and expression" (449).

⁶There are exceptions, but they are extremely rare. See, for example: Birdsell; and Leff, "Textual Criticism."

⁷As Robert Hariman suggests, "the writer is not the sole author of the work, which also is the product of inventional patterns provided by (and sustaining) the writer's dominant social organization. Academic discourse is made by the academic institution, and discovering the relationship between the rhetorical and epistemological dimensions of such discourse should include a critique of its institutional invention" (213).

⁸As Hariman notes, "professionalism has been a productive movement." Among other functions it has "[advanced] democratic access to learning within and without the academy" (223). And as Bruce Robbins notes, the professionalism decried by those like Jacoby overlooks the professional university's achievements in including and advancing the work of women. "Even in the worst instance," Robbins concludes, "professionalization is always partly achievement from below as well as co-optation from above" (xviii).

⁹See Wilshire; Jacoby; Smith; and Bledstein.

¹⁰See Wilshire; and Hariman. As Graff points out, this was only one of the possible forms professionalization might have assumed. We heed his warning that professionalization itself is not necessarily dangerous, but the form it takes may be (*Professing Literature*, 5).

¹¹Levine defines "discipline" as a "discrete body of knowledge with a characteristic regimen for investigation and analysis . . ." (522). Katrín Fridjónsdóttir suggests the mutual dependence of professionalism and disciplinarity (120).

¹²See Foucault, "Discourse." There he argues that disciplines negotiate what counts as true [*dans le vrai*]. He suggests that, "disciplines constitute a system of control in the production of discourse, fixing its limits through the action of an identity taking the form of a permanent reactivation of the rules" (224).

¹³Wilshire uses philosophy as an example: "It is symptomatic of the university's malaise, its distance from the common concerns of humans to build lives for themselves, that philosophers tend to be isolated in highly technical, verbalistic communication with professional fellows. The complexity and expertness of their language is the problem" (xxii).

¹⁴In the late nineteenth-century movement to professionalize the university, "learned societies blossomed in great profusion" (Rudolph, *Curriculum*, 156). Wilshire notes that "in the 1870s and '80s two hundred learned societies were formed in addition to teacher's groups" (64). Significant in Wilshire's description is not only the linkage of professionalism to the growth of learned societies, but also his distinction between these professional organizations and "teacher's groups." Such segregation of the professional and the pedagogical is another sign of the estrangement of civic and experiential domains from the professional.

¹⁵See Wilshire 49. As Cornelis Disco suggests, "the organization of professions across the specific peripheral institutions in which their members work provides professionals with a source of identity competitive with their identities as employees" (72).

¹⁶Certainly it is not the case that outside reviewers have completely usurped the university's evaluation function. But the outside professionals' opinions and decisions can go far in justifying a university's tenure, promotion, and merit decisions regarding individual faculty members.

¹⁷Also see: Hariman 218; Sorrell 9; and McGee and Lyne 383.

¹⁸Treatments of the question of objectivity have degenerated into something virtually useless; almost invariably, they come down to epistemological criteria, most commonly some form of empiricism (Said 14–15). The result often treads a narrow line between intellectual earnestness and farce: scholars buttressing their arguments by pointing to the impossibility of walking through walls and the like (Hikins and Zagacki 203; See also Carey 287).

¹⁹The field of history provides a well-known example of the temptations to objectivism that professionalism can create; see Novick. Hayden White points to historians' embrace of empirical method, as opposed to metaphysical reflection, as the basis for "permitting the kind of 'historical knowledge' produced by professional historians to serve as the standard of 'realism' in political thought and action in general" (123–24).

²⁰See Aronowitz ix; and Sorrell 2.

²¹Hempel, "Logic" 185. Also see his *Philosophy,* particularly Chapter 5. "Testability" in general embraces such more specific issues as replicability, quantification, operationalization, etc.

²²Toulmin uses the term "postmodern science" to describe post-Heisenberg views. He observes:

> In quantum mechanics as much as in psychiatry, in ecology as much as in anthropology, the scientific observer is now—willy-nilly—also a *participant*. The scientists of the mid-twentieth century, then, have entered the period of postmodern science. For natural scientists today, the classical posture of pure spectator is no longer available even on the level of pure theory; and the objectivity of scientific knowledge can no longer rely on the passivity of the scientists' objects of knowledge alone. In the physical sciences, objectivity can now be achieved only in the way it is in the human sciences: the scientist must acknowledge and discount his own reactions to and influence on that which he seeks to understand. (103)

²³This move toward a Catholic interpretation of the discipline had its Protestant counter-movements, functioning at the same time: Delia notes that the proliferation of professional guilds—specifically the development of individual national organizations in theatre, speech

pathology, and broadcasting—contributed to the break-up of departments of speech, which once typically housed all these subareas under one administrative roof, into their own individual administrative units (78). To the extent that scholars in these various areas once shared much in common, substantively or professionally, this centrifugal force discouraged the continuation of these ties.

²⁴And the rhetorical scholars did not always provide a gracious welcome. For example, David Berg described in 1972 the problems of publishing rhetorical criticism of the media stemming from "a very literal and limited conception within the discipline of what constitutes 'speech' " (255). He describes his attempt in the late 1960s to get an article accepted in *Quarterly Journal of Speech*—an article that was later published in *Journalism Quarterly*. Berg was told by the editor of the *Quarterly Journal of Speech* that an article on the persuasive functions of newspapers was inappropriate for the journal. Stretching the definition of speech to cover newspapers would, according to that editor, lead ultimately to the loss of the "unique quality" of *Quarterly Journal of Speech* (255).

²⁵Also see Cohen; and Benson, "History."

²⁶Berlo, in 1955, lamented the absence of a "hypothetical-deductive (to use the Hullian term) theory of rhetoric," but insisted that "it is the responsibility of any experimenter to attempt to provide a theoretical rationale for any piece of research not exploratory in nature" (4). He concluded that "only through training competent experimentalists and securing the presence of a skilled methodologician on the editorial review boards of our journals will research in Speech secure the academic respect of our colleagues in the social sciences, and aid in the development of a realistic theory of rhetoric" (8). That this determination still is a dominant concern is clear in Berger's attempt to account for the "high level of fragmentation" he takes to be a difficulty of communication research and the so-called problem of "relatively little commerce among the various sub-areas of the field" (101). This despite Arthur Bochner and Eric Eisenberg's sensible, if obvious, objection:

> Not only is coherence an unrealistic objective but, even worse, the search for coherence militates against cohesion. Consider what happens when a discipline looks for a single framework, perspective, or paradigm capable of making the field as a whole seem coherent. Promoters of particularized points of view are given license to make outrageous claims about the range of issues to which their largely unspecified perspective apply . . . to universalize a perspective is to ask that "reality-under-a-certain-description" be viewed as accommodating all possible descriptions of reality. . . . No field of knowledge has ever been able to settle on a final set of terms under which all its inquiry could be subsumed." (314–15)

²⁷Also see Arnold, "Rhetorical and Communication Studies"; Brockriede, "Toward a Contemporary Aristotelian Theory"; Brockriede, "Trends"; Clevenger; and Thompson.

²⁸This approach will therefore tend to favor the voice of rhetorical critics over that of media critics, but to the extent that they share overlapping disciplinary histories, the difference is not as crucial as might be supposed. Our choice was driven by the fact that there are presently comparatively few textbooks on media criticism associated with speech communication—as opposed, for example to film criticism, for which numerous texts are available but which has shared little disciplinary history with speech communication. To attempt to reconstruct a disciplinary voice from such a small body of work strikes us as unfair. Where reference to those available works in media criticism, for example, Vande Berg and Wenner, is appropriate to highlight either important differences or significant convergences between media criticism and rhetorical criticism, we have attempted to do so.

²⁹Leff describes "modernist rhetoric" as "an approach based in conventional social scientific notions of theory," and "probably best articulated by Roderick Hart" ("Things" 230n). Whether or not that is an accurate label, we think Leff is correct in suggesting that practitioners of both "textual criticism" and "critical rhetoric" can agree in their resistance to this main-

stream criticism. The two groups pursue different, competitive routes in their desires to supplant it, however. "Textual criticism" represents a particular position within what has been called a "renaissance" in public address scholarship. "Critical rhetoric" is but one specific stance among an array of similar but nonidentical positions that thematize discourse as power and that view criticism as a vehicle of change, sometimes radical change. Representatives of the former group include: Iltis and Browne; Leff, "Textual Criticism"; Lucas; Mohrmann; and Zarefsky. Representatives of the latter include: Biesecker; Blair, "Contested Histories"; Blair, " 'Meta-Ideology' "; Charland; Condit; McGee, "Text"; McKerrow; and Ono and Sloop.

[30]Our observations that the critic-artist does not seem to fare as well as the critic-scientist in the Committee's descriptions should not be taken as a statement of support for the critic-artist as an appropriate model. We agree with Klumpp and Hollihan's observation, that "both of these self-images alienate." They explain:

> The social scientist must alienate him/herself from his/her own involvement in the act and the artistic critic must alienate him/herself from the obvious social context and impact of the rhetorical and critical act. The result has been a criticism that seems sterile. One reads Martin Medhurst's criticism of the anti–gay rights campaign and his defense of the criticism and feels an estrangement from the morality of consequences that alienates all but the professional critic sharing the social science orientation. One reads Robert L. Scott and Wayne Brockriede's study of Harry S. Truman's elegant use of counterpoint musical form and feels the dominance of a rarified technical theory of art estranged from the impact of a rhetor who fundamentally changed our world. (92)

Also see Medhurst; and Scott and Brockriede 10–43.

[31]This despite the "Conclusion" of the National Developmental Project:

> The issue becomes: shall there be concerted action to "rhetoricize" rather than to "scientize" social and humanistic study and action? Our conferences have suggested that intolerance of differences, exacerbation of disagreement, and distrust of the content of modern education are at least in part the consequences of educational and other public policies which imply that objective, depersonalized conclusions or "truths" are or should be possible, though indeed no such possibilities do or can exist. In the tons of print and hours of sound expended upon "the cause of the present malaise," one finds almost no attention given to the fact that decision-making in a vast array of problem areas has been culturally misrepresented (as scientific) to several generations. (Bitzer and Black, eds. 244)

[32]See also Brockriede, "Trends"; Farrell, "Beyond Science"; Fisher, "Rhetorical Criticism"; and Wallace.

[33]Also see: Campbell, "Criticism" 11; Hart, "Contemporary Scholarship"; and Hart, "Theory-Building." In this context, Vande Berg and Wenner stake out a moderate position, citing Foss with approval on the goal of theory building in criticism, but listing "theory builder" as only one of several roles the critic may play, the others including interpreter, teacher, and judge (6–8).

[34]The attempt to ascribe "pre-scientific" status to critical research has its counterpart in media research as well, beginning with Paul Lazarsfeld's attempt to introduce European critical theory into American media research by bringing Theodor Adorno into collaboration with his research team in 1938. Lazarsfeld had hoped that Adorno's critical theory could generate ideas that would be empirically testable by the methods of Lazarsfeld's team. As Slack and Allor report, "attempts at convergence failed essentially because it proved impossible to translate Adorno's critical analysis into the methods and goals of other members of the radio project" (210).

[35]Brummett's references are to: Gronbeck 328; Black, "A Note" 333–34; McGee, " 'Social Movement' " 233; Zarefsky 245; and Swanson 210.

³⁶See Chaffee and Berger 104–5. They list seven criteria for evaluating theory, the first of which is explanatory power: "Here we are concerned with the theory's ability to provide plausible explanations for the phenomena it was constructed to explain. Also considered here is the range of phenomena that the theory explains; the greater the range, the more powerful the theory" (104).

³⁷We will take up the issue of criticism's audience and "proper" outlet further on. However, Wander and Jenkins's observation, that "the critic is but one human being trying to communicate with other human beings," is suggestive of the problem in Campbell's analysis. The division of academic criticism, which addresses professionals, from social criticism, which addresses people at large, forgets the fact that critics are also people at large and not *just* professionals.

³⁸The confusion is exacerbated by one of Brock, Scott, and Chesebro's predictions: "We anticipate that the ideological nature increasingly attributed to rhetorical criticism may be perceived as a denial of the social ends and functions traditionally attributed to rhetorical criticism" (512). That criticism, which has devalued judgment as a principal operation for almost thirty years, does not now appear to *have* much of a social function is one source of confusion. But to suggest that it would be the ideological turn that might divert criticism away from a social end that it currently does not have is even more puzzling. As Wander suggests, "criticism takes an ideological turn when it recognizes the existence of powerful vested interests benefiting from and consistently urging policies and technology that threaten life on this planet, when it realizes that we search for alternatives" (18).

³⁹Black would later soften his position. In the preface of the 1978 reissue of his book, he claims that, "these reflections on the subjectivity of criticism are recorded here as a corrective to this book's excessive deference . . . to an ideal of objectivity" (xiv). Two observations are in order regarding Black's modification. First, it almost certainly came too late to change the scientistic course that had been set. That is *not* to suggest that Black was singly responsible for that course, nor that he should have modified his position earlier. Black's, like other critics', statements are ones of a discourse community as much as of any individual. Had Black not made the 1965 statements or had he modified them sooner, it is quite unlikely that the course taken in criticism would have been materially different. Second, apparently trapped within the Cartesianism that so pervades modernist thought, Black simply chose the other half of the dualism in his revision. His 1978 account discusses *subjectivity* as a corrective to the overemphasis on objectivity, thus remaining within the same dualist vision with a change of emphasis. We believe that there are other options available, if only we are able to think outside of Descartes' moment. It is worth noting also, however, that Black is not alone in his occupation of the Cartesian system. See, for example, Rybacki and Rybacki 13.

⁴⁰The only examples we can think of are: Benson, "Another Shooting"; Hill, "Reply"; and Pacanowsky. The Benson and Pacanowsky essays are clear departures in this respect and others from the norm. Hill's claims to being a McGovern supporter and a liberal were in a "Forum" essay, where presumably the norms governing such self-reference are more lax than in the typical critical article.

⁴¹See: Megill; Rosenfield, "Ideological Miasma"; Hill; Campbell, "Response"; McGee, "Another Philippic"; Francesconi; and Corcoran. Not all of the respondents disagree with Wander. However, the apparent need or desire to defend his position itself points to the recalcitrance of the view attacked by Wander. Wander responded to these critics in "The Third Persona."

⁴²Classifications seem a potent weapon for those who would resist some forms of criticism. Sillars divides critical approaches into two general categories—"the objectivist and the deconstructive" (10). "Deconstruction" in Sillars's text consists of virtually all types of criticism done in the last thirty years, *except* that kind which most of us would recognize as deconstruction. On Sillars's classification, Kenneth Burke, Walter R. Fisher, and Sillars himself would be decon-

structionists; those most typically associated with deconstruction—Jacques Derrida and Paul de Man—never appear in Sillars's account. Such classification *is* a way of making deconstruction seem safe, if not a means of actually carrying out the spirit of the pluralist project Sillars advocates (10).

⁴²Hart's description here is not by any means the worst representation in the discipline. There are moments of understanding and sympathy with these projects to be found in his chapter. Donald Ellis's essay is an even more resistant rendition and it is founded upon a serious misreading and reduction of poststructuralist projects.

⁴⁴To so construe reliability, however, is a reach, and a potentially dangerous one. It suggests that a critic is "right" if the reader cannot disconfirm the critic's argument, and that a critic is "wrong" if the reader disagrees or casts doubt on the argument.

⁴⁵See Clevenger 175; and Farrell, "Critical Models."

⁴⁶See, for example: Andrews 12; Brock, Scott, and Chesebro 17; Brockriede, "Rhetorical Criticism" 169; Foss, *Rhetorical Criticism* 11; Hart, *Modern Rhetorical Criticism* 34–35; Rybacki and Rybacki 23; Sillars 22; and Sloan, et al. 226, 227.

⁴⁷See Thonssen and Baird v, 4. Also see Brigance, ed; and Hochmuth, ed.

⁴⁸For a broader justification of the political-ethical obligations of the critic, see Thonssen and Baird 467–71. It is worth noting that, by 1948, when *Speech Criticism* was published, the signs of professional, scientized criticism were evident. For example, Thonssen and Baird advocated a "dispassionate, objective attitude toward the object of investigation" (20). Nonetheless, the older connection of the academic to the culture was still much in evidence.

⁴⁹It is a sad irony: Modern criticism's life is completely intertwined with the college and university, yet modern critics are producing criticism often described as "inaccessible" to their own students—"inaccessible" being an apparent euphemism for "incomprehensible," but carrying with it as well an unintended slur against the competence of the students. Indeed, a reservation voiced by more than one reviewer of the proposal for *this* anthology was that the critical essays to be reprinted herein, drawn from academic journals, would be inaccessible to their undergraduate students.

⁵⁰For example, Rosenfield characterizes the moment of appreciative encounter between critic and text in terms bordering on the erotic; it is tempting to describe the energetic efforts to conceal this moment of pleasure (or pain) from the public gaze as a kind of intellectual puritanism. See Rosenfield, "Experience."

⁵¹Indeed, we find that a significant part of the problem is that the question of critical invention, and its relation to critical practice, to theory, and to the politics and pedagogy of criticism, is a disciplinary pariah: As the modern university has divided up boundaries, our question is not *in* any discipline, by definition. The reflection on the disciplinary structures of knowledge and their implications for practice in any critical field is no one's responsibility (with the arguable exception—heaven help us—of university administrators). This is even true of "interdisciplinary studies," which may fashion curricula or research programs crossing the boundaries of several disciplines but which in almost every case assume the reality and propriety of those boundaries (Wilshire 113–14; Said 21; Graff, "Pseudo-Politics" 70).

⁵²Factional rivalry exists even within the communication borders, for example between those whose loyalties are to the Speech Communication Association and those who give allegiance to the International Communication Association. Notwithstanding their nominal association with communication and the fact that they frequently work in the same departments, these two groups—and other groups affiliated with broadcasting, journalism, etc.—often have little professional communication. Reeves and Borgman's 1983 network analysis of citations of nine journals nominally related to communication found that the three Speech Communication Association-related journals (*Quarterly Journal of Speech, Central States Communication Journal,* and *Communication Monographs*) were strongly linked to one another, citing

one another's research frequently, but found no such links to any of the other tested journals, except to *Human Communication Research* (130). The other journals in their sample were *Journalism Quarterly, Communication Research, Public Opinion Quarterly, Journal of Communication,* and *Journal of Broadcasting.*

[53]The number of times that Berger refers to "one's theory," "one's own theory," and "ego," in the span of two pages, may be enlightening on this point.

[54]Burton Bledstein expresses the consequences of this tension well: "Historically speaking, the culture of professionalism in America has been enormously satisfying to the human ego, while it has taken an inestimable toll on the integrity of individuals" (xi).

[55]See: Nelson, Megill, and McCloskey, eds.; Simons, ed. *Rhetoric;* and Simons, ed. *The Rhetorical Turn.* Also see Blair, "Contested Histories."

[56]Graff recounts an example of precisely this problem. In a literature course, he assigned his students a short story whose ending apparently contradicted the well-established motivations of the main character. He then asked the students to write about this ending.

> The students had grasped the contradictions of the tale, but when they came to write their papers they had no terms for talking about contradictions except as things to be resolved. Their interpretations had been predetermined by an assumption drilled into them since high-school English, namely, that when you encounter an apparent anomaly in a literary work—especially if it's a canonized one—it's not a real anomaly. The students who read the ending as ironic did so because that is the only plausible way to make it cohere with the rest of the story. That there are occasions when the elements of a literary work *don't* cohere was a possibility they either hadn't been led to consider or had no terms to express, at least not in formal writing. Not surprisingly, it was the *better* students in the class who were least able to treat the story's contradictions *as* contradictions. This makes depressing sense: it's the students who have best mastered a particular interpretive strategy who figure to be most its captive. ("University" 76)

Graff's encounter with the professionalization of criticism among his students is doubtless far more typical than either teacher or student would care to admit. The same is probably true of his observation that it is often the "better" students who most quickly discipline themselves to keep a safe distance from critical inventiveness.

[57]Foss does identify a different reason for these difficulties than we would. Analyzing the possibilities open to critics with Burke's pentad, she suggests that the difficulties are a result of focusing too much upon method. We believe the problem goes much deeper than that, into the heart of the institutions in which we practice and into our own motivations to maintain them. Overemphasis on method, in that larger context, is as much a symptom of the problem as a cause.

▪ Works Cited

Almond, Gabriel A., Marvin Chodorow, and Roy Harvey Pearce, eds. *Progress and Its Discontents.* Berkeley: University of California Press, 1982.

Andrews, James R. *The Practice of Rhetorical Criticism.* 2d ed. New York: Longman, 1990.

Arnold, Carroll C. "Reflections on the Wingspread Conference." Bitzer and Black, eds. 194–99.

———."Rhetorical and Communication Studies: Two Worlds or One?" *Western Speech* 36 (1972): 75–81.

Aronowitz, Stanley. *Science as Power: Discourse and Ideology in Modern Society.* Minneapolis: University of Minnesota Press, 1988.

Barthes, Roland. "From Work to Text." *Image-Music-Text.* Trans. Stephen Heath. New York: Hill and Wang, 1977. 155–64.

Becker, Samuel L. "Marxist Approaches to Media Studies: The British Experience." *Critical Studies in Mass Communication* 1 (1984): 66–80.

Benson, Thomas W. "Another Shooting in Cowtown." *Quarterly Journal of Speech* 67 (1981): 347–406.

———. "History, Criticism, and Theory in the Study of American Rhetoric." *American Rhetoric: Context and Criticism.* Ed. Thomas W. Benson. Carbondale: Southern Illinois University Press, 1989. 1–17.

———, ed. *Speech Communication in the 20th Century.* Carbondale: Southern Illinois University Press, 1985.

Berg, David M. "Rhetoric, Reality, and Mass Media." *Quarterly Journal of Speech* 58 (1972): 255–63.

Berger, Charles R. "Communication Theories and Other Curios." *Communication Monographs* 58 (1991): 101–13.

Berger, Charles R., and Steven H. Chaffee, eds. *Handbook of Communication Science.* Newbury Park, CA: Sage, 1987.

Berlo, David K. "Problems in Communication Research." *Central States Speech Journal* 7 (1955): 3–8.

Biesecker, Barbara A. "Towards a Transactional View of Rhetorical and Feminist Theory: Rereading Hélène Cixous's *The Laugh of the Medusa.*" *Southern Communication Journal* 57 (1992): 86–96.

Birdsell, David S. "Ronald Reagan on Lebanon and Grenada: Flexibility and Interpretation in the Application of Kenneth Burke's Pentad." *Quarterly Journal of Speech* 73 (1987): 267–79.

Bitzer, Lloyd F., and Edwin Black, eds. *The Prospect of Rhetoric.* Report of the National Developmental Project Sponsored by the Speech Communication Association. Englewood Cliffs, NJ: Prentice-Hall, 1971.

Black, Edwin. "A Note on Theory and Practice in Rhetorical Criticism." *Western Journal of Speech Communication* 44 (1980): 331–36.

———. *Rhetorical Criticism: A Study in Method.* New York: Macmillan, 1965.

———. *Rhetorical Criticism: A Study in Method* [reissued]. Madison: University of Wisconsin Press, 1978.

Blair, Carole. "Contested Histories of Rhetoric: The Politics of Preservation, Progress, and Change." *Quarterly Journal of Speech* 78 (1992): 403–28.

———. " 'Meta-Ideology,' Rhetoric and Social Theory: Reenactment of the Wisdom-Eloquence Tension After the Linguistic Turn." *Rhetoric and Ideology: Compositions and Criticisms of Power.* Ed. Charles W. Kneupper. Arlington, TX: Rhetoric Society of America, 1989. 21–29.

Bledstein, Burton J. *The Culture of Professionalism: The Middle Class and the Development of Higher Education in America.* New York: Norton, 1976.

Bochner, Arthur P., and Eric M. Eisenberg. "Legitimizing Speech Communication: An Examination of Coherence and Cohesion in the Development of the Discipline." Benson, ed. *Speech Communication* 299–321.

Bormann, Ernest G. "Generalizing About Significant Form: Science and Humanism Compared and Contrasted." *Form and Genre: Shaping Rhetorical Action.* Ed. Karlyn Kohrs Campbell and Kathleen Hall Jamieson. Falls Church, VA: Speech Communication Association, 1977. 51–69.

Bové, Paul A. "Discourse." *Critical Terms for Literary Study.* Ed. Frank Lentricchia and Thomas McLaughlin. Chicago: University of Chicago Press, 1990. 50–65.

Bowers, John Waite. "The Pre-Scientific Function of Rhetorical Criticism." *Essays on Rhetorical Criticism.* Ed. Thomas R. Nilson. New York: Random House, 1968. 126–45. Rpt. in Ehninger, ed. 163–73.

Brigance, William Norwood, ed. *A History and Criticism of American Public Address.* 2 vols. New York: McGraw-Hill, 1943.

Brock, Bernard L., Robert L. Scott, and James W. Chesebro, eds. *Methods of Rhetorical Criticism: A Twentieth-Century Perspective.* 3d ed. Detroit: Wayne State University Press, 1989.

Brockriede, Wayne. "Rhetorical Criticism as Argument." *Quarterly Journal of Speech* 60 (1974): 165–74.

———. "Toward a Contemporary Aristotelian Theory of Rhetoric." *Quarterly Journal of Speech* 52 (1966): 33–40. Rpt. in Johannesen, ed. 39–49.

———. "Trends in the Study of Rhetoric: Toward a Blending of Criticism and Science." Bitzer and Black, eds. 123–39.

Brown, William R. "Mass Media and Society: The Development of Critical Perspectives." Benson ed. *Speech Communication* 196–220.

Brummett, Barry. "How to Propose a Discourse—A Reply to Rowland." *Communication Studies* 41 (1990): 128–35.

———. "Rhetorical Theory as Heuristic and Moral: A Pedagogical Justification." *Communication Education* 33 (1984): 97–107.

Campbell, Karlyn Kohrs. "Criticism: Ephemeral and Enduring." *Speech Teacher* 23 (1974): 9–14.

———. "Response to Forbes Hill." *Central States Speech Journal* 34 (1983): 126–27.

Carey, James W. "Graduate Education in Mass Communication," *Communication Education* 28 (1979): 282–93.

Carroll, Raymond L. "Context in the Study of Mass Communication: The Cases of 'Telecommunications' and 'Journalism,' " *Feedback* 27 (1985): 3–8.

Chaffee, Steven H., and Charles R. Berger. "What Communication Scientists Do." Berger and Chaffee, eds. 99–122.

Cherwitz, Richard A., and John Theobald-Osborne. "Contemporary Developments in Rhetorical Criticism: A Consideration of the Effects of Rhetoric." Phillips and Wood, ed. 52–80.

Clevenger, Theodore, Jr. "The Interaction of Descriptive and Experimental Research in the Development of Rhetorical Theory." *Central States Speech Journal* 16 (1965): 7–12. Rpt. in Ehninger, ed. 174–78.

Cohen, Herman. "The Development of Research in Speech Communication: A Historical Perspective." Benson, ed. *Speech Communication* 282–98.

Condit, Celeste. "Rhetorical Criticism and Audiences: The Extremes of McGee and Leff." *Western Journal of Communication* 54 (1990): 330–45.

Corcoran, Farrel. "The Widening Gyre: Another Look at Ideology in Wander and His Critics." *Central States Speech Journal* 35 (1984): 54–56.

Davis, Bernard D. "Fear of Progress in Biology." Almond, Chodorow, and Pearce, eds. 182–201.

Delia, Jesse G. "Communication Research: A History." Berger and Chaffee, eds. 20–98.

Disco, Cornelis. "Intellectuals in Advanced Capitalism: Capital, Closure, and the New-Class Thesis." Eyerman, Svensson, and Söerqvist, eds. 50–77.

Eagleton, Terry. *The Function of Criticism: From* The Spectator *to Post-Structuralism.* London: Verso, 1984.

Ehninger, Douglas, ed. *Contemporary Rhetoric: A Reader's Coursebook.* Glenview, IL: Scott, Foresman, 1972.

Ellis, Donald G. "Post-Structuralism and Language: Non-Sense." *Communication Monographs* 58 (1991): 213–24.

Eyerman, Ron, Lennart G. Svensson, and Thomas Söerqvist, eds. *Intellectuals, Universities and the State in Western Modern Societies.* Berkeley: University of California Press, 1987.

Farrell, Thomas B. "Beyond Science: Humanities Contributions to Communication Theory." Berger and Chaffee, eds. 123–39.

———. "Critical Models in the Analysis of Discourse." *Western Journal of Speech Communication* 44 (1980): 300–14.

Feigl, Herbert. "The Scientific Outlook: Naturalism and Humanism." *Readings in the Philosophy of Science.* Ed. Herbert Feigl and May Brodbeck. New York: Appleton-Century-Crofts, 1953. 8–18.

Feinberg, Gerald. "Progress in Physics: The Game of Intellectual Leapfrog." Almond, Chodorow, and Pearce, eds. 161–81.

Fisher, Walter R. "Rhetorical Criticism as Criticism." *Western Speech* 38 (1974): 75–80.

Foss, Sonja K. "Constituted by Agency: The Discourse and Practice of Rhetorical Criticism." Phillips and Wood, eds. 33–51.

———. "Criteria for Adequacy in Rhetorical Criticism." *Southern Speech Communication Journal* 48 (1983): 283–95.

———. *Rhetorical Criticism: Exploration and Practice.* Prospect Heights, IL: Waveland, 1989.

Foucault, Michel. *The Archaeology of Knowledge.* Trans. A. M. Sheridan Smith. New York: Pantheon, 1972.

———. "Critical Theory/Intellectual History." Trans. Jeremy Harding. *Michel Foucault: Politics, Philosophy, Culture—Interviews and Other Writings, 1977–1984.* Ed. Lawrence D. Kritzman. New York: Routledge, 1988. 17–46.

———. "The Discourse on Language." Lecture at the Collège de France. December 2, 1970. Trans. Rupert Swyer. Appendix to *The Archaeology of Knowledge.* 215–37.

———. "Questions of Method." *The Foucault Effect: Studies in Governmentality.* Ed. Graham Burchell, Colin Gordon, and Peter Miller. Chicago: University of Chicago Press, 1991. 73–86.

———. "Two Lectures." *Power/Knowledge: Selected Interviews and Other Writings, 1972–1977.* Ed. Colin Gordon. Trans. Colin Gordon, Leo Marshall, John Mepham, and Kate Soper. New York: Pantheon, 1980. 78–108.

Francesconi, Robert. "Heidegger and Ideology: Reflections of an Innocent Bystander." *Central States Speech Journal* 35 (1984): 51–53.

Fridjónsdóttir, Katrín. "The Modern Intellectual: In Power or Disarmed? Reflections on the Sociology of Intellectuals and Intellectual Work." Eyerman, Svensson, and Söderqvist, eds. 110–26.

Gibbons, Reginald. "Academic Criticism and Contemporary Literature." Graff and Gibbons, eds. 15–35.

Graff, Gerald. *Professing Literature: An Institutional History.* Chicago: University of Chicago Press, 1987.

———. "The Pseudo-Politics of Interpretation." Mitchell, ed. 145–58.

———. "The University and the Prevention of Culture." Graff and Gibbons, eds. 62–82.

Graff, Gerald, and Reginald Gibbons, eds. *Criticism in the University.* Evanston, IL: Northwestern University Press, 1985.

Gregg, Richard B. "The Criticism of Symbolic Inducement: A Critical-Theoretical Connection." Benson, ed. 41–62.

Gronbeck, Bruce E. "Dramaturgical Theory and Criticism: The State of the Art (or Science?)." *Western Journal of Speech Communication* 44 (1980): 315–30.

Haber, Samuel. *The Quest for Authority and Honor in the American Professions, 1750–1900.* Chicago: University of Chicago Press, 1991.

Hariman, Robert. "The Rhetoric of Inquiry and the Professional Scholar." Simons, ed. *Rhetoric.* 211–32.

Hart, Roderick P. "Contemporary Scholarship in Public Address: A Research Editorial." *Western Journal of Speech Communication* 50 (1986): 283–95.

———. *Modern Rhetorical Criticism.* Glenview, IL: Scott, Foresman/Little, Brown, 1990.

———. "Rhetorical Research: The Most Traditional Tradition." *Spectra,* 20, February 1989: 2–3.

———. "Theory-Building and Rhetorical Criticism: An Informal Statement of Opinion." *Central States Speech Journal* 27 (1976): 70–77.

Head, Sydney W. "The Telecommunication Curriculum: A Personal View." *Feedback* 27 (1985): 9–12.

Hempel, Carl G. "The Logic of Functional Analysis." *Readings in the Philosophy of Science.* Ed. May Brodbeck. New York: Macmillan, 1963.

———. *Philosophy of Natural Science.* Englewood Cliffs, NJ: Prentice-Hall, 1966.

Hickson, Mark, III, Don W. Stacks, and Jonathan H. Amsbury. "An Analysis of Prolific Scholarship in Speech Communication, 1915–1985: Toward a Yardstick for Measuring Research Productivity." *Communication Education* 38 (1989): 230–36.

Hikins, James W., and Kenneth S. Zagacki. "Rhetoric, Philosophy, and Objectivism: An Attenuation of the Claims of the Rhetoric of Inquiry." *Quarterly Journal of Speech* 74 (1988): 201–28.

Hill, Forbes. "Reply to Professor Campbell." *Quarterly Journal of Speech* 58 (1972): 454–60.

———. "A Turn Against Ideology: Reply to Professor Wander." *Central States Speech Journal* 34 (1983): 121–26.

Hochmuth, Marie, ed. *A History and Criticism of American Public Address.* Vol. 3. New York: Russell & Russell, 1955.

Holton, Gerald. "Toward a Theory of Scientific Progress." Almond, Chodorow, and Pearce, eds. 202–25.

Iltis, Robert S., and Stephen H. Browne. "Tradition and Resurgence in Public Address Studies." Phillips and Wood, eds. 81–93.

Jacoby, Russell. *The Last Intellectuals: American Culture in the Age of Academe.* New York: Basic Books, 1987.

Johannesen, Richard L., ed. *Contemporary Theories of Rhetoric: Selected Readings.* New York: Harper & Row, 1971.

Johnstone, Henry W., Jr. *The Problem of the Self.* University Park: Pennsylvania State University Press, 1970.

Kerlinger, Fred N. *Foundations of Behavioral Research.* New York: Holt, Rinehart, and Winston, 1946.

Klumpp, James F., and Thomas A. Hollihan. "Rhetorical Criticism as Moral Action." *Quarterly Journal of Speech* 75 (1989): 84–97.

Klyn, Mark S. "Toward a Pluralistic Rhetorical Criticism." *Essays on Rhetorical Criticism.* Ed. Thomas R. Nilsen. New York: Random House, 1968. 146–57.

Krupnick, Mark. "The Two Worlds of Cultural Criticism." Graff and Gibbons, eds. 159–69.

Kuhn, Thomas S. *The Structure of Scientific Revolutions.* 2d ed. University of Chicago Press, 1970.

LeFevre, Karen Burke. *Invention as a Social Act.* Carbondale: Southern Illinois University Press, 1987.

Leff, Michael C. "Interpretation and the Art of the Rhetorical Critic." *Western Journal of Speech Communication* 44 (1980): 337–49.

———. "Textual Criticism: The Legacy of G. P. Mohrmann." *Quarterly Journal of Speech* 72 (1986): 377–89.

———. "Things Made By Words: Reflections on Textual Criticism." *Quarterly Journal of Speech* 78 (1992): 223–31.

Levine, Arthur. *Handbook on Undergraduate Curriculum.* San Francisco: Jossey-Bass, 1978.

Lucas, Stephen E. "The Renaissance of American Public Address: Text and Context in Rhetorical Criticism." *Quarterly Journal of Speech* 74 (1988): 241–60.

McGee, Michael Calvin. "Another Philippic: Notes on the Ideological Turn in Criticism." *Central States Speech Journal* 35 (1984): 43–50.

———. " 'Social Movement': Phenomenon or Meaning?" *Central States Speech Journal* 31 (1980): 233–44.

———. "Text, Context, and the Fragmentation of Contemporary Culture." *Western Journal of Speech Communication* 54 (1990): 274–89.

McGee, Michael Calvin, and John R. Lyne. "What Are Nice Folks Like You Doing in a Place Like This? Some Entailments of Treating Knowledge Claims Rhetorically." Nelson, Megill, and McCloskey, eds. 381–406.

McGuckin, Henry E., Jr. "The Experimentalist as Critic." *Western Speech* 32 (1968): 167–72.

McKerrow, Raymie E. "Critical Rhetoric: Theory and Praxis." *Communication Monographs* 56 (1989): 91–111.

Medhurst, Martin J. "The First Amendment vs. Human Rights: A Case Study in Community Sentiment and Argument from Definition." *Western Journal of Speech Communication* 46 (1982): 1–19.

Megill, Allan. "Heidegger, Wander, and Ideology." *Central States Speech Journal* 34 (1983): 114–19.

Miller, Gerald R. "Humanistic and Scientific Approaches to Speech Communication Inquiry: Rivalry, Redundancy, or Rapprochement." *Western Speech Communication* 39 (1975): 230–39.

Mitchell, W. J. T., ed. *The Politics of Interpretation.* Chicago: University of Chicago Press, 1983.

Mohrmann, G. P. "Elegy in a Critical Grave-Yard." *Western Journal of Speech Communication* 44 (1980): 265–74.

Nelson, John S., Allan Megill, and Donald N. McCloskey, eds. *The Rhetoric of the Human Sciences: Language and Argument in Scholarship and Public Affairs.* Madison: University of Wisconsin Press, 1987.

Newcomb, Horace M. "American Television Criticism, 1970–1985." *Critical Studies in Mass Communication* 3 (1986): 217–28.

Nilsen, Thomas R. *Essays on Rhetorical Criticism.* New York: Random House, 1968.

Nothstine, William L. " 'Topics' as Ontological Metaphor in Contemporary Rhetorical Theory and Criticism." *Quarterly Journal of Speech* 74 (1988): 151–63.

Nothstine, William L., and Gary A. Copeland. "Against the Bureaucratization of Criticism." *Pennsylvania Speech Communication Annual* 45 (1989): 19–28.

Novick, Peter. *That Noble Dream: The "Objectivity Question" and the American Historical Profession.* Cambridge: Cambridge University Press, 1988.

Ono, Kent A., and John M. Sloop. "Commitment to *Telos*—A Sustained Critical Rhetoric." *Communication Monographs* 59 (1992): 48–60.

Pacanowsky, Michael E. "Slouching Towards Chicago." *Quarterly Journal of Speech* 74 (1988): 453–67.

Pearce, W. Barnett. "Scientific Research Methods in Communication Studies and Their Implications for Theory and Research." Benson, ed. *Speech Communication* 255–81.

Phillips, Gerald M., and Julia T. Wood, eds. *Speech Communication: Essays to Commemorate the 75th Anniversary of the Speech Communication Association.* Carbondale: Southern Illinois University Press, 1990.

Pirsig, Robert M. *Zen and the Art of Motorcycle Maintenance: An Inquiry into Values.* New York: Bantam New Age Edition, 1981.

Reeves, Byron, and Christine L. Borgman, "A Bibliometric Evaluation of Core Journals in Communication Research." *Human Communication Research* 10 (1983): 119–36.

Robbins, Bruce. "Introduction: The Grounding of Intellectuals." *Intellectuals: Aesthetics, Politics, Academics.* Ed. Bruce Robbins. Minneapolis: University of Minnesota Press, 1990. ix–xxvii.

Rogers, Everett M., and Steven H. Chaffee, "Communication as an Academic Discipline: A Dialogue." *Journal of Communication* 33 (1983): 18–30.

Rosenfield, Lawrence W. "The Anatomy of Critical Discourse." *Speech Monographs* 25 (1968): 50–69. Rpt. in Brock, Scott, and Chesebro, eds. 96–116.

———. "The Experience of Criticism." *Quarterly Journal of Speech* 60 (1974): 489–96.

———. "Ideological Miasma." *Central States Speech Journal* 34 (1983): 119–21.

Rudolph, Frederick. *Curriculum: A History of the American Undergraduate Course of Study Since 1636.* San Francisco: Jossey-Bass, 1977.

Rybacki, Karyn, and Donald Rybacki. *Communication Criticism: Approaches and Genres.* Belmont, CA: Wadsworth, 1991.

Said, Edward W. "Opponents, Audiences, Constituencies, and Communities." Mitchell, ed. 7–32.

Scott, Robert L., and Wayne Brockriede. *Moments in the Rhetoric of the Cold War.* New York: Harper & Row, 1970.

Sillars, Malcolm O. *Messages, Meanings, and Culture: Approaches to Communication Criticism.* New York: HarperCollins, 1991.

Simons, Herbert W., ed. *Rhetoric in the Human Sciences.* Newbury Park, CA: Sage, 1989.

———. ed. *The Rhetorical Turn: Invention and Persuasion in the Conduct of Inquiry.* Chicago: University of Chicago Press, 1990.

Slack, Jennifer Daryl, and Martin Allor. "The Political and Epistemological Constituents of Critical Communication Research." *Journal of Communication* 33 (1983): 208–18.

Sloan, Thomas O., Richard B. Gregg, Thomas R. Nilsen, Irving J. Rein, Herbert W. Simons, Herman G. Stelzner, and Donald W. Zacharias. "Report of the Committee on the Advancement and Refinement of Rhetorical Criticism." Bitzer and Black, eds. 220–27.

Smith, Page. *Killing the Spirit: Higher Education in America.* New York: Penguin, 1990.

Sorrell, Tom. *Scientism: Philosophy and the Infatuation with Science.* London: Routledge, 1991.

Swanson, David L. "A Reflective View of the Epistemology of Critical Inquiry." *Communication Monographs* 44 (1977): 207–19.

Thompson, Wayne N. "A Conservative View of a Progressive Rhetoric." *Quarterly Journal of Speech* 49 (1963): 1–7. Rpt. in Johannesen, ed. 9–17.

Thonssen, Lester, and A. Craig Baird. *Speech Criticism: The Development of Standards for Rhetorical Appraisal.* New York: Ronald Press, 1948.

Toulmin, Stephen. "The Construal of Reality: Criticism in Modern and Postmodern Science." Mitchell, ed. 99–117.

Vande Berg, Leah R. and Lawrence A. Wenner, *Television Criticism.* New York: Longman, 1991.

Wallace, Karl R. "The Fundamentals of Rhetoric." Bitzer and Black, eds. 3–20.

Wander, Philip. "The Ideological Turn in Modern Criticism." *Central States Speech Journal* 34 (1983): 1–18.

———. "The Third Persona: An Ideological Turn in Rhetorical Theory." *Central States Speech Journal* 35 (1984): 197–216.

Wander, Philip, and Steven Jenkins. "Rhetoric, Society, and the Critical Response." *Quarterly Journal of Speech* 58 (1972): 441–50.

Weber, Samuel. *Institution and Interpretation.* Minneapolis: University of Minnesota Press, 1987.

White, Hayden. "The Politics of Historical Interpretation: Discipline and De-Sublimation." Mitchell, ed. 119–43.

Wichelns, Herbert A. *A History of the Speech Association of the Eastern States* (Speech Association of the Eastern States, 1959).

Wilshire, Bruce. *The Moral Collapse of the University: Professionalism, Purity, and Alienation.* Albany: State University of New York Press, 1990.

Winans, J. A. "The Need for Research." *Quarterly Journal of Public Speaking* 1 (1915): 17–23.

———. "Should We Worry?" *Quarterly Journal of Public Speaking* 1 (1915): 197–201.

Zarefsky, David. "A Skeptical View of Movement Studies." *Central States Speech Journal* 31 (1980): 245–54.

———. "The State of the Art in Public Address Scholarship." *Texts in Context: Critical Dialogues on Significant Episodes in American Political Rhetoric.* Ed. Michael C. Leff and Fred J. Kauffeld. Davis, CA: Hermagoras Press, 1989. 13–27.

CHAPTER 3 ⬚

WANDERING WITH RHETORICAL CRITICISM

Roderick P. Hart

In this essay, Roderick P. Hart describes assumptions that have guided his work as a critic for the past two decades. Hart locates his interest in rhetoric, understood as "how people use language to narrow the policy options of others," and traces three sets of assumptions that characterize his criticism: political (liberal/capitalist), epistemological (investigating "the American audience through texts prepared for their consumption"), and procedural (from "fishing expeditions" to perfecting the "incomplete arguments" of scholars in other fields).

Nobody knows where ideas come from. Certainly nobody I know, at least. To suggest the contrary is folly of the highest order. I most certainly do not know where my ideas come from. I am just grateful that they come along often enough to keep my family fed. (At the moment, I would not mind if a Really Big Idea arrived in time for me to pay a certain young woman's tuition bill.) And so I am uncomfortable even speculating about the source of critical invention. I fear that to think too much about invention will cause it to suddenly drift off on the winds, never again to waft in my direction. Like some obedient native of a pre-technological culture, I fear that raising my eyes to scrutinize the godhead of ideas will result in my being blinded for my hubris. What to do?

I have chosen to press on here, not because I know where ideas come from but because the questions the editors of this text pose are intriguing: What sorts of people do rhetorical criticism? Why do they do it? What do they do when doing it? Because all criticism is autobiographical, as George Bernard Shaw has said, I have no choice but to respond personally when trying to answer such hard questions. This, too, is a kind of hubris, but perhaps one less deserving of permanent sensory deprivation. To lose one's eyes for poetry is conceivable; for God or love, perhaps even noble. To lose one's eyes for rhetoric is daft.

Rhetoric can, however, steal one's heart. It has mine. Studying how people use language to narrow the policy options of others¹ became my occupation twenty years ago and it has preoccupied me ever since. Criticism is not something I do; it is something I am. I am a critic because I often do not like the language my contemporaries speak nor the policy options they endorse. I am a critic because I feel that rhetoric should move a society forward rather than backward, that it should open and not close the public sphere, that it should make people generous and not craven. I am a critic, ultimately, because I am a citizen.

In this essay, I shall attempt to point up three different sets of assumptions that have guided my work as a critic. As a collection of assumptions, they may not make much sense. They are the sorts of rag-tag beliefs that a person picks up without noticing, beliefs that lie safely out of range until that person is forced to confront them as I have been asked to do here. These assumptions spring from my personal upbringing, from the thinkers who influenced me along the way, and from a bevy of personality quirks that I do not fully understand but which I cannot reasonably deny. Sensible or not, these assumptions have made my criticisms. Sensible or not, they have made me as well.

▓ Political Assumptions

For me, all critical work is political work. The critical essay is part of an intertextual world of statement-and-response and the critic is part of a political cadre: advancing this agenda or that agenda, criticizing this use of power or that use of power, offering a new take on the world or reminding us of an older one. Over time, the critic's brow becomes almost permanently furrowed as he or she scrutinizes what people say and how they say it. And yet the best critics refuse to descend into cynicism, that hell-hole reserved for skeptics without imaginations. Instead, the best critics remember that rhetoric—the language of policy—is infinitely self-corrective and self-generative, an art of the possible. To reword the world is to remake the world, at least in part. People respond to words and to things-like-words—symbols—because they have no choice. They can, however, choose from *among* the symbols they see and hear. The critic's job is to help them do the choosing.

To be a political worker is not necessarily to be a partisan worker. Alas, not everyone agrees with this statement. Some would argue that the critic is either part of the patriarchy or opposed to it, collusive with the forces of hegemony or committed to undermining them. Such thinkers feel that a culture's rhetoric can trap a critic even before the critic traps a text. They urge a kind of radical self-awareness in criticism, a constant examination of the critic's own social, economic, and epistemological assumptions. Conducting political inventories of this sort is said to keep the forces of repression from being unwittingly reproduced in the critic's oeuvre. Guided by such inventories, words like "struggle," "marginality," "commodification," and "resistance" interpenetrate much of the work produced by contemporary critics.

And then there is postmodernism. The postmodern critic is a wag who comments breezily on the surfaces that pass for realities in modern social life. For the postmodernist, "meaning" is a problematic animal, one not worth stalking since meaning is so often deferred in day-to-day life. As a result, postmodernists explain how a text "embarrasses" itself with its inconsistent premises and linguistic absurdities. Such critics do not actually deconstruct texts as much as they oversee the inevitable self-deconstructions that texts produce. Postmodern politics, if there is such a thing, embraces radical individuality and multiperspectivism and fiercely interrogates a society's overarching myths and narratives.

I have always admired the clarity of purpose and sense of mission found in Marxian, feminist, and postmodern researches. My own criticism, alas, has been far more muddled. In part this is because of my own politics: liberal/capitalist. Because I subscribe to that agenda, I have also subscribed to much of the modernist project—that economic achievement is theoretically possible for all; that excellence, not tradition, should be society's sole measuring rod for advancement; that enduring institutions can be beneficent; that technologies, wisely used, make people's lives better.

Because modernism so powerfully determines what happens in the United States, I have studied statist discourse almost exclusively during my career. In a series of books and essays I have explored the rhetoric of the American presidency simply because executive politics matters so much in the real world. But I have also felt, perhaps because of my coming-of-age in the tumultuous sixties, that institutional politicians do not always tend the modernist hearth as I would have them tend it. This assumption has compelled me to look over the presidents' shoulders when they talk.

One of the assumptions I have made as a citizen-critic is that the most important discourses in U.S. society are deliberative in nature. If a given text is not policy-impinging, I do not study it. For many, this is an overly constraining assumption since it rules out so much cultural politics: images of women in second-grade textbooks; emancipatory themes in MTV videos; protectionist themes in commercial advertising; the xenophobic rhetoric of the cable televangelist; the crypto-Freudian overtones of modern cinema. Surely these everyday messages also affect people's political visions. Surely they open up a world of subtle insinuations that are persuasive precisely because people feel so superior to them. Surely the prosaic, but portentous, rhetoric of *Donahue* does more to mold the American mindset each day than the president of the United States does each year.

So it seems to the critic of popular culture. I do not wish to gainsay these assumptions entirely since I have learned much from cultural critics. But I make a different set of assumptions: (1) that deliberative, not cultural, discourse most powerfully affects the policy options available to the average citizen; (2) that discourse about the disbursement of public monies, and about the statutory regulation of private monies, ultimately constrains all other discourse in a modernist society; (3) that it takes a certain kind of expertise to track policy-impinging rhetoric.

Subsumed beneath these assumptions are still more assumptions: that people's cultural perceptions are constraining but that law constrains them even more tightly; that it is good to have symbolic capital (for example, Madonna) but that it is better to have capitalist capital (for example, Ross Perot); that the off-site rhetoric of *Murphy Brown* empowers women but that the on-site rhetoric of the Thomas-Hill Senate hearings empowers men even better; that African-American rap lyrics help that community deal with its frustrations, but that a new urban policy in the United States would do so far more expeditiously; that having a rainbow coalition of newscasters at 6:00 P.M. is good but that being an actor in the news is better; that the rhetoric of campus multiculturalism is stimulating but that the rhetoric of congressional redistricting is determinative.

All of this is to say that the move in the 1970s and 1980s to expand rhetorical criticism into the cultural domain carried with it a hidden danger: that the economic and regulatory clout of deliberative politics would become occluded in the academic community. With that as my worry, what do I do as a critic? Answer: I find a policy-relevant reason to launch any rhetorical investigation. Thus, the rhetoric of *Larry King Live* became important to me when it served to launch a presidential campaign in 1992. *Murphy Brown* became relevant when the star's purported offspring bedeviled the reigning vice president as well as the anti-abortion lobbies in Washington. MTV became important when it was used more advantageously by a progressive political candidate than by a conservative.

In other words, my political assumptions make me distinguish between the *policy sphere* and the *public sphere*. The latter is more encompassing than the former and therefore has a certain natural attraction to critics, especially since the pyrotechnics of popular culture are included within it. But the former is where law is made and law, it seems clear, determines *precisely and irrevocably* what people can and cannot do in their everyday lives.

My choice as a critic, therefore, has been to remember this sobering dictum when choosing which texts to study. Happily, I have not found this to be a noxious constraint since it has kept my eye trained on the modernist substratum—materialist advancement. Like other critics, I am often fascinated by the policy-distant rhetorics of popular culture but I generally steel myself against them. I do so because they distract me from the nation's bottom line—who gets what. They distract me, also, from the groups in society who have profited most from that bottom line. Historically, my Irish Catholic ancestors in Massachusetts were not among the profiteers. The scars of those denials still reside within me and they affect what I do as a critic.

▓ Epistemological Assumptions

What one studies inevitably affects how one studies it. Because politics is a functional art, I study quotidian texts. Because politics is a situated art, I specialize in Americanist texts. Because politics is a populist art, I typically avoid the ersatz text. Unlike many of the critics who preceded me in the field, that is, I have been comparatively uninterested in the signal oration. Politics is an art of central tendency, I have reasoned, not an art of dispersion from the mean. Democratic politics lives or dies by its ability to corral 51 percent of the vote. And so the most common text—the 51-percent text—has always had special appeal for me.

Thus, while I, like all rhetorical critics, appreciate Marie Hochmuth Nichols's magisterial analysis of Lincoln's first inaugural,[2] I have never mounted such an Olympian platform myself. Instead, I became intrigued by Ronald Reagan's first inaugural precisely because it was so undistinguished—a hodgepodge of rhetorical forms and functions that captured the hodgepodge of the Reagan presidency itself: angry rhetoric cum expedient politics.[3] Similarly, I was one of the few critics interested in Jimmy Carter's much reviled "Malaise speech" of 1979.[4] The electorate's critical reactions to Carter's address, I have argued, exposed their disapproval of theoretical politics and exposed, also, certain faultlines between Eastern and Western values. Examining an allegedly banal text like Carter's can sometimes produce uncommon insight. Or so I have felt.

Any text—exalted or ordinary—tells only what the critic asks it to tell. That is, although I have spent a great deal of time studying American presidents, I have never been terribly interested in the forty-odd chief executives themselves. Their personality tics are intriguing, to be sure, but psychobiography seems at best an arcane science. A far more productive operation is to read the American audience through the texts prepared for their consumption.

That is, the presidential tableaux can legitimately be viewed as a record of the nation's wishes and dreams and nothing more. Because presidents virtually never stray from their political leashes, it is curious that the chief executive is so often accused of "being political." Translated, that means that the president has responded with supreme delicacy to the pressure groups he has been asked to superintend. His too-careful rhetoric betrays that delicacy and it betrays, also, the public's impatience with the serial compromises required in a complex polity. In short, the real news trapped in the presidential text may well be sociological, not psychological. If read insightfully, that text can tell us who we are and who we wish to be. The president himself, in such a scheme, becomes little more than a spectacular afterthought.

When doing criticism, then, I have always tried to "read large" rather than "read small." No doubt, I have read too large for some tastes. But a given piece of rhetoric has only intrigued me if it seems to have a broader story to tell. And so I simultaneously studied the rhetoric of the American Communist Party and the John Birch Society because they had so much in common rhetorically (doctrinal constraints, for example) even though they are political antipodes.[5] In addition, I have patiently tracked the linguistic choices made by Richard Nixon, not because he alone warranted such patience but because his collected discourse revealed a fissure in American politics between absolutism and compromise.[6] In another study, I examined the pragmatic and sentimentalist motifs displayed in sharply different forms of American ritual and discovered that a nation imbeds both its conclusions and its indeterminacies in its most sacred texts.[7]

Because I see rhetorical criticism as cultural work, I have consistently oversampled rhetoric, basing most of my scholarly arguments on patterns discerned *across* texts and across a *large number* of texts at that. Such a procedure is not unique to me. Indeed, it is a hallmark of the social-scientific method. But it is a rather rare procedure for a critic to use and, in some people's eyes, it is reason enough to drum me out of the corps. Traditional critics feel that such procedures violate the integrity of the historical moment. "A discourse exists in a special time and place and then is gone forever," they claim. "The critic must show full allegiance to the phenomenology of that moment," they argue further, "and abandon forthwith any feckless grab for universal truth."

Maybe. But is it not also the case that people—audiences—live in many moments of time and that, through human memory, they are able to live again in the past (emotionally) even though the past is no longer present (literally)? In other words, is it not plausible that rhetorical effects *aggregate* within us over time and that the wise critic accounts for their cumulative influence?[8] By examining forty years worth of *Time* magazine's political coverage, for example, I and my colleagues were able to show how the institutional superstructure of the presidency—the collective unconscious, if you will—impinges upon whoever happens to be sitting in the Oval Office.[9] Similarly, by documenting the verbal and nonverbal features of television news across three presidencies in another study, we detailed how executive politics is *remade* for the American people each night and how sharply different priorities within the first and fourth estates are continually reinscribed by the nation's media.[10]

Perhaps my greatest heresy as a critic can also be laid at the social scientist's door. I have counted things. Many things. For example, I have noted the frequency with which speakers use certain kinds of words. Again using the logic of additivity, I have speculated about how unconscious rhetorical habits might affect public opinion. So, for example, I found that sitting presidents use much more optimistic and cautious language than do political campaigners.[11] This suggests two principles: (1) a president must be happy even when the electorate is angry, and (2) it is easy to pontificate when the buck stops on someone else's desk. The regularity of such patterns across very different presidencies was surprising, suggesting that institutional constraints are much more powerful than previously thought. The subtlety of these patterns is also noteworthy, suggesting that rhetoric may affect us in a variety of unconscious ways. Numbers did not reveal these things. Critical interpretation did.

The importance of a critic's epistemological assumptions was driven home for me by a team-teaching experience I had several years ago in a graduate seminar on "Persuasion and the Presidency." My colleague and I often set ourselves the task of separately analyzing the same presidential message and then presenting our results in class. Although my team-teacher and I shared much in common, we almost never agreed on what was most important about the sample text. She emphasized speaker and I audience; she featured argument and I language; she the visual and I the verbal; she the administrative and I the cultural. Because our thoughts began in such different places, we almost always arrived at different destinations. Happily, for the most part.

Such is the nature of criticism. And such is the nature of rhetorical experience. *How* we come to know greatly affects *what* we come to learn. Because rhetoric is such a vast repository of truths and visions, it takes many hands to understand it. When analyzing discourse, not everyone should feature the political over the aesthetic, the normative over the idiosyncratic, or the quantitative over the qualitative as have I. But all critics, it seems clear, should know where they started and why they started there.

▓ Procedural Assumptions

The doing of criticism is an individual thing. No two critics represented in this volume are exactly alike and none of them operates in the same way. Moreover, a given critic may be interested in one sort of text on Monday and a different sort on Wednesday. Likewise, critics change their modes of operation from project to project since sterility means the death of criticism. The best critic chooses the right way to examine the right text. What could be simpler?

Criticism is hardly ever this simple. Each project I have taken on over the years has surprised me (usually by taking longer than anticipated). The experienced critic becomes experienced only because he or she has traveled down so many blind textual alleys and been proved wrong on so many occasions. The critic has a hunch. He or she checks it out. The hunch proves wrong. The critic becomes intrigued by something else.

When retracing my own steps as a critic, I seem to have stumbled down four different paths. Each has proved fruitful, but only hindsight has shown me that. When I was actually doing the criticism I wandered around a great deal. My wanderings began in these places:

1. *The Fishing Expedition.* Confession is said to be good for the soul. Here is my confession: I began a book-length project without knowing exactly why. Here is what I did know: (a) that it was possible to find each of the 10,000 texts spoke by American presidents between 1945 and 1985; (b) that no critic had ever bothered to record the date, place, occasion, genre, etc. of these remarks; (c) that a computer database could be built that would let me discover the rhetorical patterns of the modern presidency; (d) I had tenure, so time was on my side.

Five years later I wrote a book, *The Sound of Leadership.*[12] When one looks at that book now, it seems as if I knew what I was doing from the beginning. Clearly a lie. I did, of course, have my hunches. I knew that a voracious mass media industry had developed in the United States and that it was pressuring the chief executive. Both, it was clear, were now locked in a battle for opinion leadership in the country. I reasoned that while presidents were being victimized by the whims of fate, by a recalcitrant Congress, and by a pesky press, presidents had the scheduling of rhetoric on their side. My book details how the presidents used that advantage and how they changed the face of American politics as a result. The book also shows that patience is the critic's greatest ally.

2. *The Curious Text.* Many critical projects begin because the critic is baffled. I, for example, became baffled when collecting the rhetoric of American atheists.[13] Atheists, I was to learn, have always been part of the American landscape even though 95 percent of the American people profess belief in God. Atheists in the United States must be a hardy lot, I imagined, but until I read what they wrote I had no inkling of how hardy they really were.

To put the matter simply, atheists use discourse like a blunt instrument. Everything I had been taught about rhetoric—that it ingratiates itself with its audience, that it adapts to audience members' needs so as not to offend them—proved untrue of the atheists. They excoriated the Church, which was to be expected, but they also excoriated teachers, scientists, legislators, novelists, painters, patriotic organizations, and others. Theirs was a scorched-earth policy. To understand why, I had to learn that rhetoric is both a social and an auto-reflexive activity and that expression often feels better than communication. I would not have appreciated these principles unless I had first noticed how silly the atheists seemed.

3. *The Bold Assertion.* A particularly good reason to do criticism is to find out if some elegant conceptual vessel really holds water. This sort of "empirical" instinct motivates the work of many critics as they treat popular texts as "proof" of some hypothesized trend or phenomenon. As I have argued elsewhere, the extra dividend of this approach is that it enriches a given body of theory even as it opens doors for yet more inquiry.[14] When the work of the wide-ranging theorist is joined with that of the careful critic, everyone profits.

One of the most compelling books ever written on American politics is James David Barber's *The Presidential Character.*[15] In that book, Barber examined the lives of modern American presidents and constructed a compelling model of presidential character. He then proceeded to categorize each chief executive on the basis of their active or passive natures and their negative or positive predispositions. Barber's work intrigued me, but I felt that he had not been systematic or comprehensive enough, nor as precise as he needed to be. Seven-hundred textual analyses later, I published *Verbal Style and the Presidency*[16] which in part operationalized Barber's notions and in part dealt with other matters. As in so many studies of this sort, I found much in the presidents' discourse that intrigued me far more than Barber's notions, but I would not have strayed into this particular thicket if Professor Barber had not blazed the trail some years earlier.

4. *The Incomplete Argument.* I remember the exact moment when one of my critical projects began. It was after reading Robert Bellah's groundbreaking essay "Civil Religion in America."[17] In that essay, Bellah argues that the American people, because of their enormous diversity, have had a special need to work out their church-state relations amicably. He traces the religious antagonisms that had flourished in the Old World and then shows how the American establishment found ways of building a "civil religion" that would bind them together as a people and provide a usable social structure for their new nation.

In 1968 Robert Bellah was an esteemed sociologist and I was a lowly graduate student. But even in that profound state of humility I knew there was more to Bellah's tale than he had told and that it was a quintessentially rhetorical tale as well. It took me nine years to get around to telling it, but I eventually did so in *The Political Pulpit.*[18] There, I argued that Bellah's civil religion was a *rhetorical* phenomenon, not an historical or sociological phenomenon, and that that was its genius. I argued further that church and state in America have decided to talk in certain ways about one another, that there are clear and definitive rules about how that conversation should go, that there are penalties associated with any significant deviation from those rules, and, most important, that these accommodations provide the sense of community a mottled nation like the United States needs in order to survive. Even today, I like to think that only a rhetorical critic could have extended Bellah's story in precisely the way it needed to be extended.

▓ Conclusion

Compared to most of the authors in this volume, my take on criticism is probably the most linear. I normally begin an assignment because I am vaguely troubled by some unanswered theoretical question or because a given body of texts stubbornly resists conventional modes of interpretation. My world is probably more orderly than it needs to be but I have tried to turn that weakness into a strength by reading the work of less orderly critics. Within their imaginative flights and noisy expostulations, I have often found food for thought as well as a researchable hypothesis or two. Often, my reductions of their work probably get me into a special kind of trouble. But all critics get into trouble. Getting out of trouble is what inspires their work. Mine included.

The clearest way of staying out of trouble, of course, is to read wisely and well. Therein lies the importance of a critical community. When many persons toil in the same vineyard, good wine gets made. The wanderings I have described above are unique to me and surely constitute no iron law of critical inquiry. It is not necessary for all rhetorical critics to study the policy sphere as intently as I have studied it. There are other spheres of human activity and they have their uses. My own opinion, to be sure, is that all roads lead to Rome and, more particularly, to the Roman *polis*. That is why I have positioned myself on the *Via Maximus* and why I refuse to be distracted from how laws are made, who makes them, and for whom they are made. Unquestionably, there are other kinds of critical projects to be done. And there are other kinds of critics to do them.

There are also as many ways of doing criticism as there are critics. Because of my interests and training, I choose to think of all critics as unwitting mathematicians, as persons who study a particular population of items and who learn the most when an element within that population behaves oddly. In such a scheme, the perceptive critic becomes one who (1) notices a rhetorical pattern that nobody had noticed previously, or (2) who finds a textual variation, a break in pattern, that surprises. It is at these two moments—at moments of odd continuity or sudden deviation—that the two most powerful critical questions emerge: Why this? Why now?

Rhetoric exists because people differ from one another and because rhetoric can be used to bridge the chasms between them. Not all rhetoric builds bridges, of course. Some of it creates chasms. The critic's job is to distinguish the bridges from the chasms, but that is not always easy. Did the rhetoric of the Equal Rights Amendment help or hurt the women's movement among blue-collar workers? Did Ronald Reagan's saber-rattling promote or end the Cold War? Did the Catholic church's pronouncements create the pro-life movement, the pro-choice movement, or both? None of these questions is easy to answer. Only the critic is trained by temperament and education to call a bridge a bridge and a chasm a chasm. No society can call itself humane, however, unless someone performs that function. That is what gives the critic a reason to be.

▓ Notes

¹This is an abbreviated form of my definition of rhetoric. For an expansion of this definition see R. P. Hart, *Modern Rhetorical Criticism* (New York: Harper, 1990), 4.

²M. H. Nichols, "Lincoln's First Inaugural," in R. Scott and B. Brock (eds.), *Methods of Rhetorical Criticism: A Twentieth Century Perspective* (New York: Harper, 1972), 60–101.

³See R. P. Hart, "Of Genre, Computers, and the Reagan Inaugural," in H. Simons and A. Aghazarian (eds.), *Form, Genre, and the Study of Political Discourse* (Columbia: University of South Carolina Press, 1986), 278–98.

⁴R. P. Hart, "Culture, Rhetoric, and the Tragedy of Jimmy Carter," in J. Andrews and J. Lucaites (eds.), *Rhetorical Practices: Theory and Criticism* (in press).

⁵R. P. Hart, "The Rhetoric of the True Believer," *Communication Monographs*, 38 (1971), 249–61.

⁶R. P. Hart, "Absolutism and Situation: Prolegomena to a Rhetorical Biography of Richard M. Nixon," *Communication Monographs*, 43 (1976), 204–28.

⁷R. P. Hart, "The Functions of Human Communication in the Maintenance of Public Values," in C. Arnold and J. Bowers (eds.), *Handbook of Rhetorical and Communication Theory* (Boston: Allyn and Bacon, 1984), 749–91.

⁸I have defended this notion more fully in R. P. Hart, "Systematic Analysis of Political Discourse: The Development of DICTION," in K. Sanders, et al. (eds.), *Political Communication Yearbook: 1984* (Carbondale, IL: Southern Illinois University Press, 1985), 97–134.

⁹R. P. Hart, D. Smith-Howell and J. Llewellyn, "The Mindscape of the Presidency: *Time* Magazine, 1945–1985," *Journal of Communication*, 41 (1991), 6–25.

¹⁰R. P. Hart, P. Jerome and K. McComb, "Rhetorical Features of Newscasts about the President," *Critical Studies in Mass Communication*, 1 (1984), 260–86.

¹¹See R. P. Hart, "The Language of the Modern Presidency," *Presidential Studies Quarterly*, 14 (1984), 249–64.

¹²R. P. Hart, *The Sound of Leadership: Presidential Communication in the Modern Age* (Chicago: University of Chicago Press, 1987).

¹³R. P. Hart, "An Unquiet Desperation: Rhetorical Aspects of Popular Atheism in the United States," *Quarterly Journal of Speech*, 64 (1978), 33–46.

¹⁴See, for example, R. P. Hart, "Theory-Building and Rhetorical Criticism," *Communication Studies*, 27 (1976), 70–77; and "Contemporary Scholarship in Public Address: A Research Editorial," *Western Journal of Communication*, 50 (1986), 283–95.

¹⁵J. D. Barber, *The Presidential Character: Predicting Performance in the White House* (Englewood Cliffs, NJ: Prentice-Hall, 1972).

¹⁶R. P. Hart, *Verbal Style and the Presidency: A Computer-Based Analysis* (New York: Academic Press, 1984).

¹⁷R. Bellah, "Civil Religion in America," *Daedalus* (Winter, 1967), 1–21.

¹⁸R. P. Hart, *The Political Pulpit* (W. Lafayette, IN: Purdue University Press, 1977).

CHAPTER 4

THE INVENTION OF RHETORICAL CRITICISM IN MY WORK

Michael M. Osborn

In this essay, Michael M. Osborn reflects on his own critical scholarship as an entry-point into three central issues: What is the nature of rhetorical criticism? What stance should the critic assume? What questions should the critic ask? Osborn's answer characterizes an approach to criticism that is concerned with "the recovery of the rhetorical moment," the fullest appreciation of the products of the art of rhetoric. Osborn describes the influence of his background in literary studies as making him "more at home with the texture of vital images in discourse than with skeins of practical reasoning."

This chapter promises consideration of three central and related issues: (1) what is the proper nature of the object of rhetorical criticism? (2) what critical stance should the critic assume in response to this object? and (3) what questions should the critic ask? In this essay I will reflect on these questions, especially as they pertain to my own scholarship.

I

The question of "proper object" for rhetorical criticism goes to the genesis of my life as a scholar. After I had graduated with a master's degree in literary studies, I had to choose between continuing in that field or going into what was then called "Speech." I decided on Speech, and one of the factors in that decision, I now realize, was the nature of the texts studied in the two disciplines. Literary texts, at least in that time, were regarded as art objects. They were to be contemplated as self-contained and self-sufficient verbal masterworks, complete in themselves, standing out of time. Hemingway presented the point of view well in *Death in the Afternoon*, as he commented that the value of a "major art" can only be assessed after its timeliness has faded and "the unimportant physical rottenness of whoever made it is well buried," revealing finally its gleaming virtues.[1] Obviously this view has an honorable antiquity, reaching back to Longinus, who suggested that only the tests of time and diverse audiences could decide the excellence of artistic works. Hemingway and Longinus, it is clear, would reject *timeliness* and *intensity of appeal* for specific audiences as significant criteria for deciding on discursive excellence. Indeed, it is the secondary, inferior nature of intense but ephemeral appeal that requires Hemingway to consign reluctantly his beloved bullfighting to a minor place within the pantheon of the arts. Yet typically, it is these very criteria that loom large in the assessments of rhetorical critics.

As art objects, literary works do command attention in and of themselves, and finely wrought, enduring novels often can be more intrinsically engaging than discourse that is primarily rhetorical, that exists to confront life around it and to play a role in the fate of change. But if the literary art object is often more intrinsically interesting, the same cannot be said for the nature and significance of the critical questions one poses in response to literary and rhetorical creations. At least it was true for me that the literary criticism practiced during my neophyte scholarly days too often seemed to trivialize the objects of its interests. What books was Byron reading while writing *Childe Harold's Pilgrimage*, and what is the evidence of their influence, are questions that fascinate a fairly restricted audience at a relatively specialized level of interest. Rhetorical criticism, on the other hand, seemed to open a new field of inquiry, one that might contribute substantially to knowledge about human behavior. Of course the objects of rhetorical criticism were different kinds of objects—they were actually not objects but agents, engines of influence. They courted listeners, seeking not esthetic distance but strategic closeness. Whereas literary art objects had a certain density, themselves being the termini of attention, rhetorical productions were translucent. Through them one might see dimly configurations of power, prejudice, and piety, all witnessing and manipulating the courtship ritual. Rhetorical productions themselves had an enthymematic quality, in that they rested on foundations of faith and taste that were outside themselves, presumably in the audiences they addressed. They had, to use a term happily offered just recently by Michael C. McGee, a *fragmentary* quality. To reconstruct a sense of that wholeness in which they once participated is a major task of rhetorical critics, just as paleoanthropologists often must seek to reconstruct an entire lost species from a few fragments of bone. Except that the work of the rhetorical critic is as much a matter of art as it is of science. Indeed, one of the special joys of rhetorical criticism is its essential creative function. Recently, as I labored to recapture the wholeness of that rhetorical energy-field to which Martin Luther King's last speech in Memphis made dynamic contribution, I commented on the artful nature of rhetorical criticism in this way:

> Criticism itself must participate in the final fate of the rhetorical event. Rhetorical artistry is not preserved entire in a monument of words; any surviving text must be fragmentary, dependent for its appreciation on the critical gloss. The critic becomes an archaeologist of the meaning surrounding the rhetorical moment. Therefore, rhetorical criticism is essential to the symbolic after-life of the artistry it contemplates. Such criticism freezes an evanescent moment for lasting contemplation: on the rhetorical critic's urn, forever shall they speak and listeners be moved.[2]

While the critic's own art work seems integral to the recovery of the rhetorical moment, it is also true that the critic's obligation as scholar is not diminished. The practice of rhetorical criticism must be marked by integrity as well as imagination; it must be a *faithful rendering of events*. The critic does not become the primary artist in the rhetorical production; rather the critic functions as the medium through which that production is preserved. If the critic wishes to argue, and to use rhetorical performance itself as evidence for a case, then in that moment the criticism itself transforms into a rhetorical performance that invites its own critical appreciation.

Obviously, this view will not be acceptable to those who argue that the criticism *ought to* or even *must* function as advocacy. Clearly, criticism can motivate advocacy, and can itself become evidence in the case we create, but some distinction may yet be desirable between the critical and rhetorical enterprises. Despite the subjectivity of all experience, the critic *qua critic* strives as much as possible to see rhetorical events through eyes unimpeded by political or personal interest. Objectivity may be an unreachable star, but nevertheless it can still guide the critical quest.

If I was drawn initially to rhetorical criticism by some intimation of its urgency in recapturing and preserving vital discursive events, I was also schooled initially to think of these events primarily in terms of speeches. I am still comfortable in giving much of my critical attention to speeches, perhaps because I remain fascinated by the power, sense of public ritual and ordeal, complexity of challenge, and risk this form of expression seems to entail. Moreover, I was much influenced early in my career by the following reflections from Hegel's *Reason in History:*

> Speeches are actions among men and, indeed, most effective ones. . . . Speeches from peoples to peoples or to peoples and princes are integral parts of history. Even granted, therefore, that orations like those of Pericles—that most profoundly accomplished, most genuine, and most noble of statesmen—had been elaborated by Thucydides, they were yet not foreign to Pericles' character. In these orations these men expressed the maxims of their people, of their own

personality, the consciousness of their political situation, and the principles of their moral and spiritual nature, their aims and actions.[3]

When we realize that the advancing species-consciousness that so fascinated Hegel often glimmers first in the minds of great orators and leaders, then the importance of significant speeches seems all the more underscored. Finally, I accepted the centrality of speeches as objects of critical concern for the simple reason that no other departments of academic study seemed inclined or equipped to deal with them as serious and unique forms of expression. If they were to be appreciated and preserved *as rhetorical events,* then rhetorical scholars must assume that moral as well as academic duty.

Having established the piety of my concern with significant speeches, I now confess that my first exercise as a fledgling rhetorician came as I studied Swift's passionate *Drapier Letters.* I never believed in making speeches the *exclusive* objects of rhetorical criticism; such misplaced sense of loyalty as one used to encounter in our discipline succeeded only in distorting the study of rhetoric by featuring a form at the expense of the function. That function, which is to form, reinforce, and dissolve the bonds of social consanguinity, can work through forms as disparate as blatant letters to the editor or television situation-comedies masquerading as entertainments as they subvert orientations and model proper actions. A considerable irony for me was to return recently to certain prominent novels, and to discover that literary critics had too often botched the job of reading their significance, because that significance was inscribed in the language of rhetoric.[4]

II

These thoughts on the "proper object" of rhetorical criticism also suggest appropriate stances for the critic. By "stance" I mean how the critic positions her- or himself vis-à-vis the critical object in order to perform the task of criticism. This task is to appreciate as fully as possible the nature of some rhetorical interaction, taking into account the constraints of *in vivo* rhetorical performance. This appreciation enables the critic to realize the magnificence or meanness of rhetorical behavior, its summons to greatness or its outright exploitation of those whom it addresses. And the critic can then perform the creative and re-creative duties described in the previous section.

The critical object we have described can only be characterized as unstable and ephemeral, losing its original coloration as the moment of its production fades, assuming new colorations as it passes into new situations and performs new functions for new audiences. If the object is unstable, then the critic's work is correspondingly precarious. Always, rhetorical critics risk deceiving themselves and others. For these reasons, we ought to especially admire critical performance when it is well executed.

As I reflect upon my own critical stance with respect to objects of rhetorical criticism, I detect two opposing extremes of position. My first strategy was to assume that if specific rhetorical efforts resist responsible critical reading, then one ought to survey large numbers of such efforts to detect patterns of repetition or similarity as preserved in the fragmentary texts. This strategy is clearly akin to a scientific orientation, for it assumes the unreliability of single instances while it also privileges the importance of "constants" that emerge across a field of critical inspection. My point of entry into rhetorical scholarship was the *metaphor,* which at that time had only begun to impinge significantly upon the world of rhetorical scholarship.[5] To that point, literary critics had dominated the study of figuration, regarding it usually as a phenomenon within the art objects they contemplated. Therefore, they studied metaphorical meaning more as an intrinsic contextual phenomenon.[6] The realization that metaphor might also tap into deep communal and archetypal susceptibilities, that it might move mass audiences to action as well as invite individual esthetic response, had not yet dawned in the world of rhetorical scholarship. Sensing the fragility and instability of the rhetorical object, I sought to read widely among speech texts, especially as I sought to describe patterns of archetypal behavior. Thus I sought to describe certain prominent forms of metaphor in speeches across time, or I sought to identify patterns of metaphorical usage across the corpus of a rhetorician's work.[7] Perhaps I sensed that the enduring stability of archetypal meaning might somehow compensate for the instability of a given instance of rhetorical practice. For this reason, much of my early rhetorical scholarship might better be described as metacritical, on the border between theory and criticism, as it sought to identify reliable features in such fleeting phenomena.

At the other extreme from a stance so distant from specific instances and events is my recent effort to criticize King's "Mountaintop" speech. I assumed the risk—and to some extent the presumptuousness—of such criticism because I had been part of the scene of that speech. I thought I might be unusually qualified to transcend the fragmentary text to capture the largeness of the interactive process to which that speech contributed. Here I was performing what I had earlier called *close criticism,* "which engages specific rhetorical actions," in contrast with *perspective criticism,* "which places specific actions within some overall frame of rhetorical process."[8] I had gone on to describe the aims of close criticism as follows: "Close criticism aspires to an enlightened understanding of *challenges* confronted by rhetors in the moment, the *options* available in confronting these challenges, an assessment of the rhetor's *performance,* a description of the rhetoric as *consummated* in that moment when rhetor, audience, and message converge, and the various *consequences* of the interaction." Note that the close critic of rhetorical events should be singularly qualified by circumstance and preparation to perform justly and with circumspection. Ideally, close critics will have breathed the air of that rhetoric; their nerve ends will have resonated with its tensions. Such critics always run the danger of a kind of shallow impudence that offers facile judgments without a real under-standing of the terrible, sometimes contradictory forces that can drive the behaviors of rhetors locked within some desperate moment. The urn for such criticism, which we described earlier, must be quite large, its colors rich and subtle, its brushwork informed by the wholeness of the events depicted.

I am aware as I write that these reflections on critical stance may raise serious questions about the efficacy of much that has passed for rhetorical criticism in our field. Of course, nothing better answers such ruminations than examples of excellent critical work, and fortunately there seem to be more and more of these as rhetorical scholarship continues to mature.

▓ III

What forces have shaped the critical questions I have asked and continue to ask? This difficult question requires a degree of self-understanding I am not certain I possess. The questions we ask spring from inventional processes that run deep in our natures. Moreover, each vital day in the production of scholarship brings countless small frustrations and illuminations that make up the inventional history of any scholarly production. Re-creating that kind of history in connection with any one of my published essays would be impossible at this point. Nevertheless, as I reflect upon the general trajectory of my work as rhetorical scholar, I can recall important factors and moments that might help explain the questions I have asked.

One such factor was the background of training and orientation I brought to my graduate work in rhetoric. In my literary studies I had concen-trated on the make-believe world of fiction and drama and on the world of feeling and insight expressed in poetry. From the very beginning I would be more at home with the texture of vital images in discourse than with skeins of practical reasoning. A second factor was the environment I encountered during my training at the University of Florida. I was fortunate to find there a compatible group who were eager to examine new conceptions of rhetori-cal scholarship. Among them was Gerry Mohrmann, who shared my interest in the intersection of literary and rhetorical studies and became a lifelong friend. Douglas Ehninger, my first mentor, encouraged innovative scholarly work, and made me believe that I might make a contribution to knowledge. As my research program began to develop, Charles Morris, a philosopher who pioneered in the field of semiotics research, shared my excitement over my discoveries, convinced me that they had value, and took over the direc-tion of my dissertation when Ehninger moved to Iowa. All in all, it was a heady environment for a fledgling scholar.

Much of what we were reacting against at that time was unimaginative criticism, since critiqued very nicely by Edwin Black,[9] that imposed an obligatory formula on scholars assessing the speaking careers of individual rhetors. I found most such work deadly dull, and thought it offered little to what Bacon had called "the advancement of learning." Moreover, I decided early that I did not want to focus my study on a "man." Such studies seemed to make the mistake of treating speeches as art objects rather than as translucent expression. In the world of art objects, speeches would always be doomed to inferior status. Even worse, their discursive nature and values would be distorted. But as *means* of study rather than *objects* of study, speeches in their unique translucence might reveal configurations of behavior and culture not otherwise visible. So I decided that I would isolate an interesting rhetorical phenomenon and study its manifestations across speeches. Ehninger encouraged this inclination and suggested I might want to consider the seemingly rich but lightly explored subject of rhetorical symbolism. While excited by that possibility, I was at the same time bothered by its complexity and vagueness. I sensed that it might open onto a vast field of study, that there might in fact be many forms of powerful rhetorical symbolism that would require serious and disciplined investigation. So my inclination was to concentrate on one such form to see where this might lead me. I was convinced that metaphor might be such a form, and that the metaphor in rhetoric and the rhetoric in metaphor had been generally neglected. So I set out on a long, personal odyssey in quest of rhetorical metaphor.

From the very beginning I rejected the study of metaphor as a surface textual phenomenon. The metaphor I wanted to study, I wrote in 1961 in my first convention paper, functioned not as "ornament" but as "argument."[10] If we were to understand the thought patterns that flowed visibly in the speech, we would have to find or reconstruct the fundamental, often implicit metaphors that generated thought, both in speakers and in the cultures they represented. Indeed, argumentation might be studied often as the clash of basic metaphors. Such metaphors must be studied as inventional phenomena. The paper was controversial, and I was advised, probably wisely, to let my thoughts ripen more before I ventured into print. I continued reading and thinking, and I do remember the evening when it occurred to me that one might form a visual model of the process of metaphor I. A. Richards had described.[11] Before I could even begin to sketch the model on paper, I could see it vividly as though it were printed on the wall of my study. It was an electric moment. I presented my discovery in a research paper before Morris's seminar in the philosophy of language, and his reaction was one of the great moments of my life: "Paul Henle [another philosopher] once commented that there is nothing new to be said on the subject of metaphor," he told the group. "I no longer believe that statement." Susie and I were living on my fellowship at the time, but we had steak that evening!

Once the model was in place, my thinking began to develop very rapidly. Soon I had progressed from a static to a process model, because as a rhetorician I was sensitive to the role of audience in creating metaphorical meaning.[12] Indeed, I relocated metaphor as an "adventure in meaning" within the minds of listeners, and began thinking, beyond Richards, about the forces that might constrain the interaction of tenor and vehicle. This led me to form a theory of *qualifiers*, forms of influence that might shape this interaction. In my dissertation, I emphasized the following kinds of qualifiers: *contextual, situational, communal, archetypal,* and *personal.*[13] One of these forms, the archetypal, struck me as especially interesting. I had learned that rhetoric was indeed timely, powerful but ephemeral, and it was clear that the study of rhetoric belonged more to specific situations and audience interactions. It was the fate of rhetoric most often to become quickly dated. How then might one reconcile the presence within many rhetorical documents of metaphorical forms that appeared timeless, that appealed across many audiences and situations? My curiosity over this question turned my research in a decisive direction, leading to essays on metaphors of light and darkness, space, and the sea. Eventually I saw that metaphors that depend more on communal qualification, meanings that belong to a specific culture of usage, form a nice contrast with archetypes. I began to describe these figures as *culturetypes.*[14]

To this point it was clear that the direction of my research was towards a finer, increasingly narrow focus. It was while completing a writing assignment with the SRA company that this direction began to turn. The challenge seemed simple enough: I had merely to summarize and simplify the traditional principles of rhetorical style in a small book for an anticipated readership of advanced undergraduates. What I quickly rediscovered was the truth of nineteenth-century philosopher Herbert Spencer's observation: *no one had ever identified such principles within a comprehensive theory.*[15] There were a few scattered observations about the rhetorical functions of language, most of them admonitions to be simple, clear, etc., accompanied by a catalog of figures of speech. Inclusion within this catalog seemed more by tradition than by principle. What I had to do then was to pick up the challenge where Spencer had left it—I had to discover and construct these principles, and the meta-principles that in turn tied them together into a coherent theory. I must say that I *felt* this challenge more than I was able to articulate it for myself; that is, until I was finally able to solve the problem.

What I did was to study the more prominent figures of speech in various contexts until I was able to see underlying categories of functions that they performed and to which they variously belonged. Moreover, it was clear that these functions were related, in the sense that one such function would seem to be preparatory to the next in a sequential, circular pattern that one might read across an entire campaign of related discourses. The arc of the circle began with strategic depiction, as rhetors sought to influence the way that auditors perceived the subjects of discourse. Most vital metaphors, it seemed to me, did much of their work within this basic function. But this function led to another, the control of feeling, as rhetors sought to fan audience response to what they perceived. The next task was to transform these feelings into a shared sense of group membership as rhetors sought to mobilize audiences into action groups. To achieve this group identity, it would be necessary to develop a kind of folk theater that would be accepted as truth, and that would include images of heroism, villainy, martyrdom, and ideal identity. The rhetor also must cultivate a specific vocabulary of vital symbols that expressed the values of group membership. Linking with the group function was the rhetoric of action, both implementing and sustaining concerted behaviors toward desired ends. The final point on the arc was ritual behavior that celebrated and affirmed group values and accomplishments, and that reinforced vital forms of perception. Thus the linkage back to strategic depiction would be effected.

When I was able to frame, identify, and describe this interlocking structure of functions, then for the first time I was able to state the significance of metaphor within a more comprehensive theory of style. As this theory has developed in subsequent writings, the focus of my thought has continued to broaden. From stating the function of metaphor within a theory of style, I have gone to stating the theory of symbolic action within a larger theory of rhetorical process,[16] and that theory I am now contemplating within an even larger frame of social organization. Thus the trajectory of my scholarly life has tracked into specialization and out again into generalization, and as I have traced that curve the kinds of critical questions I have asked of discourse have varied accordingly.

IV

While many of the critical questions I have asked have been suggested by my own scholarly interests, I have been constantly influenced by the work of other rhetorical scholars. Recent theoretical discoveries have created a profusion of ways to assess rhetorical practice, enriching and expanding the inventional processes of rhetorical criticism. In this final section I wish to sketch a way to access these expanded options through four propositions which center on the nature and work of rhetoric itself.

1. *Rhetoric fashions an integrated system of evidence, proofs, and arguments.* This view of rhetoric's identity suggests that the critic view rhetoric more as a rational system created in quest of assent and consent. It presumes that people are often susceptible to an overall arrangement of evidence, combined into proofs, combined again into arguments, which seeks to convince listeners of the fundamental rightness and soundness of a position in con-

ns is that of story-telling.[19] He insists that
propositional perspective) is at best only
nse of the wholeness of experience. The
g in fiction—there must be engaging
satisfying conclusions or denouements,
et what they deserve—spill over into life
our most intellectual activities, as when
lectical inquiries, should be viewed as
the stories we are living.
ful symbols. This perspective offers a
f communication resources in which
elop and move. The effectiveness of
rhetor engages these systems. Here
ypal metaphor, for it postulates a
their attachment to fundamental
ed that this system might include
he most potent metaphors within
spatial contrasts, mountains, war,
re, and the family.
contrasting category of powerful
essence of this contrast is that
They evolve and change along
of symbols was described by
devil terms, defined by the way
ure. Writing for his own time,
such words as "progress,"
trast with such devil-terms
rds, he suggested, ha
d successfully in
lturetypal catego
cGee. McGee has
nd expressions tha
rated expressions o
e. Rhetor

mous
into the
onents from
closeness.
[18] Humans con-
their cocoons become

Bcof pu   supply exciting visions of
stantly models of disciplined, pious living. To
their re rect these organic fantasies and examine
purpose conditions developed in response to their
underst the extent to which reality conformed to the
he exte
lines

he calls the *narrative paradigm*, suggesting that

the fundamental nature of huma
the rational perspective (our first
partial, and that it robs us of a se
requirements for good story-tellin
beginnings, exciting conflicts, and
in which the characters in the story g
narratives as well, Fisher insists. Even
we engage in debate and pursue dia
episodes within the wider context of

3. *Rhetoric activates arrays of powe*
view of language-in-use as a universe o
certain powerful systems of symbols de
rhetoric often depends on how artfully a
obviously belongs my notion of archet
system of powerful metaphors defined b
forms of experience. An examination of
fifty-six world-historical speeches suggest
metaphors of light and darkness, the sea,
the human body, sexuality, disease and cu

As I noted earlier, there may be also a o
symbols that one might call *culturetypes.* The
culturetypes are timely and culture specific.
with the drift in culture. One such group
Richard Weaver as *ultimate terms* or *god-and-*
they express deeper value tendencies of a cult
the decade of the 1950s, Weaver pointed to
"scientific," "modern," and "efficiency," in con
"communism" and "un-American." Such wo
unusual power to move audiences when invoke

Another, more recent discovery within the cu
erful symbols has been made by Michael Calvin M
what he calls *ideographs,* certain abstract words a
tion as compressed ideology. They offer concen
underlying ideology or political beliefs of a peopl
as ultimate sanctions for courses of action. Thus
"liberty," "rugged individualism," and "We the Pe
rich with potential to move audiences. McGee's disc
useful when applied in rhetorical criticism. When I
combine it with the study of *icons,* defined as picto
ments of ideographs. Such images may seem to
quality, precisely because they are so laden with
of Liberty and the frontiersman as an icon f

flict. This proposition derives from the integrated systems approach outlined in Aristotle's *Rhetoric*. In addition to considering specific forms of evidence, proofs, arguments, and the relations among them, the critic responding to this perspective may also examine patterns of arrangement that structure a single discourse or the many discourses within a rhetorical campaign. The critic may well be alert to the presence of enthymemes, formed often by the interplay of premises both developed in discourse and embedded within the culture of the audience. As joint creations, enthymemes can connect rhetor, discourse, and audience in a sense of shared meaning.

2. *Rhetoric structures experience in terms of plotlines.* The conception of human existence as an aimless, drifting iteration of births and deaths, beginnings and endings, without destination or meaning beyond its own immediate needs and satisfactions, is intolerable in public rhetoric. The tendency of such rhetoric is to cast public life in terms of a melodrama, heavily moralistic, replete with two-dimensional heroes and villains (simply observe the rhetorical displays in a typical political campaign). I first encountered this perspective on rhetoric in an intriguing observation in George Campbell's *The Philosophy of Rhetoric,* in which he described metaphor as "an allegory in miniature." Campbell's observation suggests to me that the language of public discourse is deeply embued with moral colorations, and that it is replete with potential stories, either waiting to be told in discourse or to be played out implicitly in the minds of an audience. This perspective has been popular among contemporary critics, especially as developed in the ideas of Kenneth Burke, Ernest Bormann, and Walter Fisher.

For Burke, rhetoric is a *drama* of competing identifications in which speakers strive to overcome division and separation and to draw near their listeners by sharing visions, experiences, images, values, pieties, hierarchies, emotions, dialects. The critical vocabulary that has developed around this hub of dramatistic conception invites critics to consider rhetorical performance in terms of actors, scenes, agents, agencies, and purpose—the famous Burkean "pentad."[17] Competing rhetors try in turn to drive wedges into the identification rituals, to discredit them, to distance their opponents from listeners and to replace them in such positions of esteemed closeness.

Bormann emphasizes the fantasy-play of experience.[18] Humans constantly spin out fantasies to surround themselves—their cocoons become their reality. The prevailing fantasies of public life supply exciting visions of purpose and destination and offer models of disciplined, pious living. To understand a people we must resurrect these organic fantasies and examine the extent to which actual life-conditions developed in response to their plotlines—in short, determine the extent to which reality conformed to the folk art of their fantasies.

Fisher has pursued what he calls the *narrative paradigm,* suggesting that the fundamental nature of humans is that of story-telling.[19] He insists that the rational perspective (our first propositional perspective) is at best only partial, and that it robs us of a sense of the wholeness of experience. The requirements for good story-telling in fiction—there must be engaging beginnings, exciting conflicts, and satisfying conclusions or denouements, in which the characters in the story get what they deserve—spill over into life narratives as well, Fisher insists. Even our most intellectual activities, as when we engage in debate and pursue dialectical inquiries, should be viewed as episodes within the wider context of the stories we are living.

3. *Rhetoric activates arrays of powerful symbols.* This perspective offers a view of language-in-use as a universe of communication resources in which certain powerful systems of symbols develop and move. The effectiveness of rhetoric often depends on how artfully a rhetor engages these systems. Here obviously belongs my notion of archetypal metaphor, for it postulates a system of powerful metaphors defined by their attachment to fundamental forms of experience. An examination of the most potent metaphors within fifty-six world-historical speeches suggested that this system might include metaphors of light and darkness, the sea, spatial contrasts, mountains, war, the human body, sexuality, disease and cure, and the family.

As I noted earlier, there may be also a contrasting category of powerful symbols that one might call *culturetypes.* The essence of this contrast is that culturetypes are timely and culture specific. They evolve and change along with the drift in culture. One such group of symbols was described by Richard Weaver as *ultimate terms* or *god-and-devil terms,* defined by the way they express deeper value tendencies of a culture. Writing for his own time, the decade of the 1950s, Weaver pointed to such words as "progress," "scientific," "modern," and "efficiency," in contrast with such devil-terms as "communism" and "un-American." Such words, he suggested, had an unusual power to move audiences when invoked successfully in discourse.

Another, more recent discovery within the culturetypal category of powerful symbols has been made by Michael Calvin McGee. McGee has isolated what he calls *ideographs,* certain abstract words and expressions that function as compressed ideology. They offer concentrated expressions of the underlying ideology or political beliefs of a people. Rhetors may use them as ultimate sanctions for courses of action. Thus words like "freedom," "liberty," "rugged individualism," and "We the People" may be especially rich with potential to move audiences. McGee's discovery has proved most useful when applied in rhetorical criticism. When I use the concept, I often combine it with the study of *icons,* defined as pictorial or concrete embodiments of ideographs. Such images may seem to possess a secular-sacred quality, precisely because they are so laden with political values. The Statue of Liberty and the frontiersman as an icon for individualism are good examples. My suggestion is that the *combination* of ideograph and icon may be especially potent in popular discourse, because it offers the virtues of both abstract and concrete rhetorical expression.

4. *Rhetoric is an instrument of power.* The rhetorical critic who responds to this perspective has an inherent distrust of popular discourse. The assumption may be that power itself is usually malevolent, in service to its own selfish interests, and that popular discourse simply places a pleasant mask on ugly motivations. The function of the critic is to strip away the mask of the implicit structure of interests and assumptions we have come to accept without question that in effect constrains us. The aim of such criticism is emancipation.

To illustrate the assumptions undergirding this critical perspective, we need only cite one of its more influential proponents, Michel Foucault: "Truth isn't outside power, or lacking in power . . . truth isn't the reward of free spirits, the child of protracted solitude, nor the privilege of those who have succeeded in liberating themselves. Truth is a thing of this world. . . . And it induces regular effects of power. Each society has its regime of truth, its 'general politics' of truth. . . ."[20]

One remarkable feature of this perspective is that it places the critic in a heroic, even Promethean position. The critic brings the fire of her or his superior knowledge of rhetoric and its stratagems to the unmasking of discourse, to the end that readers might be saved from possible victimage. To engage in such criticism is by necessity to assume an activist posture and to renounce the traditional role of the scholar who is a mere observer upon life. (It is these critics who would insist on the "mere"; their position is that the old scholarly robe was itself designed by power sources so that the pursuit of knowledge—always dangerous to established power—might be relegated, enfeebled, and controlled.)

Within the activist posture required by this critical perspective, the old academic values of detachment and objectivity are scorned. One such critic asks feelingly "why ignoring the murder of men, women, and children following from actions justified in public address should count as a triumph of scholarly restraint."[21] Why, indeed. One of the major contributions of the "rhetoric is power" perspective may well be the restoration of passion and personal engagement in the critical act. And that is no small gift.

As I reflect upon this plenitude of perspectives on the nature of rhetoric, and how they enrich the inventional processes of criticism, I become aware of the spiritual distance we have traversed in the thirty years since I began work in this discipline. There is a marvelous human story here, to which so many have contributed so substantially. As a collective human enterprise, scholarship is surely a noble venture.

▓ Notes

[1]Ernest Hemingway, *Death in the Afternoon* (New York: Scribner's, 1960) 99.

[2]"The Last Mountaintop of Martin Luther King, Jr.," *Martin Luther King, Jr., and the Sermonic Power of Public Discourse,* eds. Carolyn Calloway-Thomas and John Louis Lucaites (Tuscaloosa, AL: University of Alabama Press, in press).

[3]Georg Wilhelm Friedrich Hegel, *Reason in History: A General Introduction to the Philosophy of History,* trans. Robert W. Hartman (New York: Liberal Arts Press, 1953) 4–5.

[4]"Rhetorical Depiction," *Form, Genre, and the Study of Political Discourse,* ed. Herbert W. Simons and Aram A. Aghazarian (Columbia: University of South Carolina Press, 1986) 79–107.

[5]Kenneth Burke, that trailblazer in rhetorical and literary studies, had laid the foundations for an appreciation of the rhetorical significance of metaphor in *Permanence and Change: An Anatomy of Purpose* (New York: New Republic, 1935).

[6]We first characterized contextual, communal, and archetypal forms of meaning in Michael Osborn and Douglas Ehninger, "The Metaphor in Public Address," *Speech Monographs* 29 (1962): 223–34.

[7]Examples of longitudinal studies were "Archetypal Metaphor in Rhetoric: the Light-Dark Family," *Quarterly Journal of Speech* 53 (1967): 115–26, and "The Evolution of the Archetypal Sea in Rhetoric and Poetic," *Quarterly Journal of Speech* 63 (1977): 347–63. An example of focus upon the overall production of a speaker was "Vertical Symbolism in the Speeches of Edmund Burke," *Studies in Burke and His Time* 10 (1969): 1232–38.

[8]"A Philosophy of Criticism," remarks at the Eastern Communication Association Convention, 1988.

[9]*Rhetorical Criticism: A Study in Method* (New York: Macmillan, 1965).

[10]"The Use of the Image in Great Debate," paper presented to the Southern Speech Association Convention, April 1961.

[11]*The Philosophy of Rhetoric* (New York, 1936) 89–114.

[12]Both forms of model appear in the Osborn and Ehninger essay.

[13]"The Functions and Significance of Metaphor in Rhetorical Discourse," unpubl. Ph.D. diss., University of Florida, 1963.

[14]This term first appears in my *Orientations to Rhetorical Style* (Chicago: SRA, 1976).

[15]*Philosophy of Style: An Essay* (New York: Appleton, 1892).

[16]See my "Rhetorical Depiction" essay.

[17]See his discussions in *A Grammar of Motives* (New York: Prentice-Hall, 1945) and *A Rhetoric of Motives* (New York: Prentice-Hall, 1950).

[18]Ernest G. Bormann, *The Force of Fantasy: Restoring the American Dream* (Carbondale: Southern Illinois University Press, 1985).

[19]Walter R. Fisher, *Human Communication as Narration: Toward a Philosophy of Reason, Value, and Action* (Columbia: University of South Carolina Press, 1987).

[20]Michel Foucault, "Truth and Power," in *The Foucault Reader,* ed. Paul Rabinow (New York: Pantheon, 1984) 72–73.

[21]Philip Wander, "The Ideological Turn in Modern Criticism," *Central States Speech Journal* 34 (1983): 8.

PART II

CRITICAL INVENTION: MAXIMS, COMMENTARIES, AND CASES

MAXIM 1

CRITICISM REQUIRES UNDERSTANDING AND PURSUING ONE'S OWN INTERESTS

CHAPTER 5 ☐

FEMINIST CRITICISM AND
THE MARY TYLER MOORE SHOW

Bonnie J. Dow

In this commentary, Bonnie J. Dow locates the beginnings of her critical study of The Mary Tyler Moore Show *in the recurring presence of the show in her life: as a program she watched with her family on Saturday nights as a child, as an afternoon ritual when the show was in syndication, and even as a comfortable and comforting anchor when she moved to a new city. Her enjoyment of the program eventually merged with her growing interest in feminism and discourse.*

COMMENTARY

By 1988, when I began to write the essay that would become "Hegemony, Feminist Criticism, and *The Mary Tyler Moore Show*," I felt like I had been watching *The Mary Tyler Moore Show (TMTMS)* all my life. I almost had. It debuted on prime-time television when I was in elementary school, and watching it was a Saturday night event for my family. When it moved to syndication in the late 1970s, I watched the reruns almost daily after school. When I moved to Minneapolis in 1987, watching *TMTMS* every night comforted me during a time when I was lonely, living in a large city where I knew few people. Watching television is and always has been an immensely comfortable experience for me, one that I do not hesitate to admit that I enjoy (unlike many television critics, who hold the strange attitude that they really have no use or respect for the medium that they study—except for PBS, of course).

When I began to experiment with rhetorical criticism of fictional television in graduate school, I decided to write about *TMTMS* not only because it was an ideal artifact for exploring contemporary feminism, a prior interest of mine, but also because I knew it well enough that I was comfortable making generalizations about the entire series (which spanned seven years and almost two hundred episodes). In my experience with criticism of television series, the most useful insights apply to the series as a whole and are supported by numerous episodes. This is particularly true for an intensely generic form like situation comedy that draws persuasive power from the ability to hammer home the same message again and again.

The decision to approach *TMTMS* from a feminist perspective is a fairly obvious one, given the program's place in television history. All of the reading that I did about *TMTMS*, both in initial reviews of the show in the popular press and in more formal works on television history, commented on the program's status as the first sitcom influenced by feminism. Given the resistance to feminism in the 1970s (and since), the fact that *TMTMS* was so successful begged for a rhetorical explanation. However, few of the critical treatments of the program that I read attempted any kind of considered feminist evaluation and those that did seemed to leave out what I saw as distinctive about a *rhetorical* approach: a concern with how discourse functions for an audience. So my general question became: How was *TMTMS*, a program about a single, seemingly independent, working woman able to appeal successfully to a television audience accustomed to domestic sitcoms in which leading female characters were usually wives or mothers with little real power or independence?

As I began to watch *TMTMS* with a "critical" eye I found that my more specific inquiries about its feminist content were guided by my appreciation of the generic features of sitcoms. For example, I found myself asking: What is significant about the female characters in this show (particularly Mary Richards, of course), and what is the relationship of these characters to each other and to the male characters? How are those roles and relationships different from female roles and relationships in past sitcoms (and television in general)? Such questions reflected not just feminist concerns, but issues related to generic appeal. Given the power of genre to guide understanding, viewers are likely to understand a sitcom as much in relation to other sitcoms as in relation to their lives external to television. That is, Mary Richards's perceived atypicality would come from her difference from other female television characters more than from her difference from women in the life experience of viewers.

Moreover, the questions that began as questions about genre were also useful for investigating the feminist implications of the show. For example, a standard generic question I asked was: If all sitcoms are driven by a problem/solution narrative, then what kinds of problems occur in this show and how do they get solved? This led to: What is the role of Mary Richards, the main character, in that process? When you read the final essay, it's easy to see that these two questions, basic as they are, turned out to be the most fruitful in terms of leading me to significant patterns in *TMTMS*.

All of these questions reflect my particular bias of viewing television with an eye for comparison. For example, I've done further work on other, more recent sitcoms with feminist implications and I always find myself asking how they compare with *TMTMS.* Yet this habit has led me to understand that criticism relies on some kind of implicit or explicit comparison at every level. In the case of *TMTMS,* I specifically was concerned with generic and historical comparisons, but in most cases critics seem to ask questions that follow two general lines: "How is this discourse *like* something else (whatever that thing may be) and why is that illuminating or important?" and/or "How is this discourse *different from* something else and why is that illuminating or important?" (For more explanation of this perspective, see Adena Rosmarin, *The Power of Genre,* University of Minnesota Press, 1985.) The emphasis on comparison underscores my earlier conviction about the importance of extensive experience with the discourse—the better you know your subject matter, the more informed your comparisons will be.

To begin the process of answering the questions I had developed, I took detailed notes each time I watched an episode of *TMTMS.* I did not own a VCR at the time, so such written detail was necessary as well as helpful. Later, when I studied my collected notes on forty or fifty episodes, I found that they acted as a filter that allowed me to see patterns that I had not heretofore noticed. For instance, from repeated comments in my notes such as "Mary comforts," "Mary agrees to help," and "Mary gives advice," I began to notice the prominence of Mary Richards's problem-solving and emotional support functions across all kinds of plotlines. While I had begun this process assuming that the several episodes in the series' history that specifically addressed some kind of "feminist" issue (such as equal pay, equal opportunity, or sexual freedom) would be important to my analysis, I found that *TMTMS*'s recurring message about the role of women was as apparent in episodes that had no such feminist angle as in those that did. In fact, only one such explicitly "feminist" episode, the one in which Mary Richards hires a female sportscaster, was included in the final essay.

When I began to see these patterns across episodes, the essay began to take shape for me. The evidence that I had gathered indicated that, despite alteration in some superficial characteristics, the character of Mary Richards functioned much like female characters from past domestic sitcoms in terms of her relationships with other, specifically male, characters. Although my vital comparisons were taking shape, I had not yet found a way to discuss their importance on a more abstract level. Answering the second half of the compound question underlying criticism ("why is that illuminating or important?") gave me some trouble.

The result of this difficulty was that the version of the essay that I submitted for publication was extremely descriptive but lacked the all-important attention to "theoretical significance." The first reviews of the essay all said that I was not clear about the importance of what I was claiming. I had made an attempt to introduce the essay with a discussion of the assumptions of feminist criticism, but all of my experience with feminist criticism came from literary study and I learned, via some pointed observations from reviewers, that dealing with television was quite different from dealing with literature.

This was my first attempt at television criticism, and I was dealing with a problem of having no basis for comparison in the area of theoretical significance. My experience with the literature on women and popular culture and television and hegemony was limited, thus I was handicapped in arguing how my essay fit within this tradition. My reviewers kindly directed me to some reading, and the revised version of the essay was framed quite differently. The final version, in fact, has a paragraph devoted to the problems of transferring assumptions from feminist literary study to television.

Although it appeared at the time that the changes required were enormous, with hindsight I see that the majority of the analysis remained essentially the same as in the original version; what changed was the framing and interpretation of that analysis. In the conclusion section of the original version, I alluded to hegemony when making the claim for the limited progressiveness of *TMTMS*, but the entire mention of hegemony in that draft occupied about two sentences. The reviewers and the editor concurred that the use of hegemony should be expanded to provide an overall frame for the essay, a move that clarified the intent and the importance of the analysis enormously. *TMTMS* was, in fact, an ideal case study for making an argument about feminism and hegemony, and the reviewers directed me toward a terminology that became very useful.

Interestingly, my first revision of the manuscript, which made a strong argument for *TMTMS* as an example of hegemonic strategies working to contain feminism, opened a new area for disagreement. At least one reviewer claimed that the new version left too little room for the possibility that the show might contain *mixed* messages about feminism. I had landed myself in the middle of a current debate within media studies about how "open" texts were, how "active" audiences were, and how possible it was for viewers to "resist" the hegemonic message of a text. In the next revision, I qualified my claims a bit, arguing that *TMTMS* was interesting precisely because it had the potential to be interpreted in more than one way. However, I believed (and still do) that textual analysis of hegemonic strategies is equally as valuable as audience research, particularly for feminist critics, and I was able to add a brief section to the conclusion in which I made that argument.

In general, the essay was changed in some significant ways by the review process; though most of these changes were clearly beneficial, a few still trouble me. During most of the review process I was still a graduate student, however, and I felt that I was in no position to argue with many of the demands made by the editor and the reviewers. On the other hand, I realize now that the essay was fairly raw when I first sent it to be reviewed, so I am grateful that enough initial promise was seen in it to warrant requests for revision.

In total, I did four revisions of "Hegemony, Feminist Criticism, and *The Mary Tyler Moore Show*" in the eighteen months between when I submitted it and it appeared in print. The last of those revisions was required to shorten the piece because of space limitations in the issue for which it was intended. I regret parts of that final edit because I think it weakened the coherence of the essay and eliminated some important supporting material.

Contrary to my experience since, I struggled more with this essay *after* I submitted it for publication than I did before submitting it. That is, I did not find *TMTMS* a complex text to work with in terms of finding a focus for my analysis or discerning significant rhetorical strategies. However, the work of the revision process was a valuable learning experience through which I discovered that the negotiation that occurs between an author and her reviewers/editors is, in some cases, as important to the creative process as the critic's solitary struggle with the text.

Although they challenged my patience (and my ego) at points, the inquiries and suggestions offered by the readers of "Hegemony, Feminist Criticism, and *The Mary Tyler Moore Show*" did the project much more good than harm. I was blessed with readers who were sympathetic to the purpose and potential of the analysis and who genuinely wanted to make it better. Because of this early, positive experience, I now perceive the review process as an opportunity to augment and refine my ideas rather than as a threat to their survival. While this sanguine view requires perseverance and a willingness to compromise, its reward is often a stronger and more informed piece of criticism.

CHAPTER 6 ⌑

THE CAMPAIGN
FOR CIVIL DEFENSE

**Elizabeth Walker Mechling
and Jay Mechling**

*In this commentary, Elizabeth Walker Mechling and Jay Mechling describe
how a chance to write on "Cold War campaigns" triggered questions,
images, and personal memories from their childhoods in the 1950s. Writing
criticism became the chance for them to answer some of these questions, make
sense of the images, and reconcile the memories.*

COMMENTARY

The idea to write an essay on the civil defense campaign of the 1950s–60s
and on social movements resisting the campaign came to us through the sort
of serendipity many scholars relish. One of the things scholars do at their
scholarly conventions is sit in hotel bars and in airport waiting lounges
talking about ideas and plotting together the next collaboration on a convention panel or book project. These small groups make up the larger
"invisible colleges" of colleagues who depend upon each other for thoughtful criticism, ideas, and encouragement. In this case, three critics were
working on Cold War texts and wanted to put together a panel on "The
Rhetoric of Cold War Campaigns" for the 1988 meeting of the Western
Speech Communication Association. As the conversation developed, one of
the group turned to us and asked, simply, "What would you two want to do?"
We looked at each other and began to free-associate ideas about what Cold
War campaigns might interest us. Most of the images evoked during that
stream-of-consciousness (however distracted we were by the "help" we were
getting from our friends around the table) included the bomb and its
emblematic mushroom cloud. Those images, in turn, evoked personal memories.

Snapshot: Frank Walker is worried about his family. Living in south Florida, there are constant reminders of the threat of nuclear attack. To the north is Cape Canaveral and the fledgling space program. To the west lies Miami International Airport, a natural target. To the south sits a Strategic Air Command base at Homestead. To the east, of course, is the Atlantic Ocean. Nowhere to run. Frank cannot afford to build a bomb shelter and Florida houses do not have basements. So he designates a closet in the house as the most protected shelter in case of nuclear attack, and he fills a footlocker with bottled water, canned goods, first aid supplies, books, games, and seeds. Ruth and the five children know what to do in the case of attack. The seven Walkers will huddle in that closet, a mattress against the door, for as long as it takes to hear the all-clear signal.

Snapshot: June Mechling puts in long hours through the 1956–57 school year planning with other mothers an evacuation exercise for the children at Treasure Island Elementary School in Miami Beach, Florida. The PTA decided that they needed a plan for getting children from the school to their homes in the case of imminent nuclear attack. The mothers work for months assembling the plan, creating a telephone tree, lining up drivers, and so on. On the day of the drill, everything goes smoothly. As a safety patrol officer, sixth-grader Jay leads a group of children out of the school on a march down a street, across a bridge (the traffic halted by the local police), and to a parking lot full of cars waiting to carry the children to their homes. The mothers gather in the Mechling home to have drinks and celebrate a smooth drill, the point of which (though none would say this) is that the children can die at home rather than at school.

This is the madness we sought to understand. How could our parents, perfectly reasonable people, act in this way? How could we, cynical pre-adolescents then, also take this world as "natural"? How were we so easily socialized into Lifton's "nuclear culture"? How did some people in the 1950s resist the socialization, even to the point of creating social movements engaging in civil disobedience meant to thwart civil defense planning? The questions were real and troubling. This was no mere scholarly exercise of choosing an "interesting" topic. The stakes of self-understanding were high, both in retrospect for understanding our nuclear socialization, and in prospect for understanding what possibly pathological worldviews have become normal, "naturalized," for us in the 1990s. These questions led us to settle upon the civil defense campaigns and resistances as the texts we would analyze for the panel.

Most of our ideas for essays come in just this way. Some cultural experience strikes us as odd or puzzling. After talking about it for a while and getting more excited about the puzzle the more we talk about it, we usually resolve to write about the puzzle, using writing as our way of figuring it out. Our first joint work on theme parks began with such a puzzlement, as have our subsequent essays on sugar, on animal rights campaigns, and on the ABC Persian Gulf War special for kids. Indeed, our major individual projects—Elizabeth's work on free clinics and Jay's on the Boy Scouts of America—arose out of genuine cultural questions rooted in personal experiences.

So the puzzling texts present themselves first. We do not begin with a theory or method or hypotheses and then search for a case study to demonstrate or illuminate the theory. Rather, we bring to the text a repertoire of tools and ideas and fashion an approach we think appropriate to the text. Our educations have been thoroughly interdisciplinary, Elizabeth's in English and speech communication and Jay's in the conjunction of literary criticism, art criticism, history, anthropology, sociology, psychology, geography, and more that makes up an American studies training. Our training suits our cognitive styles, which is to say we consider the interdisciplinary imagination playful, eclectic, and inventive, seeing connections everywhere. The search for workable ideas and approaches should not end at the borders of the discipline. The borders, after all, are the most exciting place to be, both in cultures and in intellectual disciplines. The interdisciplinary imagination has a good enough map of the disciplines and a good enough compass (or sense of the goal) to draw upon whatever works best to solve the puzzles of the meanings of the text. As in Wallace Stevens's poem, "Thirteen Ways of Looking at a Blackbird," there are many ways to reinscribe the "meanings" of a text, and (still in Stevens's spirit) those meanings or truths we discover will always be partial and emergent. From the pragmatic perspective, our critical practice must be in concert with our moral and political goals; the practice must take us where we want to go. And "to work best" is a comparative judgment made by and within an interpretive community. The rhetorical critic must persuade readers that a given interpretation of texts finds some "truth" about the texts and their cultural contexts.

This is not to say we do not have some familiar starting points for every inquiry. For example, it always profits us to ask what Kenneth Burke would say about the text, so it seems clear that his dramatism and his attention to symbolic narratives on the mythological level appeal to our sense of the goals of culture criticism. Similarly, we always become smarter about a text when we ask what Peter Berger, Gregory Bateson, and the symbolic anthropologists (Mary Douglas, Victor Turner, Clifford Geertz) would have to say in an imagined group discussion about the text. And, of course, we always learn something new by asking what difference gender, race, ethnicity, social class, age, sexual orientation, or other human particularities make in creating and receiving the meanings of texts.

This way of operating has become more and more naturalized in our critical writing over the years, as we realized when the first round of reviewers' reports from the *Western Journal of Speech Communication* (now the *Western Journal of Communication*) asked for, as the editor put it, "a stronger theoretical basis." The first manuscript version of our essay did not address theory. We sat down to reconstruct our theoretical perspective from our critical practices, that is, from the manuscript in front of us. We wrote a new section, "Criticism in the Pragmatic Attitude," explaining our theoretical approach, though neither pragmatism nor the neopragmatism of Rorty, Bernstein, West, and others is best described as a "theory." We had to condense a lot of our thinking in a few pages, and we wished we had a whole essay to lay out a model of rhetorical criticism in the pragmatic attitude. Perhaps we shall. But we satisfied ourselves that we had articulated something of our approach, and the reviewers seemed pleased on the second round of reading.

The new section notwithstanding, the development of theory was not our primary aim at the outset of our study. The "text" was central, but at the beginning the "text" was some generalized memory of the civil defense campaign. Rhetorical critics need texts, so our first step was to search for the rhetorical artifacts we would study. The debate was a public one, so we looked mainly at the magazine articles (and some books) that constituted the debate. The discourse of the resistance is a bit harder to come by. As Elizabeth discovered in her work on the free clinic movement, most social movements generate ephemeral printed texts unlikely to be preserved in the usual library and institutional collections. Elizabeth's study of the free clinic movement was possible largely because one of the physicians active in the movement saved every scrap of paper that came his way. Fortunately for us, the Swarthmore College Peace Collection had files of social movement materials documenting some of the resistance to the civil defense campaigns.

Culture criticism now looks at a greatly expanded range of what we would call "texts," so we knew from the outset that we should think broadly about the debate over civil defense, even if we did not include every text in our analysis. We paid attention to the maps and photographs accompanying articles in magazines, and we were struck especially by the similarities between the drawings in fallout shelter pamphlets and the drawings common in magazine advertising in the 1950s. As teenagers we had both read Pat Frank's *Alas, Babylon,* a nuclear war novel set in Florida, and we knew that Philip Wylie (author of the apocalyptic novel *Tomorrow!*) was an early proponent of civil defense measures, so we returned to the fiction of the 1950s to understand how those texts may have contributed to nuclear culture. Our assumption that film and television provided the most important grand, mythic narratives led us to survey those media. We focused our critical attention on *On the Beach* and the *Twilight Zone* episode "The Shelter," because those texts played such a large role in the public discourse, but we easily could have extended our analysis to the science fiction films of the 1950s, to nuclear apocalyptic comic books, perhaps to *Mad Magazine,* and beyond. We knew intertextual relations were some of the most interesting aspects of the debate. Believing it more important to interpret a few, key texts in depth rather than create an uncritical inventory of texts and a map of their connections, we relegated these other texts to footnotes and, sometimes, to our file drawers.

Notice that we keep saying "we" in this discussion of how the essay came to be written. We began writing together when we began living apart in the late 1970s. Teaching at universities eighty miles distant (and a hard, congested commute), we lived apart four days a week and were together for long weekends. We reckoned that it would be good to have something beyond exhaustion and institutional complaints to bring us together on weekends, and we saw writing together as a positive force in our married life.

Writing together is far more difficult than solitary authorship. Many university merit review processes diminish the importance of joint authorship, sometimes only "counting" a joint article as "one-half a publication." While such skepticism may be warranted in the natural sciences, where people are added to a list of authors for minimal contribution, joint authorship in the humanities is quite another matter. In humanistic culture criticism the writing is no mere, flat report on the research. The humanist discovers what she knows and means through the writing, and when the writing is that important, more hands do not make light work. We joke that Elizabeth writes the verbs and adjectives and that Jay writes the nouns and adverbs, and those who know us well see the inside joke. A sense of humor helps. We both read all the texts and supporting materials and then engage in lengthy discussions about how to interpret the texts and about how to organize the essay. From a very sketchy and tentative outline, we usually take responsibility for writing the first draft of different sections, though sometimes only one of us will attempt the first draft. Then the real joint writing begins, as we meld the drafts, cut, paste, fill holes, and so on until we have an essay that satisfies us both.

Even so, the first version of the civil defense essay was long, and adding the section on "Criticism in the Pragmatic Attitude" meant that we had to cut even more in subsequent drafts. Sacrificed was a description and analysis of a speech by Edward Teller, answering the Gerald Piel speech (which we did describe and analyze). We were drawn to the details of that debate and could write a whole essay comparing those two speeches; perhaps we will, someday. In earlier drafts we addressed more explicitly the racial and social class nuances of the dispersal strategy, but at readers' urgings we demoted Dean MacCannell's provocative analysis to a footnote. Similarly, our original notes toward the essay explored in greater depth the gender politics encoded in the civil defense materials, but we abbreviated this dimension, in large part because Elaine Tyler May's fine book about the American family in the Cold War had just appeared. Finally, we resisted the temptation to create a conversation between this essay and the "Hot Pacifism and Cold War" essay we were working on simultaneously (and which appeared in the *QJS* in 1992). It was tempting to take advantage of the New Class thesis emerging in the pacifism essay and fold it back into the final revision of the civil defense essay, but the final revision is no time to introduce a new argument. Still, it is relevant for understanding the civil defense essay that we were immersed at the same time in the rhetoric of 1950s pacifism.

The opportunity to revise and shorten the essay also meant that we had to reconsider matters of organization and structure. One of the things we disagreed upon early was how much of our conclusion to give away in the early pages of the essay. Jay prefers the approach Stephen Jay Gould uses in his monthly essays for *Natural History,* wherein Gould usually poses a puzzle of some sort and begins working through it, recording all the dead-ends, complications, and such before arriving finally at the solution, much as a detective arrives at the solution in the last pages of a novel. Humanists seem most comfortable with this sort of narrative, and one will find in history and literary criticism journals many essays constructed this way. Another element of the humanist's rhetoric is to write an essay without subheadings, assuming that a well-written essay makes clear its organization and coherence without artificial signposts along the way.

Elizabeth warned against this approach. In her experience the editors, reviewers, and readers of essays in rhetorical criticism like to have the full thesis up front, with clear organization and subheadings. Perhaps this is the result of too many debaters in the profession. In any case, Elizabeth knew the conventions of the genre and thought the essay should follow those conventions. Jay prevailed, against Elizabeth's better judgment, and the reviewers' comments vindicated her view. One reviewer wrote, "The whole paper is, frankly, bass-ackwards. . . . The emphasis should be on the claim, not the examples. In fact, your best statement of a thesis is in your conclusion." We revised the essay accordingly, laying out our thesis at the outset and creating subheadings meant to clarify the organization of the essay. The reviewers liked the changes. Showing uncharacteristic restraint, Elizabeth did not say "I told you so."

Now, it is true that we should not make too much of this instance. We do not write as well as Gould and what we thought was artful might have been vague and clumsy. But putting aside for the moment the question of how well we executed our intentions in the first manuscript version of our essay, our experience suggests that the discipline of rhetorical criticism might not be served well by the present rhetorical conventions for the writing of rhetorical criticism. At a time when other disciplines are posing interesting questions about the ideological implications of their rhetorical conventions and are experimenting with new forms of discourse, the practice of rhetorical criticism seems to us inordinately conservative and conventional. One reviewer thought we "intruded" into the essay "much more than is needed," but the intrusion of the critic into the scene under study is precisely what is happening in, say, the new ethnography advocated by James Clifford and others. It is hard to tell if the conservative nature of the rhetoric of rhetorical criticism is due to the gatekeepers (the editors and reviewers) or, more probably, to the self-censoring of authors. Certainly it would be healthy for some journal or volume editor to invite explicitly unconventional, experimental approaches to writing rhetorical criticism.

The purpose of sociological thinking, wrote C. Wright Mills in *The Sociological Imagination,* is "to connect private troubles with public issues," a notion later endorsed by the women's movement in its insistence that, politically, the private is public. There is no better motto for American culture criticism. The act of reflexive culture criticism—that is, the unpacking of one's own cultural assumptions, the discovery of cultural contingency in the beliefs one most takes for granted—is a political act to the extent that it links the public and private. Only when we understand the ways in which our social locations and interests work to influence our views of the world can we sort the "is" from the "ought." Approached with the right attitude, the radical relativizing, the debunking, the deconstruction of the critic's own world should leave the critic not an immobilized victim in a web of cultural determinism but a social actor who understands both the limits of his or her knowledge and the necessity of making choices about his or her own lives and about the lives we influence. We live in a William Jamesian world of "forced options," so we had best arm ourselves both with the self-knowledge of contemporary culture criticism and with clarity about the intended (and unintended) consequences of our work.

CHAPTER 7 [　　　　　　　　　　　　　　]

THE FRANKENSTEIN MYTH
IN CONTEMPORARY CINEMA

Thomas S. Frentz
and Janice Hocker Rushing

In this commentary, Thomas S. Frentz and Janice Hocker Rushing describe how their study of the "Frankenstein myth" stemmed in part from their own uneasiness about technology in their lives. The project began, they report, because various events had prompted them to reflect on their ambivalence about the role of technology in their personal and academic lives. Rushing and Frentz share the conviction that finished criticism has more integrity if these triggering experiences are not discarded once the writing is begun, but are instead preserved as a reference point to provide bearings for the critic in the refining and explaining that is to come.

COMMENTARY

"The Frankenstein Myth in Contemporary Cinema" began when we saw *The Terminator* on television. Like many who viewed this film (having been conditioned, perhaps, by *Conan the Barbarian*), we expected little more than an evening of pumped-up posing, gratuitous violence, and monosyllabic mumbling. We were not, of course, disappointed. But we were also more than a little blown away by the relentlessness of the film's twenty-first-century cyborg and the bleakness of its postapocalyptic vision. For us, criticism typically starts as this kind of gut-level, unexamined intuitive feeling about a text(s). If we don't feel intensely about it one way or another—it can be hate, love, disgust, surprise, fear, awe, perplexity—we don't write.

Although criticism must eventually develop beyond this initial reaction that Robert Pirsig refers to in *Zen and the Art of Motorcycle Maintenance* as "preintellectual awareness," we try to honor it throughout the process. For us, this intuitive feeling is the purest "moment" in which the opposition between the critic-as-subject and the text-as-object is broken down, and it generally provides the "seed crystal" for the unfolding of the more reasoned aspects of the critique. We have discovered that the finished product has more integrity if we re-member its genesis in feeling even as we inevitably dis-member it intellectually to refine, revise, and explain. In our work, criticism typically unfolds as a series of analogies between the text and us as potential critics. That is, something in the text links up with something in us to form an insight or a problem that insists upon our attention. Such analogies usually multiply and they never occur in an orderly fashion. We often talk to other people about these analogies in seeking to solve the problem, develop an idea, or test some idiosyncrasy. If the analogies are numerous and/or intriguing enough we are almost compelled to work them out in writing. Many of these efforts lose steam, are soon forgotten, and/or end up in the circular file. A few are as tenacious as the Terminator, and evolve into full-blown analyses.

In the case of *The Terminator*, all sorts of analogical connections began to occur. Janice thought of Langdon Winner's *Autonomous Technology* and Jacques Ellul's *The Technological Society*, both of which worried that technological perfection would render humans obsolete. She also remembered she had been dreaming for some time of technologically constructed men, some with neck bolts and others with missing limbs, and despite Tom's suggestion that these nocturnal events were simply residue fears that his recently repaired neck discs and "scoped" knee were but signs of things to come, she had learned over time not to dismiss such synchronistic occurrences out of hand. We also realized that just about every major appliance in and around our house had gone berserk or quit in the last few months. Not only was this irritating in and of itself, but it prompted some abashed semiphilosophical musings concerning our own dependence on our technological trappings. Furthermore, we had just purchased, only about a decade after everybody else, a personal computer. Tom was touchy about giving up his legal pad. "It has no right," he used to complain, "to ask me whether I am *sure* I want it to do something. If I wasn't sure, I wouldn't have asked!" The *coup-de-grace* came when our Imagewriter II refused to print the draft of an idea we had on technology developing a mind of its own. Consciously and unconsciously, our ambivalence about technology—the seed crystal of this paper—had infiltrated itself into our personal and academic lives.

Although we were intrigued by the above analogies, they lay fallow for awhile until Tom and his son saw *Rocky IV*. Some years earlier, we had written an essay on the original *Rocky*, and, as such, felt a curious moral compulsion to at least *see* the seeming infinity of sequels. But having endured *Rocky III*, Janice simply could not be induced into the next ring of movie Hell. And so when Tom returned from the Saturday afternoon matinee, strode into the study muttering, "Yo—Janice! Ya gotta see this one!," a condescending "Yeah—sure" was her unimpressed response. Thinking that her coauthor/spouse, who always did have a disturbing taste for the cinematically banal, was on another one of his temporary testosterone highs, Janice ignored him. Maybe he would go away. But beneath the transparently embarrassing politics of this film, Tom insisted, was an interesting subtext about the intrusion of technology into contemporary life—both Russian and American. Moreover, he noted that the similarities between the giant Russian prizefighter in *Rocky IV* and the equally inflated cyborg in *The Terminator* might index an evolutionary pattern concerning humanity's unfolding relationship to technology.

Against her better judgment, Janice saw *Rocky IV,* and although she conceded that Tom was probably right about the technological subtext and the similarities between Ivan Drago and the Terminator, the gap between this politically romanticized melodrama and its apocalyptic sci-fi counterpart seemed too great. Tom agreed, and again the project was put on hold. But we continued to be haunted by the problem of technology, and eventually two related ideas revisited us. One was the concept of "rhetorical narration," which Tom had discussed previously in his Van Zelst lecture and Janice had extended in her earlier work on the New Frontier. Rhetorical narration was the notion that cultural myths evolve slowly over time and that singular texts—be they speeches, films, or television programs—often articulate specific marker events in a larger unfolding story that tells something significant about the psyche of the culture. The second connection occurred when we recalled the character of Roy Batty, a humanly crafted replicant in the cult favorite *Blade Runner,* about which Janice had written before in another context.

We then pieced these events together with *The Terminator* and came up with the basic idea for the article. We felt that the characters of Ivan Drago, Roy Batty, and the Terminator represented important stages in humanity's evolving relationship with technology. Moreover, the three films in which these characters played central roles seemed to comprise a rhetorical narrative insofar as they charted how technology was gradually becoming independent from humanity. Should this independence ever occur, *The Terminator* at least seemed to suggest, the worst prophecy of technological determinism, whereby machines would eliminate humanity, would come to pass. We also recognized, as other critics have noted, that this general story was itself merely a recent extension of a much more widespread myth—one that began for Western civilization with the Prometheus story, which showed the consequences of stealing fire from the gods, and continued through industrial times in Mary Shelley's classic *Frankenstein.*

Given the kernel idea, writing the first draft became a matter of solving two problems. We had to integrate some fairly diverse theoretical materials—the technological determinism literature of Winner and Ellul and the rhetorical narration idea along with its rhetorical and mythic entailments—into a coherent critical framework. We then needed to allow that critical frame to illuminate meanings from the films while those meanings reverberated back and guided us to rethink the perspective at the same time. In the process, we followed our general rule to watch the films we were writing about again and again until we would begin spontaneously to speak to each other in a restricted code consisting totally of lines from the characters. A hazard of this occupation is that it does evoke odd stares when we do this in public.

On June 16, 1987, we submitted the manuscript to *Critical Studies in Mass Communication,* presumably, given its title, an ideal forum. Although most submissions undergo significant changes and the reviewing process is lengthy, this particular process was unusually protracted: Twenty-two months passed from submission to acceptance. During that time, the essay engaged the attention of seven people—the two of us, four reviewers (two original and two added later), and the journal editor—and underwent two full revisions and a third significant editing (four drafts in all). Throughout the review process, the readers and editor liked our writing and much of our analysis of the films, but questioned the rationale for addressing the technology problem and the theoretical bases of our critical framework.

On September 25, 1987, we received reactions to our initial paper from two reviewers and a letter from the editor, suggesting that while we could revise and resubmit the manuscript in accordance with the suggestions of the reviewers, we might not want to take our work in those directions. After immediately concluding (as we typically do) that the readers were massively brain-damaged for not buying every phoneme we wrote, we began to see (as we typically do) that all had read the manuscript carefully and had made excellent suggestions. One reviewer, obviously a feminist, alerted us to the literature that linked technology with gender and to implications concerning gender within these films. The second reviewer and the editor—in quite different ways—were concerned that our critical framework seemed "dated" and that its "universalist" cast was out of keeping with the literature readers of this journal would be likely to know. We interpreted these remarks to imply that our piece was not in keeping with the emerging postmodernist (in the broadest sense) orientation of *CSMC*. The challenge to us was legitimate: If we expected to publish our piece in this journal, we would have to either revise our critical framework in light of more avant garde theoretical perspectives, or show how our own perspective was superior to them.

Our second draft, resubmitted May 26, 1988, tried to meet these challenges. As we always do, we included a detailed letter in which we cited each significant objection and how we attempted to address it. This draft reflected three important modifications. First, we developed a mythic perspective that synthesized some of the work of depth psychologist C. G. Jung, moral philosopher Alasdair MacIntyre, rhetorical scholar Kenneth Burke, novelist Mary Shelley, and a wide variety of contemporary writers on gender. Second, we used this mythic frame to reconcile competing perspectives on technology—the viewpoint of neo-Marxists (likely to be familiar to readers of

CSMC), who saw technological determinism as a stance that limited action and choice, and of technological determinists like Winner and Ellul (from our first draft), who countered that technology was rapidly obliterating choice and determining action. Our argument here was that our mythic perspective "historicized" these two seemingly antithetical views of technology as different phases in an ongoing, evolutionary process—that is, technology is on its way toward autonomy, but it is possible to avert the apocalypse if certain choices are made soon. Finally, we fleshed out the gender entailments in the three films, now noting that the patriarchal myth seemed destined to separate humanity from technology, while its repressed feminine alternative exhibited the potential to reunite the human with the machine.

We received the response to our second draft on August 26, 1988. Because we had radically altered the theoretical materials making up our critical framework, the editor asked two new readers to join the original two in reviewing this version. The two original reviewers were satisfied with our revisions and both recommended publication. One of the new reviewers was not enthusiastic, saying that s/he saw nothing theoretically new in our work. The second new reader recommended publishing the piece in a condensed form, but suggested that our analysis be grounded, not in the ongoing theoretical controversy over technology, but rather in the literature of science fiction criticism. Given the lack of unanimity among the four reviewers and the fact that the editor's space in the journal was rapidly filling up, he was uncertain whether we could accommodate the competing suggestions and make the necessary changes in the time still available.

This was a "near death experience" for our project. But, as survivors of NDEs (as they are known in the trade) usually are, we were energized by this experience and decided to rise to the occasion. To this day, we don't think the editor expected us to reassemble this considerably bullet-ridden thing, itself beginning to resemble a "Frankenstein's monster" sewn together from diverse "theory parts" in several fits of less than divine inspiration. Perhaps the editor hadn't seen *The Terminator*—or at least hadn't seen it as many times as we had—and so he couldn't have known how thoroughly we had internalized Der Arnold's few lines as well as his miraculous capacity for resurrection. Promising on August 31, 1988, that "We'll be back," we sent him a third revision on September 28, 1988. In it, we dropped the theoretically oriented literature on technology and, taking our cue from one of the new reviewers, allowed the technology problem to grow out of the science fiction criticism literature. We then wove the new science fiction orientation more fully throughout the entire essay, although the critical framework and textual analysis were not changed significantly.

The editor accepted this revision on October 6, 1988. He still thought the essay was too long and asked that we cut an additional five pages. We did this and returned it to him on October 11, 1988. It appeared in the March 1989 issue of *CSMC*.

114

What do we think of this work in retrospect? We are mixed. At this writing (a little more than three years after publication), we both still like the article, which has launched us on a longer-term project in the same general area. But we do wince a little now in reading it over. We understand the space limitations all editors must work within, and that most authors have an inflated sense of the importance of their own prose. But in the spirit of self-reflection that this book invites, we will go ahead and share our own inflation: We both feel that cutting those final five pages from the last draft was unfortunate. In particular the "Critical Framework" section seems to suffer the most, appearing choppy and cryptic, with too few transitions from point to point. Because this is our theoretical contribution in this work—synthesizing several diverse approaches into a singular mythic perspective—we lament that it is not set forth as clearly as it was in earlier drafts.

The two of us do not agree on everything, however. Tom, for example, thinks that the second draft was the strongest and potentially most theoretically subversive form of the paper. That draft argued that the "dated" mythic perspective could resolve a controversy between two more current bodies of theoretical literature on technology. To the extent that that argument was sound, it would have reaffirmed the value of mythic criticism of cultural texts and, by so doing, subverted the charge that such approaches were passe. When that material was dropped and the science fiction criticism literature substituted in its place, the article, for Tom, was somewhat depotentiated because it now grew out of "aesthetic" or "poetic" materials, which, in Tom's view, are not as important theoretically as the socially and politically inspired literature they replaced.

Whereas Janice shares some of Tom's feelings on this, she—being less conspiratorial by nature—feels that the science fiction literature was relevant and provided a useful and more direct departure point for the critical framework section as well as for the analysis itself. In addition (she reminds Tom), the body of sci-fi lit-crit was fun to read and has become an important knowledge base for much of our later research. Besides, do we really have to accept the conventional wisdom that aesthetics isn't as important as politics? She may be right on this. Tom's still thinking about it.

MAXIM 2

CRITICISM IS WRITTEN TO AND FOR AN AUDIENCE

CHAPTER 8 [   ]

RHETORICAL STRUCTURE
AND *PRIMATE*

Thomas W. Benson

In this commentary, Thomas W. Benson explains his own sense of identification with his audience as a professional, a teacher, and writer-scholar, for whom critical writing discharges obligations to both students and colleagues. Benson's attraction to the documentary films of Fred Wiseman led him to search for ways to share his understanding and appreciation of Wiseman's Primate *with this community, and his commentary recounts the tensions and choices involved in revising his work for the* Quarterly Journal of Speech.

COMMENTARY

I have been interested in the documentary films of Fred Wiseman since seeing his first two films—*Titicut Follies,* at the State University of New York at Buffalo (in, I think, about 1968, in an exhibition sponsored by one of the film's backers, Warren Bennis, who was then a provost at SUNY Buffalo), and *High School,* which I saw for the first time at the 1969 San Francisco Film Festival, when I was a visiting assistant professor at the University of California, Berkeley.

I had been teaching at SUNY Buffalo since 1963, where I had introduced courses in the history and criticism of narrative and documentary film in addition to courses in rhetorical criticism and the history of public address.

I admired the intelligence and aesthetic achievements of Wiseman's work. In the late sixties, at a time of social upheaval, of distrust and protest against the Vietnam War and institutions of oppression, Wiseman's films spoke strongly to my own sense of alienation from authority. Wiseman's films also seemed to offer a rich way to tap into understandings of how people communicated in situated, face-to-face interaction and how complex discourses (his films) communicated with audiences who were treated as active and intelligent (and flattered for being active and intelligent).

Why write rather than seek some other form of expression? I define myself professionally as a teacher and writer-scholar. Bringing a piece of scholarship to written form is part of what I feel I owe my students and colleagues. It is setting aside time to do part of society's homework, in aid of shared social knowledge—monitoring our institutions and practices, and encouraging critical reflection. And scholarly writing, despite its difficulties and disappointments, I experience as deeply rewarding for its own sake in enlarging understanding, exercising mind and spirit, and satisfying the yearning for serious communication. Scholarly writing is a way to participate in the world and to attempt to make a contribution. I was raised in a family where it was a male virtue to not talk very much. Becoming a teacher and scholar has been a personally liberating experience for me, but it always carries with it, in addition to my sometimes deep stage fright, a conscientious sense of inhibition, a repugnance about talking too much and advertising myself.

The original version of this essay was written in the summer of 1981, in preparation for a presentation at the annual convention of the Speech Communication Association in Anaheim in November of that year. I had already been doing preliminary work on *Primate* when a former doctoral student and coauthor on various projects invited me to participate in a panel he was organizing for the Anaheim convention. I worked on the film over a period of weeks, constructing notes based on a detailed, scene-by-scene analysis; the analysis was accompanied by slides shot from frames of the film. The critic-respondent was an old friend, Walt Fisher, whom I had first met at the SCA-NEH Pheasant Run conference in the spring of 1970.

At Anaheim, Herman Stelzner asked me if I would submit the *Primate* paper to *The Quarterly Journal of Speech,* of which he was then editor; I said I had written the essay in the hope that it might be suitable for *QJS,* and that I would probably send it to him. But I already had another essay in press at *QJS,* which was scheduled to appear shortly after the 1981 convention. That essay, "Another Shooting in Cowtown," was by far the longest ever published in the journal and was somewhat unconventional in form. Although the essay was generally well received, I heard of some complaints that it was not fair for one author to be given so much space in the journal, thus depriving other authors of access to a resource crucial to tenure and promotion. And so I refrained from sending the *Primate* essay to Herm Stelzner during the remainder of his editorial term. I did not want to place him in the position of being doubly criticized for giving me still more space in the journal during his term. Over the period 1981–85 I presented various versions of the *Primate* paper in lectures at the University of Texas, the Eastern Communication Association, the Society for Cinema Studies, Auburn University, and the University of Maryland, as well as in classes at Penn State University. Professors and students at these occasions always provided strong encouragement and asked questions that helped in the ongoing process of rethinking and revision.

When Walter Fisher took over as the new editor of *QJS*, I figured that the clock had been reset and that it was now appropriate for me to submit the work to the gatekeeping process. I spent most of the Christmas break in 1983, and then January and February 1984, working on the essay, revising and extending it for review. I sent it to *QJS* on February 23, 1984. The reviews praised the essay as criticism but asked for clearer statements of the theory that drove the criticism and explained its general significance. There were several useful stylistic and structural suggestions. At the end of spring semester 1984 I again turned to the paper, and sent a revision to Walt Fisher at the end of June. On October 9, 1984, Walt wrote to say that the two associate editors (whose comments he included) advised publication, but that he himself was not ready to accept it without further revision. He requested that I omit or sharply condense the paper's discussions of the work of Anthony Trollope, James Agee, and Nadine Gordimer, and introduce a more compelling theoretical grounding, such as Stanley Fish's notion of "self-consuming artifacts."

I would prefer not to tell this next part, but I've started the story, at the request of the editors of this volume, so I'll finish. I did not want to take Walt's advice, which I saw as driving me away from a paper that was groping for a complex critical understanding and toward a paper that followed a text-illustrates-theory format, a format that seemed to me likely to offer a false clarity at the expense of understanding. It is hard for me, just a few years later, to sort out the merits of the situation, to tell how much was an author's appropriate defense of his vision and how much was just my own ego and stubborn self-indulgence. In any case, Walt's letter graciously invited a response: He ended his letter by writing, "If I have been unclear or wrong-headed, call and let us discuss things. Cordially, Walt." I made some changes in the manuscript, based on this latest round of reviews, where I was convinced the reviewers' suggestions improved things, then wrote Walt explaining my views. We then talked on the phone. I recall arguing pretty strongly, though in friendly terms, both in that letter and in our phone call. On December 6, 1984, I sent Walt my final, revised version, which he accepted for publication in the May 1985 issue of the journal.

In the end, Walt and his editorial readers prompted me to revise in ways that improved the essay. Some of the revisions were made simply by accepting direct suggestions by the reviewers. More often—and I think this is typical—I found myself unable or unwilling to accept a direct suggestion, but able to use the suggestion as indicating some problem with the reader's understanding that I might be able to repair in a different way. I frequently tell my students who are starting out in journal publishing to read all editorial suggestions not as absolute directives to be mechanically accepted but as symptoms of some failure of the author to be clear in substance or style, and to try and rewrite accordingly.

As I look at the essay now I cannot really say I am "satisfied" with it. There are many thousands of scholarly journals, but this essay was written specifically for *QJS*, and for no other. I worked hard over a period of years to understand how to write the essay, and in the end even lobbied a bit to have it appear in the form in which it appeared. Yet I recoil at gaps in the logic of the paper, and at its sometimes inflated and pontifical tone. I wish that there were more close textual analysis of the film, but the paper was already rather long for a journal article. I am not entirely pleased with the theoretical frame of the paper, in which, for example, the film is considered from the perspectives of deliberative, forensic, and epideictic rhetoric; these passages, though they seem to me true, also seem of less theoretical interest than some of what emerges as part of the close reading, in which I attempted to suggest Wiseman's implicit theories of how texts may induce complex and active responses in collaboration with audiences. In many ways, I am never satisfied that I have written anything as I had originally envisioned it; on the other hand, the writing and revision process always introduces happy surprises that go beyond what was originally envisioned.

I did get one more chance with the paper, when Carolyn Anderson and I decided to use it as the basis for a chapter in a book on Fred Wiseman's films, *Reality Fictions*. The chapter on *Primate* as it appears in the book adds some additional detail about the film from the perspective of its human subjects—research workers at the Yerkes Regional Primate Research Center of Emory University, where the film was made, who accused Wiseman of inaccuracy and betrayal. Carolyn became the coauthor of the paper as it was prepared for the book, and, at least from my point of view, the paper takes on a different and more meaningful shape when it appears in the context of a more extended analysis of Wiseman's films that involves both close readings and close historical attention to matters of production and reception, thus extending the purely "textual" (and intertextual) approach taken in the *QJS* version of the paper.

Well, maybe all of this amounts to no more than professional gossip and, yet again, an exercise in self-promotion. But a large and growing body of literature in the rhetoric of inquiry and the political economy of scholarly publishing argues that our shared, published knowledge is importantly shaped by institutional forces and the influence of disciplinary traditions and fashions.

The story told in these reflections may show merely that in the end an old friendship prevailed over good editorial judgment, and that despite a carefully planned system of blind reviewing, an essay that was recommended for publication by the editorial referees might in the end have been rejected, or at least radically revised, had it been submitted by a doctoral student, but

☐ Criticism Is Written to and for an Audience

instead was published as the author could be persuaded to revise it. I hope the story is more edifying than that, perhaps showing something of the complexity of the writing and reviewing process, of the urge to remain silent and the urge to speak, and of the tensions between "criticism" and "theory" in rhetorical studies as they presently express themselves in the writing and gatekeeping process.

CHAPTER 9 ⬜

CONSTITUTIVE RHETORIC AND THE *PEUPLE QUÉBÉCOIS*

Maurice Charland

Maurice Charland's commentary traces a project superficially similar to Thomas Benson's in the previous commentary: writing and revising an essay for a scholarly journal. However, in Charland's case, he was a comparative newcomer to the audience and community he addressed: a Canadian writing about Quebec nationalism for the largely American audience of the Quarterly Journal of Speech *in the "language" of the American study of rhetoric, which has no counterpart in the Canadian communication curriculum in which he began his education. Charland's commentary, compared to Benson's, is thus much more the story of initiation, as a critic, into a new community and language.*

COMMENTARY

I did not initially set out to write an essay for the *Quarterly Journal of Speech*. That came much later. I was, like many a doctoral student, struggling to develop a dissertation topic. Something to do with public culture, but what? Two things happened. The first was the rising tide of nationalism in Quebec, my home. The second was the hiring by Iowa (where I was studying for my Ph.D. in communication) of Michael McGee, a rising star in speech communication's version of rhetoric. I had never studied rhetoric, which had no presence in Canadian communication studies. But as I came to know McGee and his work and thought about the news from home, it seemed that I might be able to explain something, at least to myself, and be able to take a stand on the theoretical terrain of cultural theory that I was discovering. My intuitions were rough and unformed, but I sensed that the usual premises of rhetorical studies did not render the Quebec case well. What struck me was that, while for my American friends and fellow students, national identity was unproblematic and politics was concerned with deliberation and reasonableness, from my perspective national identity was extremely problematic and politics seemed far more linked to "being" than reason. As I read McGee's "In Search of 'The People'," I realized that much of it could be applied to Quebec.

The story of writing the thesis is one that I will not go into here, save to say that it was at times a pleasure, at times a drama, and at most times an ordeal. But I should underline that at its genesis, the project was less intended than emergent, and that once it was set in motion I often felt that the best I could do was not to let it overwhelm me as I tried to guide it to completion. I was so absorbed with that task that I never gave any thought to what might follow from it. And when it was finally defended and deposited, I had no desire to return to it, at least for a good long while.

I had pretty much ruled out turning my thesis into a book until I received an unsolicited request for a manuscript from a university press. I enthusiastically sent off my dissertation and awaited the press' review. I then started fiddling with the text until, six months later, I received the reviewer's comments. The review was perceptive and ambivalent. I would have a book, if I rewrote the text basically from scratch! After another six months of studying how it could be revised, I decided not to pursue the project. While dissertations are often laborious, the genre also permits a certain economy of detail and research. What is crucial in the doctoral thesis is the development of a specific theoretical argument within narrow disciplinary frames. The rest is incidental. Not so with a book: It must be comprehensible to general readers who bring their own agenda to it. The broad strokes in which I had drawn Quebec history from 1760 to 1980 would have been inadequate to those whose main interest was Quebec affairs, while my rhetorical concerns might have appeared arcane. Retelling the story of Quebec nationalism in the terms a Quebec historian could appreciate and a rhetorical theorist could value was not worth the effort. I wanted to keep up to date with the field, and not be dragged back into rewriting my thesis for the equivalent of another committee. So there I was, with a manuscript whose scope was too narrow for a book—but not too narrow for a journal article.

While I still did not fully consider myself a rhetorician, I decided to submit a manuscript to the *Quarterly Journal of Speech*, in part, because I thought the arguments I wished to make would be of interest to its readership, in part because it is a national journal (ego and tenure review demand the most prestigious journal possible) and in part because the journal was highly regarded by former professors and classmates to whom I could prove my academic coming of age. Also, since graduate school my interlocutors had been primarily rhetoricians, even though my arguments were usually against rhetoric's conventional principles. Better to write to them than to those who would not care about the point I was trying to make. Ultimately, in retrospect, the article was a performance, to prove something to myself,

Paper," my primary text. On a notepad and later on an outline processor, I brainstormed, I dissected my ideas, and I tried to order them. There would be a descriptive component; there would be an epistemological claim; there would be a discussion of narrative form; there would be some claim linking discourse to political action. I found myself confronting (but not of course resolving) the big questions: individual vs. collective action; materialism vs. idealism; text vs. performance. I was developing a sense of what I would need to write around. I saved paragraphs and sections in separate files; I kept alternate versions; I dated them. Slowly, a structure for the work emerged.

The essay was not written quickly. At least six months went by between beginning this revision piece and submitting it. I wanted the work to be accessible to the reader ignorant of Quebec and unfamiliar with what, at the time, I called a "structuralist" orientation, but I did not want to sacrifice theoretical substance. More than that, I did not want to face a rejection letter and so spent a great deal of time crafting sentences. I tried to keep them short. I used paraphrase and repetition for the sake of clarity. And most importantly, I sought to maintain a dialectic between my theory and my case.

I wanted the piece to be regarded theoretically, and not be considered primarily descriptive of an episode in Quebec political life. And so was born my hook and lead: I began by raising a theoretical distinction and I invoked Kenneth Burke's authority to secure its significance. Having made a few sweeping generalizations, it was necessary to elaborate specifics of the case and their relevance to my argument. My chapters would provide some of that, but again major revision was necessary. I wanted to emphasize the problem of national identity and so highlighted differences and discord.

A draft assembled, I read it over and over and over again. I checked the spelling, the flow, the clarity. Finally, I mailed it off and waited. Six months or so later, I received a response. One reviewer loved it, another felt it unfit for publication, and a third recommended publication but perceptively pointed out its weaknesses. Most notably, in the initial draft Kenneth Burke pretty much disappeared after the opening paragraph. Where had he gone? The editor assured me the essay would be published, but encouraged me to consider the reviewers' comments. Back to Burke's books. I scanned the index of each one for "rhetoric" and "ideology." I found suitable quotations that would illustrate or better state what I was attempting to say. In the process, I learned a great deal about Burke and the essay became somewhat "Burkean." Also, a reviewer asked how one could account for the emergence and success of new constitutive appeals. I had not wanted to grapple with "persuasiveness" in this essay. Indeed, the essay adopted "identification" as a counterpoint to "persuasion" as rhetoric's key term. But the reviewer's point was well taken, and so I struggled to respond. Another four months had passed. Enough was enough. I returned the corrected essay.

my colleagues, my professors, and my friends. To "get published." As a friend paraphrased Dr. Hook: There ain't no thrill like when you get your picture on the cover of the *QJS.*

My task began in earnest once I had decided to submit an article to *QJS.* To go from dissertation to journal is not just a matter of lifting a chapter, adding a beginning and concluding paragraph, and buying a stamp. Dissertations are extended works; articles offer short, self-contained arguments that address specific debates within a field. In addition, *QJS* is a disciplinary and association journal. It addresses a particular community that shares a particular literature and intellectual heritage. I needed to speak in terms that would be understood, that would establish my membership in their community. And so I reread Kenneth Burke. Also, I returned to other sources within rhetorical studies: McGee of course, for I was truly indebted to his thought, but also Edwin Black and Walter Fisher, who seemed to be addressing questions similar to my own.

I would be writing to rhetoricians, but my intent was to issue a kind of challenge. Thus, my project also required that I establish my difference. And so I framed my essay in terms of both Burke and Louis Althusser (the French Marxist philosopher). Both can be found in my dissertation's bibliography, but their explicit presence was minor. Roland Barthes and Frederic Jameson were similarly enlisted. None of these authors was absolutely necessary. I had no interest in developing a commentary or exegesis of some great thinker. My intellectual habits and writing strategy are more those of a *bricoleur,* a hobbyist-tinkerer, who crafts his works from available materials even if they are decontextualized in the process.

When I began to work on the article, I had been teaching Althusser, and realized that the concepts "subject" and "interpellation" underlay what I had been trying to say all along. Indeed, they likely influenced the dissertation itself, for I had read Althusser in graduate school. As for Burke, "identification" would provide a familiar reference point for what I had to say. But what was that exactly? I reread my dissertation and an earlier article presented at the second Alta conference on argumentation, and thought again about the initial inspiration for the thesis. My intuition was that claims were often warranted by an audience's identity, but that identities themselves are ultimately rhetorical constructs. Furthermore, it appeared to me that these were elicited through an effect of narrative. This then was what the article would be about, and I would have to develop and systematize it.

At one level, I was involved in a major "cut-and-paste" operation, but more fundamentally this was a new article, sharing only some primary texts and a few key ideas with its antecedents. My dissertation features the term "constitutive discourse," which inspired the crisper and more theoretical sounding "constitutive rhetoric" of my title. My dissertation chapters formed the basis for my description of Quebec affairs and the "White

☐ **Criticism Is Written to and for an Audience**

Six years after the Alta conference paper, more than three years after my dissertation defense, and two years after the beginning of my revisions, the essay was in print. The pleasure was great. More astounding, however, was that the essay was then read by people I did not know. I had never given any thought to what is so self-evident: Publication is ultimately a form of communication.

CHAPTER 10 ⬜[▬▬▬▬▬▬▬▬▬▬▬▬]

PSEUDO-PRIVATE AND
THE PTL MINISTRY SCANDAL

William L. Nothstine

*This commentary, by William L. Nothstine, recounts the transformations of
an essay on the role of the media in the PTL Ministry scandal: from a short
piece submitted to a magazine of political opinion, to a professional
conference paper, to a manuscript submitted and revised for a scholarly
journal. In each form, considerations of audience led to revisions of content,
style, and organization. In Nothstine's case, the impulse to express his
critical conclusions in the language of his chosen readers was in a state of
tension with his original interests in the project. Eventually he concluded
that the project had too little resemblance to what had originally prompted
him to write about the PTL scandal, and consequently he shelved the
project.*

COMMENTARY

Unlike the other critical essays in this anthology, "Public, Private, and
Pseudo-Private" was not published elsewhere, although it almost was. It
began in 1987 as a short magazine submission, was transformed into a
convention paper, and finally became a manuscript for journal submission
in 1989. Based on the cumulative effect of these incremental changes, I
decided to withdraw the manuscript from journal review and file it away.

In many ways, my original interest in the PTL Ministry scandal was
unremarkable. During the height of the scandal, roughly from March to
May of 1987, the images of Jim and Tammy Bakker seemed everywhere in
the popular media, and like many Americans I found the sideshow atmosphere fascinating. ABC's Ted Koppel compared the whole business to "a
national soap opera," but I found it to be closer to an auto accident:
Although I was a little ashamed of myself, I just couldn't resist staring. I

began collecting magazine and newspaper articles, and taping the major TV appearances of the main figures in the scandal. My collection was more than haphazard, but hardly exhaustive. Beyond satisfying the voyeuristic curiosity I shared with many Americans about the scandal, I thought perhaps the materials might be useful as a case for study in the classroom. In part because my writing interests were in a different area, I had no plans to write and disseminate a critical essay concerning the Bakkers, the media, or any of the other themes eventually played out in the following essay. That came later.

By chance, at about this time a colleague invited me to contribute a paper to a convention panel she was organizing on the intriguing-sounding subject of "scandal management." None of the writing projects I had underway seemed to fit the bill, but we discussed some possibilities, including the PTL scandal. Since it had received so much media attention, and since coincidentally I had already accumulated quite a bit of background material on the topic, we tentatively decided that I should investigate the PTL scandal, although neither of us had any particular idea yet of *what* I might have to say, as a critic, about the scandal. Convention planning deadlines being what they are, we knew I had six or seven months to research and write a paper if the panel proposal was accepted (as it eventually was). Like many of my colleagues who submit abstracts of papers for conventions when the papers are as yet unwritten, I counted on the muses of criticism to visit with inspiration in a timely manner.

I wouldn't say they visited, but they did leave me a "while you were out" note. The following week, browsing through old files, I rediscovered "Pseudo-Private Lives," a short piece by Charles Krauthammer in *The New Republic,* about the blurring of "public" and "private" in the media coverage of political figures. I had saved the article for no clear reason other than that I found it interesting and well written. I think that's important: In saving the Krauthammer article, and in collecting the materials on the PTL scandal, my choices were responses to a series of coincidences, driven by my own intellectual curiosity more than by any explicit axe to grind, whether theoretical, religious, or ideological. And had it not been for the unexpected phone call from my colleague, whatever interest I had in these issues and incidents would almost certainly never have played itself out in writing.

Rereading Krauthammer's essay, I found his observations suggested interesting conclusions about the case of the Bakkers. Since *The New Republic*'s editorial policy at that time had not yet fully turned the corner from laggard-progressive to neo-conservative, this struck me as a convenient and topical opportunity for me to write for a different (and larger) audience than the journals and conventions of my field provided. I set to work and soon turned out a 1,000-word manuscript, which I sent to *The New Republic.* Its rejection was quick and perfunctory, and (except for a handful of public presentations based on it and the few obituary remarks herein) that manuscript was consigned to oblivion and need concern no one ever again.

That original 1,000-word piece asserted that Jim and Tammy Bakker's most typical *public* appearances in the media featured the characteristic actions and implied standards of judgment associated with *private* display— hence they were, using Krauthammer's term, pseudo-private displays. The essay listed several examples of the Bakkers' behavior demonstrating this point, and concluded by observing that this shift went a long way toward explaining why the media coverage of the two focused on how tacky or tasteless they were, rather than how dishonest or impious they were. The essay was thus a simple form of criticism by analogy: The insights Krautham- mer had reached regarding several political figures recently in the news could be usefully extended to the case of the Bakkers as well. The case of the Bakkers also allowed the conceptual point to be stretched from the political arena to the religious, since the Bakkers were evangelists, but the main purpose was to demonstrate a noteworthy feature of the Bakkers' media coverage, nothing more.

However, it gradually became much more. The convention paper that followed a few months later was over twice the size of the original piece. The convention version had by no means become the essay that follows in this volume, since convention papers are normally not accountable to the same professional and rhetorical demands that journal articles are. This was most noticeable in the style and tone of the language, which still showed my enjoyment of irony and word play. In fact, one sentence I wrote for the convention paper delighted me so much that I called a col- league up, long-distance, and dictated it into her answering machine for her amusement. (By contrast, I can't imagine reading a single sentence written for the version in this book into anyone's answering machine, even if it was a local call.)

Nevertheless, the differences between the convention version and the original version are striking. The *New Republic* version was organized induc- tively, building to its thesis in what I fancied to be a crescendo; the conven- tion paper was organized deductively, with the thesis first and the proof deployed afterward. Elliptical arguments, some of them little more than familiar allusions, were replaced for the convention by more complete syllo- gisms. The most important difference, however, was in the substance and justification of its main argument. What began as an assertion about the seemingly bullet-proof media personae of the Bakkers gradually but undeni- ably became a study of the changes worked by the modern media upon our culturally shared sense of the true and the good. The Bakkers' case, once in the spotlight by itself, now shared the stage with this evolving theoretical argument. As the form and content were recast from social criticism to scholarly criticism, the paper's voice changed, too: Where once it spoke in a simple and vigorous public idiom, intended for the audience of *The New Republic*, it now spoke in an intricate and brittle professional dialect in- tended for a scholarly audience. A bristling layer of citations formed over the top, protecting the delicate inner argument and deflecting blows outward onto such targets as Aristotle and Hannah Arendt, both of whom made their first appearance in this version of the manuscript.

After the convention, I sent a slightly revised version to a journal in my field for editorial consideration. It went through two rounds of revisions and began a third, a process dragging on for eighteen months. The reviewers were always encouraging, but their strong suggestions for revisions moved the essay in directions I found less and less interesting, and in some cases philosophically offensive. One change, not specified by my reviewers but driven by the same process, was the gradual transformation of the tone from cynical to moral. The last few paragraphs of the version included in this book would have been incongruous in the original *New Republic* piece, but they were consistent with the tone of the final version. And as I revised, I gained appreciation for the complementary rhetorical functions that Jim and Tammy Bakker served in their public appearances, and—yes—even a kind of grudging respect, or at least sympathy, for Tammy Bakker.

But the most noticeable change was that the case of the PTL Ministry scandal no longer shared center-stage with the theoretical argument about public media; the Bakkers were being escorted quickly but firmly off to the side. In part this is because scholarly journals in my field prefer academic criticism to ephemeral social criticism. The fact that a year and a half had passed since I first submitted the manuscript to the journal became a disadvantage, because during that time the Bakkers had mostly faded from the public eye. As the editor wrote to me in October 1989, "Partly, I believe, because of the most recent news about the theatrics of Jim Bakker's trial, I am not convinced that these people really *matter* very much." Rather, the editor suggested, the Bakkers were "a soon-to-be-forgotten minor blip on the radar trace of the late 1980s." Theoretical issues are less fleeting than public notoriety (and, one suspects, more in keeping with the dignity of a scholarly journal). The choice was clear: If I wanted to pursue the publication of the paper, Jim and Tammy could be no more than a convenient example of a theoretical point.

Following this shift, the strictures of formalized method—rather than whether I had said anything useful to know about the PTL Ministry scandal—became central in justifying my critical conclusions. Little by little, the responsibility for my critical claims was taken out of my hands and turned over to "method" and "system." The editor wrote to me, "One part of the argument for significance, given that you have chosen a scholarly arena in which to make it, has to be a more careful statement about your research methods." The easiest way to make such a statement, of course, is if one has followed the dictates of a critical method—recognized, identified, elaborated, and formalized. But this I had not done. Instead, my claims were based to an embarrassing extent on my own observation, intuition, and judgment. I had attempted to clarify the premises and principles of my reasoning, and I worked to clarify them further, but recasting that explanation as a section entitled "Research Methods" would have been absurd and not entirely honest.

Another comment by the editors illustrates the problem from another direction: "Neither the reviewers nor I expect social-scientific defense of your 'sample size,' but we are looking for a little more evidence that you went about your 'data-gathering' (i.e., your selection of communication events on which to focus) *systematically.*" A process that had not been "methodical" or "systematic," *as the editor meant those terms here,* had now to be described after the fact as if it fit that mold. (And, of course, since the manuscript had by now swollen to 10,000 words, this *post hoc* discussion of "methodology" should not increase the length of the manuscript. . . .)

At about this time I found myself taking on unwelcome and time-consuming administrative duties, and I put the PTL scandal on the back burner with few regrets. Perhaps one more round of revisions would have gotten it into a journal, perhaps not—hardly an inconsequential consideration for an untenured professor—but it now bore little resemblance to the piece I had originally been interested in writing. I believe both the original essay and the final version made defensible arguments, albeit very different ones. But the manuscript was moving farther and farther from my own research and writing interests in the philosophy of criticism. This meant additionally that the PTL essay, if published, would not appreciably advance my "research program." There were few benefits to be derived from continuing to revise a manuscript I felt so little connection with, and I gladly diverted my energy toward more interesting and rewarding projects. The version in this anthology is the last full revision before I withdrew the essay from editorial consideration.

Public, Private, and Pseudo-Private: Ethics and Images in the Collapse of the PTL Ministry

William L. Nothstine

At the zenith of its power in the mid-1980s, the PTL ("Praise The Lord") Ministry represented the focus of an enormous media empire.[1] The Ministry's founders, Pentecostal evangelists Jim and Tammy Bakker, recognized earlier than most the incredible power the electronic media offered to evangelists. Perhaps it is fitting, then, that the slow collapse of the PTL Ministry—beginning in the spring of 1987 and featuring widely flung accusations of deceit, adultery, homosexuality, blackmail, embezzlement, fraud, and hostile corporate takeovers—was played out in all of its garish detail before the cameras and microphones of the media. So natural was the fit between the Bakkers and the media that, a year later, when a similar sex scandal engulfed rival televangelist Jimmy Swaggart in the spring of 1988, it was inevitable that the media would seek some reaction from the already beleaguered Bakkers, after the round-robin of denunciation and accusation between the two sides during the PTL scandal. Even amid the flurry of indictments handed down in the spring of 1989, leveling criminal charges of mail and wire fraud against Jim Bakker in connection with Ministry activities, the Bakkers themselves—stripped of their network, their ministry, and their expensive lifestyle—still seemed to have ready, if not always friendly, access to the media.[2]

The Bakkers' durability stems from their status as forerunners of what political commentator Charles Krauthammer has called pseudo-private display.[3] ABC interviewer Ted Koppel pronounced the daily stream of revelations and charges around the Bakkers "a national soap opera."[4] Yet the intrusive presence of the media can actually work to the advantage of those who suffer it. Many celebrities before the Bakkers have capitalized on the diminishing privacy they enjoy by manufacturing pseudo-private lives—thoroughly public media images packaged and presented as glimpses into private lives. But, though they did not invent it themselves, the Bakkers took this effect to lengths without recent equal.

Krauthammer's suggestive observations are worth clarifying and extending in their own right. The same is true of understanding the ignominious collapse of the once-powerful PTL Ministry. But the full implications of the phenomenon of pseudo-privacy go markedly beyond Krauthammer's initial sketch, and reach past the downfall of one television ministry. A fuller elaboration will show the importance of this phenomenon in understanding the evolution of public communication within the rhetorical tradition. This elaboration will require clarifying the transformation worked by the electronic media upon the traditional categories of public and private discourse. This transformation makes possible the emergence (and dominance) of a third mode of display and experience, the pseudo-private. A discussion of the characteristics of pseudo-private display will show how this transformation may be exploited to alter our perceptions of both the candor and the morality of the persons and events we come to know this way. This last is of importance beyond the fate of the Bakkers. The dislocation of public and private has implications for our perceptions of all celebrities and political or religious figures. The PTL scandal, in this sense, is merely a theoretically egregious instance of a larger issue that I intend to explore: the consequences of the media-induced transformation of "public" and "private" from descriptions of *physical* places to descriptions of *metaphorical* places.

▨ PUBLIC, PRIVATE, AND PSEUDO-PRIVATE

Pseudo-privacy represents a third kind of communicative experience, separate from the public and the private. Though we do not widely recognize or appreciate its significance and character, it is pervasive in our media society, the inevitable consequence perhaps of the fifteen minutes of celebrity Andy Warhol assured us we would each someday be guaranteed. Pseudo-private display has recognizable features, and can alter, subtly or radically, our perceptions and judgments of those whom we experience in this way.

In our culture we respect as a matter of custom the difference between public and private. Political philosopher Hannah Arendt notes that this distinction "corresponds to the household and the political realms, which have existed as distinct, separate entities at least since the rise of the ancient city-state."[5] Moreover, Arendt reminds us that from the Greek tradition we have come to regard public and private not as realms that differ merely in degree, but as different orders of experience, and as practical contraries. "The 'good life,' " observes Arendt in her discussion of Aristotle's commentary on civic life, ". . . was not merely better, more carefree or nobler than ordinary life, but of an altogether different quality."[6] The dimensions of this qualitative difference include the communicator's role, the audience's expectations, and the standards of rationality and morality thought applicable to the communicator's role.

Yet the precise nature of the correspondence that Arendt notes—between public and political, and between private and household—has been transformed in a most fundamental way since Aristotle drew upon his observations of ancient Athens. In Aristotle's world, the correspondence was metonymic: physical location determined one's communicative persona or role. There were physical sites (the legislature, the courtroom, the public gathering) where one went to enact one's public role, and one could not sensibly be called a *public* figure anywhere else. When one retreated to the household, one gave up one's public persona and became a private figure—"private" because deprived of the physical and communicative arena for being most-fully human, to the classical way of thinking.[7] Joshua Meyrowitz argues that this difference resulted directly from the limits that physical space placed upon the flow of information. That is, one had to position oneself in certain places to see and hear certain things.[8]

At approximately the same time as Arendt's reflections on the public tradition, sociologist Erving Goffman first demonstrated the extent to which our role behaviors change as a result of the various ways in which space may be bounded by barriers to perception.[9] As examples, Goffman's analysis suggests the following: Theatrical performers who drop their role when backstage; medical personnel who adopt their professional demeanor upon entering the examination room with the patient and abandon that role as soon as the patient is gone; garage mechanics whose deference to the customer ends when they leave the front office and return to the working area; or political candidates whose on-stage or on-camera behavior is carefully modulated and "presidential," yet who maintain informal rapport with staff members and reporters aboard the campaign jet between stops.[10] Goffman links role performance directly to the influence of physical space upon perception, as when he notes, "Very commonly the back region of a performance is located at one end of the place where the performance is presented, being cut off from it by a partition and guarded passageway."[11] In all of these cases, perceptual barriers—even something as seemingly transparent as a partly drawn curtain or a half-closed door—mark the location for a change from public to private role.

Goffman discusses not "public" and "private," but rather "front region" (that is, "the place where a performance is given")[12] and "back region" (that is, "a place, relative to a given performance, where the impression fostered by the performance is knowingly contradicted as a matter of course").[13] However, the parallels between the elements of Goffman's analysis and our traditional understanding of "public" and "private" are clear. In this regard it is most significant that Goffman relates front region and back region as practical contraries—not merely *different* orders of performance, as Arendt describes them, but *opposite and antithetical* ones. The image created through social performance in one region is "knowingly contradicted" in the other. This nuance of Goffman's analysis is essential to our traditional, largely unexamined view of "public" and "private."

However, in contemporary Western life—and perhaps nowhere more so than in the United States—electronic (and, in a different way, print) media have transformed the relationship between physical location and communicative persona. Because our physical location no longer has the same power to limit our access to information, the physical location of the person no longer predicts the persona or role that individual will assume. As a consequence, "public" and "private" have lost their metonymic connection to physical location, and have instead become spatial metaphors. We continue to speak of them as "realms," as if they were concrete places, but they have become "modes," ways of performing and experiencing essentially independent of physical location.

As metaphor, "public" and "private" carry with them systems of associated commonplaces.[14] With "public," we typically associate elements from one or both of two clusters of commonplaces. The first cluster stresses the artistic dimension of things public, such as *strategic, formal, contrived, inauthentic, or onstage.* The second cluster features the moral dimension of public life, including such associations as *noble, exemplary, representative, or popular.* With "private" we typically associate the opposites of these commonplaces, such as *spontaneous* rather than strategic, *informal* rather than formal, *natural* rather than contrived, or *backstage* rather than onstage. Similarly, the moral ideals implied by our typical sense of "private" are *graciousness* rather than nobility, *charm* rather than greatness, being *typical* rather than being exemplary. However, because these terms are no longer anchored in physically distinguishable settings, interaction among these systems of commonplaces is changing the meaning of our communicative practice even as we maintain our earlier habits of thinking and speaking about "public" and "private." We thereby live up to Marshall McLuhan's characterization of the limits on modern self-understanding in an electronic society: We live mythically and integrally, but continue to think in language that has not kept pace with change.[15]

As a consequence of this dislocation, although we continue to pay lip service to the public/private distinction, this observance is frequently blurred almost beyond recognition in contemporary practice. Many Americans feel, for example, that former presidential candidate Gary Hart's private indiscretions are of a different realm, a different order of action and experience, than are his public campaign tactics. Yet when Americans are pressed to account for the collapse of Hart's 1988 presidential campaign in the wake of the Donna Rice scandal, the typical answers almost immediately begin to confuse the two categories. For example, one sometimes hears the waning of Hart's popular support explained by reference to the maxim that a man who lies to his wife would probably also lie to the American voter—an explanation that succeeds by failing to distinguish between public and private standards of conduct. Only slightly more discriminating are those explanations beginning from the premise that a man who would actually encourage reporters to catch him in a scandalous indiscretion, as did Senator Hart, is probably unfit for the demands of high office. Our consensus that the public and the private are realms of different stature, values, and truths has become a fuzzy consensus at best.

This dislocation of public and private has also undermined a second, related, consensus that we share: the consensus that what is public can no longer be private, and vice versa. In Aristotle's Athens, this assertion would have been the nearly literal equivalent of "what takes place outdoors can no longer be indoors." However, the truth of that innocuous claim becomes a good deal less self-evident today when, by turning on my television, I can be both "in my living room" and "at a Cubs game" at the same time. Meyrowitz's argument applies once again: Physical location no longer determines the information we have access to, the experiences we can have, or the communicative roles we can play. Yet, significantly, the commonplaces embedded in our everyday language-use preserve the worldview of an age when this distinction still applied. While we talk of public and private as the practical opposites of one another, a more accurate and useful description would be that "public" and "private" are metaphors whose *associated commonplaces* are clustered in consistently antithetical patterns: strategic/spontaneous, noble/gracious, formal/informal, contrived/natural, inauthentic/authentic, intimate/distant, "onstage"/"backstage."

Out of this dislocation, based on the confusion of physical space with communicative role, emerges the hybrid realm of the pseudo-private, within which the opposite of "public" is no longer "private," but rather "genuine," "spontaneous," or "authentic," the commonplaces *associated with* private. At the heart of this third communicative realm is suspicion of technique. Krauthammer writes,

> Political imagery derives mainly from public actions. But public actions are suspect, precisely because they are undertaken in the knowledge that they will be observed. A glimpse of private life can shape a public image far more powerfully [than can a public statement], not just because the private revelation is more titillating, but because it has what public action can never have: the air of unself-consciousness, and thus the stamp of sincerity.[16]

From this practical paradox has emerged a potent weapon in the armory of the public figure: pseudo-private display, presenting the *appearance* of private action through the public media. This widespread phenomenon has recognizable features, features that bring home with ironic vengeance Arendt's characterization of public life as "better or nobler than ordinary life."

Pseudo-private disclosure is, of course, thoroughly public in at least one sense. It does not include the "high government official who has been saying one thing for weeks," notes Krauthammer, nor even the fact that the official "is reported to believe 'privately' the opposite." Rather, this disclosure enters the realm of the pseudo-private only when "this private confession . . . appears on the front page of *The New York Times.*"[17]

Pseudo-private disclosure is identified by framing cues, traces at some level asking us to overlook how the message has been shaped and timed and processed for popular consumption, and to focus instead on what appears to be spontaneous and uncontrived—hence, seemingly private. As the familiarity of Krauthammer's example shows, the delivery of these cues often need not be overburdened with subtlety; simply labeling a disclosure "private" is often enough to achieve the effect, even when this labeling is done in glaringly public circumstances. Overall, however, the effect of framing cues tends to be incremental and additive: One framing cue does not necessarily make a display pseudo-private, and one pseudo-private display does not necessarily transform a media image. Further, these framing cues may be nondiscursive as well as linguistic and discursive: scenic elements, dress, audio and video editing, all can become tokens of spontaneity, candor, or intimacy.

These framing cues, verbal or nonverbal, are the means by which the dislocation of public and private is accomplished. Just as any metaphor may be evoked by the systematic appearance of its associated commonplaces, aspects of the roles and rules appropriate to private settings can be evoked in public communication by framing cues—traces of either physical settings or role behaviors normally associated with the private sphere. If traces suggestive of a particular *physical location* or a particular *role or figure* traditionally considered as belonging to the public realm are shown packaged together with the verbal or nonverbal tokens of the private realm—whether language, behaviors, settings, or objects—our tendency is to experience them through the lens of the commonplaces of privacy. Therefore, one may identify framing cues by examining mass-mediated messages for traces of, or references to, physical situations or communicative roles strongly associated with the private sphere.

Pseudo-private display titillates its audience with the possibility of a revealing peek behind a mask, around a facade, over a transom, or beneath a skirt. And as with all such peekaboo games, what we see in pseudo-private disclosure usually matters less than our conviction that we were not meant to see it. Pseudo-private display has unique rhetorical power to the extent to which it is made to appear artless and uncontrived. The posture of the pseudo-private disclosure is antirhetorical; it implicitly claims kinship with the documentary genre, purporting to show a reality that is unaffected by strategic political considerations or technical manipulation. It seeks to be regarded as inartistic proof, as evidence that does not require artifice to be persuasive, whose truth is self-evident and whose ethical character is unproblematic. And yet pseudo-private display is thoroughly rhetorical—it is persuasion seeking to be effective by donning the guise of nonpersuasion.[18]

As such, its power represents the McLuhanesque extension of our well-established trust in the nonverbal over the verbal, especially when the two are perceived as incongruent.[19] Just as we tend to rely on nonverbal indicators of sincerity, on the conventional wisdom that they are harder to manufacture than the verbal, so we rely on pseudo-private portraits of motives or values because they are presented together with traces suggesting that they are intimate or revealing.

This is the first of two ways in which pseudo-private display can influence our judgments: by appearing more genuine or candid than "purely" public display, seeming to have "the stamp of sincerity." The case of Jim and Tammy Bakker demonstrates this function.[20] In the following two sections, framing cues typically associated with the Bakkers' discourse will be discussed, followed by an analysis of these cues' influence on the Bakkers' apparent sincerity.

▓ RECOGNIZING FRAMING CUES: THE BAKKERS "AT HOME"

Under the temporarily ignored supervision of the media, we were allowed many glimpses at the Bakker lifestyle, before and during the PTL scandal. A PBS *Frontline* documentary on the Bakkers, broadcast in January 1988, featured an excerpt from an informal video tour of their Palm Springs home, given to the PTL faithful by the Bakkers before the scandal broke in the spring of 1987:

Jim: (seated on a couch in the living room) We're kind of taking you into our secret hideaway.

Tammy: (clutching a stuffed animal, walking into the bedroom) Not very many people get a chance to show you their bedroom, but you never know what you're going to see in PTL.

Jim: (on couch) Tammy's out in the kitchen now.

Tammy: (off-camera) Lunch is almost ready, Jim![21]

There have been many such moments, all having little homey touches that project the illusion of nontechnique. The same documentary included another clip originally shown to PTL viewers, in which Jim Bakker proudly, one might almost say gleefully, showed off his vintage Rolls Royce, one of a collection, taking the reporter and camera operator for an evidently impromptu ride through the desert near the same Palm Springs redoubt.[22] The framing cues apparent in these instances include tokens seeming to suggest spontaneity, if not sheer amateurism: The camera following Jim into his Rolls is hand-held and wobbly; for the home-tour scenes a single camera is used, panning stiffly between the two; the sound is miked poorly and often hollow and tinny. The overall effect certainly denies the supporting presence of a sophisticated worldwide, satellite-based telecommunication network. By seeming to deny the contrived and "onstage" character of the events, the framing cues contribute to the seeming rejection of public display. The wobbly camera, perched on the camera operator's shoulder, is also reminiscent of the subjective point-of-view any of us would experience, were we actually there with Bakker—thus not only denying the presence of a *sophisticated* public medium, but of *any* public medium whatsoever.

Other traces indicative of pseudo-privacy may be found in these scenes, as well. Our commonplace sense of "public" figures is that we would not normally be given a tour of their bedroom or a joyride in their favorite car; we too strongly associate distance and formality with such figures and their roles to expect such behaviors. Therefore, the seeming inclusion of the audience in informal, even intimate, activities such as these further reframes the televised presence of these persons from public to pseudo-private, by providing traces of both private locations and behaviors appropriate to private roles. These examples all serve to help identify framing cues; their cumulative effect on our perceptions of the Bakkers will be considered below.

The Palm Springs home was the setting for a variation on this theme after scandal drove the Bakkers from their residence at Tega Cay. The Bakkers invited the media into their home again, letting themselves be seen *au naturel* to demonstrate that the scandalous publicity was not disrupting their household. Tammy chatted and giggled, and Jim wielded a hammer in some light repair work around the house, while the cameras whirred and clicked. The reader has only to imagine the national networks descending on his or her own home, with vans, lights, cables, microphones, and the rest, to imagine how intimate and spontaneous such a moment could possibly have been.

Production techniques alone are not the only means by which framing cues may be delivered; another tactic for pseudo-private display focuses our attention more directly on the communicative personae of the persons involved. A feature of the examples noted above, one that could easily be multiplied by examining televised images of the Bakkers before, during, and after the PTL scandal, is a certain naiveté, and (despite the polish of some aspects of technical presentation), aesthetic amateurism.

▨ PSEUDO-PRIVACY AS SIGN OF CANDOR: BELIEVING THE BAKKERS

Nowhere is this aesthetic amateurism better seen in the present case than in Tammy Bakker's media persona, a persona that has let the Bakkers push pseudo-private display toward limits that were, before now, only theoretical.

Certainly Tammy Faye Bakker is an inviting target for the cynic. But this misses the source of much of her appeal: Tammy's on-air demeanor is tailor-made for pseudo-private display. On *Nightline,* in May 1988, while Jim Bakker's responses to interviewer Ted Koppel usually advanced a case, Tammy veered away from the abstract and complex, toward the simple and concrete. For example, compare the responses by Jim and Tammy, when Koppel asked about their plans for the future:

Jim: . . . Ted, you know, I hope that people will let us move on into God and not spend the rest of our life in, as you said, a soap opera that the whole world has looked on. I feel so sad that I've been a part of something to bring this much, you know, pain and sorrow to the body of Christ.

Tammy: Well, you know, Jim, well, the thing I can't believe is that we are the— probably the most normal people there ever was [sic], and I just look—I wake every morning, and I say, "I can't believe this has happened. I'm the oldest of eight kids. We had an outdoor bathroom all the time I was growing up. I mean, me, just the normal of normal that this happened to. Or that anybody would be that interested in us. It's just hard to believe."[23]

Granted, a determined reader could impose quasi-syllogistic order on Tammy's answer, but her utterance clearly seems to lack the argumentative directness of Jim's reply—especially when we remember that Koppel's question was about their future plans. Tammy Bakker's habits of explanation borrow from cinema verite, if not the home movie: They favor detail and uninterpreted image, presented one after the other, rather than abstraction; they prefer verbal montage rather than argument.[24] Here it was not within production values that the framing cues were embedded, even Tammy's references to what Goffman would certainly call "back region" elements are not decisive in reframing the event; rather the framing is accomplished by the role Tammy plays, or the persona she assumes.

Tammy's persona is one far more readily associated with the private sphere than with the public, and therefore functions as a framing cue just as surely as manipulation of recording technique in previous examples. Although her public reputation is, in part, derived from her fame as the author of books on how to keep sexual excitement alive in marriage, and as what *Newsweek* has called "the flashy-trashy *femme fatale* in a leopard-skin pantsuit and four-inch stiletto heels," Tammy Faye Bakker's pseudo-private image is naive and childlike.[25] Like a child, Tammy under fire on camera is apparently without guile, especially compared to Jim's more straightforwardly rhetorical posture. On *Nightline*, while Jim rebutted charges and built a case in support of their actions, Tammy often interrupted, contributed *non sequiturs*, or added chatty ornament to remarks by others. She frequently broke into nervous giggles at inappropriate moments, suggesting a desperate eagerness to please. Her remark above captures the absence of guile: The persona we see in such moments of contrived candor probably *cannot* believe that the public would be so interested in anyone as normal as she. Whether Tammy actually sees herself that way is beside the point; what seems clear is that her pseudo-private persona *does*.

And that is the key: Tammy's on-air naiveté, like that of any child, promises us that her displays in the public media are nevertheless candid and authentic—hence, it frames her presence as not "really" public at all. A revealing example comes from the Koppel interview, in response to Koppel's first question: Why had the Bakkers ended their seclusion from the media? Jim Bakker's two-minute reply began with a reading of verses 12–16 of Psalms 38, then concluded with a list of reasons, both for their seclusion and their decision to end it:

> We wanted to protect our children. We wanted to really just cling to each other and see God. But it won't stop, and we're getting, really, thousands of letters. And people say, "We want to hear from you, Jim and Tammy. We want to know what went on. We want to know where you are or how you feel." And we chose to come out today, and we actually chose your program. We even had—I guess we had invitations just to about every program to come on, but I felt that you're not only tough, but I felt you would be fair and give us a chance to share with people all over the country.[26]

Koppel's irritation with Bakker's answer was obvious. As soon as Bakker finished answering, Koppel quickly attempted to corner the two, mistakenly expecting Tammy Bakker to be an easier target than her husband. Koppel retorted, "All right, well, I hope I live up to both of your expectations. Let's start with the tough. You may consider this to be a tough question, Mrs. Bakker: Is it going to be possible to get through an interview with both of you without you wrapping yourselves in the Bible? . . ."[27]

Tammy Bakker's answer picked up Koppel's mixed metaphor and ran with it, in a triumph of stream-of-consciousness over the syllogism. "Well the Bible is a protection. It's a very real protection. It's a comfort. That's, I think, the biggest reason we wrap ourselves in the Bible—it's so comforting. Jesus said, 'When I go away I'll send a comforter to you,' and he has, that's been our comfort during this."[28]

Koppel's remark to Tammy was two-leveled. At a semantic level, it could be paraphrased roughly as a *question:* "How likely are you to bring up the Bible throughout the rest of this interview?" Yet even without the advantage of hearing and watching Koppel deliver this line, it is evident here from the transcript alone—for example, his mock-polite remark, "You may consider this to be a tough question, Mrs. Bakker"—that Koppel was being sarcastic. His intended meaning was much closer to an *injunction:* "Answer my questions directly and without quoting the Bible during this interview." Conversational context, conventional idiom, and nonverbal cues all pointed very strongly to this second interpretation; it seems fair even to say that only someone with a childlike lack of conversational skills would have missed the second interpretation. By answering as she did, Tammy left Koppel with two choices: Either he could assume that she recognized his sarcastic intent and chose to respond by begging the question (that is, by invoking scripture yet again); or he could assume that she failed to recognize his sarcasm for what it was and had tried to answer the literal meaning of the question as best she could. Although he was demonstrably suspicious to the point of hostility when Jim Bakker had invoked scripture not a minute before, Koppel now chose to ignore the same from Tammy and quickly shift tactics, drifting on to the feud between the Bakkers and the Reverend Jerry Falwell. Koppel's rout demonstrates that what appears *strategic* coming from Jim Bakker—invoking scripture as a response to a hard question from an interviewer—is shrugged off as *naive* coming from Tammy Bakker.

The general principle underlying the discussion of pseudo-privacy so far may be formulated as follows: The presence of framing cues, transforming our experience of individuals' public or private actions into the pseudo-private, tends to make those individuals' claims and actions more plausible, their motives less suspect; if their utterances are not strictly *believed*, at least they are not as likely to be challenged.

But Koppel's rhetorical predicament was not simply that Tammy Bakker's presence on *Nightline* was reframed as pseudo-private display; he was doubly hamstrung by the fact that his own presence there was *not* pseudo-private, but rather more traditionally public. Koppel was clearly bound by the rules of public decorum (bear in mind the explicit spatial connotations of this word), and was thereby unable to respond to Tammy's answer in the manner he (or anyone) might do privately. *Informally*, or *backstage*, or *off-the-record*, Koppel might have challenged Tammy Bakker's pseudo-private performance: Are you serious? Do you expect me to believe this from you? But such informal, private rejoinders would only be available in public to Koppel if he had the availability of framing cues to discount *his own* publicness. He did not; and, as an interviewer whose role was a public (not pseudo-private and definitely not private) one, he could only respond within the communicative limits of his own role. Therefore he had little practical choice except to pass over Tammy's obtuse answers, regardless of his private opinion as to her motives.[29]

An equally glaring example of this principle was provided a month later, on 18 June 1987. The preceding days had seen media coverage awash in claims of betrayal made by Jim and Tammy Bakker, claims that rival televangelist Jerry Falwell had broken his promise to act only as "caretaker" of the troubled PTL Ministry in March of that year. When Falwell assumed full control over the ministry and its holdings (including the right to evict the Bakkers from their Tega Cay parsonage), it was a tearful Tammy who defended her family in a meeting with the press on the parsonage grounds. Jim Bakker was not present, except by implication. The following lament by Tammy was replayed frequently by the networks that afternoon and evening. "I would like to say I hope that Jerry Falwell and his family never have to suffer the way that they've made our family suffer. I wake up every morning wishing that they had killed me. And Jim does, too."[30] Such melodramatic stuff might be greeted with derision if it were to come from a public figure in a public setting. But such a remark from Tammy, a woman who has spent years as a television figure and yet apparently never mastered the codes of decorous behavior one expects of television personalities, appears plausible; at the very least, it is passed along by the media without comment.

Thus, examining the Bakkers' media images during 1987 and 1988 suggests that our experience of any figure can be removed from the public to the pseudo-private by reframing the presence of the media to discount its publicness. When this happens, a measure of rhetorical invulnerability is bestowed upon that figure's discourse: Not that the figure becomes more credible, but rather that serious challenge to his or her claims becomes much more difficult and unlikely. One obvious but effective way of accomplishing this transformation is by manipulating production values to downplay technical sophistication. More cunning tactics involve bringing the media into the home for a share in ostensibly private conversations, as one would with any friend. These techniques are most familiar to us, perhaps, as staples of political campaign spots; the Bakker's peculiar genius has less been in the technical staging of their pseudo-private display than in their ability to keep a seemingly naive and garrulous Tammy in the spotlight.

It is important to qualify my argument at this point. I do not contend that all of the examples of framing cues I have used here to illustrate my thesis are the result of deliberate calculation, although doubtless many of them are. To claim that Tammy Faye Bakker is *deliberately* as ingenuous as she appears to be would be as nonsensical as claiming that Ronald Reagan was *deliberately* more photogenic than Walter Mondale during the 1984 presidential campaign. Not all of the framing cues to which we were exposed in our experience of the Bakkers were contrived, nor is it decisive for my argument to prove that they are. My argument so far rests only on the function of these cues, when present, and on the tendency of all of us to view persons and events through these framing cues whenever we are exposed to them.

▦ PSEUDO-PRIVACY AND MORAL STANDARDS: JUDGING THE BAKKERS

Pseudo-private display influences our judgments of the figures involved, in ways both obvious and subtle. The first of these functions, as Krauthammer has indicated, is that information presented in this way is granted a claim to plausibility and sincerity that is not available to explicitly public messages. Yet pseudo-privacy is more than a collection of techniques for manipulating perceived truth-value, or defending against attack upon utterances whose truth-value is dubious. It is also a mode of action and experience, within which we may come to "know" such figures as the Bakkers. The function of this mode of action and experience is the suspension of customary (that is, public) grounds for moral and ethical judgment of the persons we witness this way.

Koppel's irritation with the Bakkers was clear from the tone of his question, above; equally clear from his tone there and throughout the interview was that he rejected the Bakkers' piety as hypocritical, if not downright dishonest. But Koppel's censure misses the point. In the pseudo-private, the categories of judgment that count are not simply honesty and piety, as we might consider appropriate for public figures, but also (and, sometimes, little other than) grace and taste. Pseudo-private display has the tactical advantage of inviting judgment primarily on aesthetic standards, rather than exclusively on moral or ethical ones. While the public realm is the realm where, as Hannah Arendt wrote, individual greatness and nobility matter most, greatness is an unsuitable standard for the private realm, and—by extension—for the pseudo-private.[31] In the pseudo-private sphere, where these two worlds collide, we frequently judge not how great or noble a person is (as would be appropriate to public display), but rather how charming or enchanting (as would be appropriate in one's private home). True, many of the Bakkers' less-friendly observers might maintain that they failed dismally the tests of grace and taste, but what of it? The point is that time thus spent decrying the Bakkers as tasteless is time during which the issues of honesty and piety (in which the critics' judgment of the Bakkers might be far more damning) are not even being raised. Many a scandal-ridden celebrity, politician, or religious leader would count that trade as a bargain.

Here the Bakkers—especially Tammy—are in their element.[32] Because their television career has, for years, played down the difference between onstage and backstage, the transition from one category of judgment to the other is far simpler for the Bakkers than it would be for, say, Jimmy Swaggart, whose backstage (private) life is more sharply separated from his onstage (public) performance.[33]

In this regard, Jim and Tammy Bakker enjoy a peculiar rhetorical advantage in that they represent a conjunction of different styles of display: Of the two, Jim is the more comfortable with and adept at the discourse and manners of traditionally public display, while Tammy is obviously more naturally at home in pseudo-private display. Thus, Jim Bakker's argumentative exchanges with Koppel, for example, were always conducted from comparative rhetorical safety, because of Tammy's presence alongside him. In the extended exchange below, notice how Koppel must repeatedly attempt to extricate himself from discussion of "shopping" with Tammy to force Jim back into a discussion of PTL Ministry finances. The excerpt begins with Jim Bakker's reply to charges made earlier that day by Jerry Falwell, and repeated by Koppel, that the Bakkers had asked for six-figure lifetime salaries (and more) from the financially racked Ministry:

Jim: Well, that was just some suggestions of where to start, and honestly, if—we'd go back to PTL and work for nothing, if God wants that.

Koppel: Yeah, well, maybe you would, but you didn't, and the fact of the matter is, not only did you not work for nothing, you worked for a great deal. Jerry Falwell today claims that now that the accountants are beginning to sort their way through all the paperwork, that they have found that over the past year, for example, you paid yourselves, or the board paid you, in salary and in dividends and in bonuses, a total of $1.9 million. Now, that's a far cry from working for nothing, isn't it?

Jim: Uh huh. Yes, and I'm not sure of those figures, but I think we've made a lot of mistakes, and I'm very sorry about it, and the—the board of directors, with me out of the room, always voted our salary. We—Tammy and I had nothing to do with our salary. And that doesn't excuse it, because we are the president, or were the president of the ministry, and we should have said, "No." And we did say, "No" many times, but our board cared about us, and they would tell us that Jim and Tammy, you earn every penny that we give you. In one week, I raised $30 million, at one time last year, and Tammy's records and our books and all have brought in literally millions of dollars, and instead of royalties, we took a salary controlled by the board of directors, and I feel that we—we should have said, "No, we'll just—we will not receive this." And the board did it out of love, they cared about us, they really did.

Koppel: Well, let's just talk numbers.

Tammy: And they told us they thought we were worth it.

Koppel: I'm sorry?

Tammy: They told us that they thought we were worth it, because I would go every time and tell them, you know, we don't deserve it, and they will all tell you I have said that to them. And they said, "Listen, you guys, you're worth it to us," you know, so—

Koppel: They also said you were kind of like a shopping machine. I mean, you would go out and—

Tammy: I do like to shop. I probably am well-known for my shopping.

Koppel: Yeah, it's—

Tammy: But I am a bargain-hunter.

Koppel: Extravagantly, though, I mean we're not talking about a little item here and a little item there, or a couple of dresses—how many mink coats, how many cars, you know what I mean, we're talking—

Tammy: I don't shop for cars, and I don't shop for mink coats. I do a lot of my shopping at places like T.J. Maxx's and the outlet stores. I shop outlet stores an awful lot, and I enjoy shopping. It's kind of a hobby to help my nerves.

Koppel: Jim Bakker—

Tammy: Better than a psychiatrist.

Koppel: Well, it may not be cheaper, the way you've been going at it, but let me—

Tammy: Maybe not.

Koppel: Let me—let me come back for a moment to the overall question of finances here. . . .[34]

Once Tammy has blithely repositioned the Bakkers in the pseudo-private, even a self-described "tough" questioner like Koppel must concentrate his energy to keep the implicit standards of judgment in the realm of honesty and ethics, not taste and materialism. Perhaps it is no coincidence, in connection with this principle of "safety" or "invulnerability," that while it was not uncommon for Tammy Bakker to appear in the media without her husband during the PTL scandal, for example on interview shows, rarely if ever did Jim Bakker appear without Tammy.

The Bakkers' ministry has always been associated with an upwardly mobile Pentecostalism that paralleled their own lives. Two features identify this Pentecostalism: a charismatic focus on the lives and times of the evangelists themselves, and a gospel of material pleasures as the sign of God's special blessing. Yet, despite Jim's occasional lapses into high display such as his vintage Rolls Royce, the Bakkers' materialism was mostly middle class: Sears and T.J. Maxx, not Saks and Neiman-Marcus.[35] What is of critical importance here is not *where* the Bakkers shop, but rather that—unlike with Gary Hart or Jimmy Swaggart, Ollie North, or other figures who faced scandal at about the same time—we *know* where they shop, and that this has been made somehow relevant in forming a judgment of them.

The trappings of this materialism, their household and lifestyle, have always been near the center of popular debate about the Bakkers. It is striking that during the scandal itself they were rarely asked to respond substantively to the many allegations of fraud, embezzlement, and so on— certainly Koppel did not ask them to do so; his idea of a "tough question" was handled rather easily by the Bakkers, as we saw in the exchange above. Rather, the popular treatment of their fall from grace was more often about the features of their pseudo-private lifestyle; about their charm rather than their piety; about their taste rather than their honesty. A newspaper article in March 1988, syndicated by Knight-Ridder Newspapers, commemorating the first anniversary of the PTL scandal, is typical of this pattern: The story devoted two paragraphs to the indictments against the Bakkers; the remaining seventy-three paragraphs focused on such details as the price of the ring Tammy wore at the interview, the age of Jim's unemployed parents, and the treatment of Jessica Hahn (Jim Bakker's alleged lover-turned-blackmailer) by the same cosmetic surgeon who transfigured pop superstar Michael Jackson.[36] Even wire service coverage of the impending collapse of the PTL ministry and the forced sale of all its assets in bankruptcy, in April 1988, was scarcely seen as an occasion to pass, invite, or even suggest moral judgment upon the Bakkers' actions.[37] By publicly playing up the Bakkers' private quirks and tastes, media coverage has moved our dominant image of them to the pseudo-private. Because of this shift, the harshest popular judgment ever passed against the Bakkers during the scandal seems to be that their taste failed to measure up to a level appropriate to the wealth they accumulated—that they are, in a word, tacky. Ethics, piety, and virtue dropped almost completely out of the picture.

▓ CONCLUSION: PSEUDO-PRIVACY AND PUBLIC ACCOUNTABILITY

The results of pseudo-private display can be impressive. Our pseudo-private experience of Jim and Tammy Bakker gives us a sense of intimacy with them that no amount of nude photo layouts in *Playboy* will ever win for Jessica Hahn. If, indeed, it were only a question of creating a greater sense of intimacy through the electronic media, then the case of the PTL scandal might be simply one more case, albeit a slightly offbeat one, of celebrities manipulating the media to their advantage.

What deserves our concern is not simply that pseudo-private display can blunt the seriousness of charges raised by interlocutors, although this is demonstrably true: During 1987, a year of seemingly perpetual scandal, perhaps only Lt. Col. Oliver North dodged the noose of civic accountability with equal panache. Indeed, the likes of Gary Hart and Joseph Biden, who saw scandal quickly derail their 1988 presidential ambitions, must look with wonder upon the ease with which the Bakkers blunted our sense of the seriousness of the (far more grave) accusations they faced by transferring our experience of them to a wholly different realm in which what we see is less important than what we agree to ignore. Rather, we should be troubled, as citizens and as observers of public discourse, to find that public discussion, through which we expect to hold public figures to standards of public accountability, may so easily be degraded to pseudo-private display—taking with it the centrality of honesty, piety, and integrity upon which the very idea of public accountability is founded. Pseudo-private display does something worse than make figures appear more honest or pious than perhaps they are; continued exposure makes less likely even the attempt to challenge figures on these grounds.[38] Suspicion of technique, upon which pseudo-private display is founded, has not made us wiser or more critically discerning; instead it tempts us to lower our expectations for public discourse in general.[39]

We therefore risk being betrayed by our own language: Pseudo-private display is *not* simply public display with minor, updated variations in technique. True, it is commonly found in physical locations traditionally considered public, and it involves persons we would ordinarily consider public figures. But the dislocation of "public" and "private" by the electronic media—by which both terms have been transformed into metaphors—means that physical location is no longer decisive in differentiating the two. Failure to recognize that "public" and "private" are now metaphors provides the opening within which pseudo-privacy operates. While the two terms were anchored metonymically in physical sites, they could sensibly be discussed as practical contraries. But when the media allow the commonplaces of one to interact with the other, allow the traces of sites and roles appropriate to the private to become mingled with messages traditionally expected to be public, the result is not merely more artful public display, but something quite different: a mode of display in which argumentative standards change, as do the appropriate standards for judgment of conduct.

After all, what has made the term "public" so important to us in our culture is not the mere physical trappings of public spaces, but rather its association with codes our culture considers important: standards of rationality, rules of conduct, precepts of morality. Display ungoverned by these rules, even when it occurs in sites traditionally considered public, is not simply a new kind of public display; it is in fact no longer public display at all, at least as we traditionally or conventionally understand that word "public."

So long as we cannot rethink the relationship within which our expectations about "public" and "private" now stand with respect to contemporary communicative practice, adequate standards for acting and judging in our communicative world will continue to elude us.

▨ Notes

[1] At its peak, the PTL Ministry's worth was estimated at $203 million, including the income from the 161 stations that aired its programming. David Brand, "God and Money," *Time* 3 August 1977: 48.

[2] The examples used to illustrate my analysis, below, were drawn chiefly from three sources, beginning after the scandal reached public proportions in March 1987: television news coverage of the Bakkers (primarily on Cable News Network); talk-show interviews with the Bakkers, including the Bakkers' 27 May 1987 appearance on *Nightline* and Tammy Bakker's 12 December 1988 appearance with talk-show host Sally Jesse Raphael; and televised documentaries related to the scandal, including "Praise the Lord" (PBS, 26 January 1988), and "Thy Will Be Done" (PBS, 6 April 1988). Other sources, such as on-line information searches, were also relied upon and are identified below. It is not the purpose of this essay to produce an exhaustive accounting of all media appearances, public or pseudo-private, by the Bakkers; obviously the total of their media appearances during the height of the scandal is far too great to treat here.

[3] Charles Krauthammer, "Pseudo-Private Lives," *The New Republic* 23 May 1983: 12–14.

[4] *Nightline*, Executive Producer Richard Kaplan, ABC, 27 May 1987. Transcription of Show no.1567 (New York: Journal Graphics, Inc., 1987) 2.

[5] Hannah Arendt, *The Human Condition* (Chicago: University of Chicago Press) 28.

[6] Arendt 36–37.

[7] I have relied upon Arendt's more elaborate discussion of the relationship between "private" and "privation"; see: Arendt 58–73.

[8] Joshua Meyrowitz, *No Sense of Place: The Impact of Electronic Media on Social Behavior* (New York: Oxford University Press, 1985). See, for example, his "Introduction: Behavior in Its Place," 1–9.

[9] Erving Goffman, *The Presentation of Self in Everyday Life* (New York: Doubleday Anchor Books, 1959) 106–140.

[10]Goffman 106–10.

[11]Goffman 113.

[12]Goffman 107.

[13]Goffman 112.

[14]Max Black, *Models and Metaphors* (Ithaca: Cornell University Press, 1962) 38–47. See also: George Lakoff and Mark Johnson, *Metaphors We Live By* (Chicago: University of Chicago Press, 1980). The argument developed here, with respect not only to metaphor in general but also to spatial metaphor in particular, relies upon William L. Nothstine, " 'Topics' as Ontological Metaphor in Contemporary Rhetorical Theory and Criticism," *Quarterly Journal of Speech* (May 1988) 151–163.

[15]See: Marshall McLuhan, *Understanding Media: The Extensions of Man,* 2nd ed. (New York: Signet Books, 1964) 19.

[16]Krauthammer 12.

[17]Krauthammer 12.

[18]Two useful discussions of the denial of persuasive intent as a persuasive strategy have guided me here: Herbert W. Simons, *Persuasion: Understanding, Practice, and Analysis,* 2nd ed. (New York: Harper and Row, 1986), Chapter 15 "Analyzing Persuasion in the Guise of Objectivity," 307–328; and F. G. Bailey, *The Tactical Uses of Passion: An Essay on Power, Reason, and Reality* (Ithaca: Cornell University Press, 1983).

[19]Mark L. Knapp, *Essentials of Nonverbal Communication* (New York: Holt, Rinehart, and Winston, 1980) 12–13.

[20]We might as appropriately look at the stream of "kiss-and-tell" books that flooded the bookstores during the summer of 1988, written by former Reagan administration officials. Perhaps the most notorious of these were: Donald T. Regan and Charles McCarry, *For the Record* (New York: Harcourt, Brace, Jovanovich, 1988); and Larry Speakes and Robert Pack, *Speaking Out* (New York: Scribners, 1988). The thesis of this essay is equally applicable—indeed, perhaps even more urgently so—to political figures as to religious figures. This is sharply demonstrated by *Time* magazine's excerpting of Regan's titillating accounts of President Reagan's deference to the First Lady's obsession with astrology. The publisher's assertion that "the decision to print excerpts of *For the Record* had less to do with personality than history" faces tremendous evidence to the contrary: not only the circus atmosphere surrounding the publication of the excerpts, but also the fact that history had all but forgotten the revelations a year later. See: "A Letter from the Publisher," *Time* 16 May 1988: 4.

[21]"Praise the Lord," Producers William Cran and Stephanie Tepper, *Frontline,* Executive Producer David Sanning, PBS, 26 January 1988. Transcription by the author.

[22]"Praise the Lord," 26 January 1988. This scene, and the one described immediately above, were broadcast to the audience of the PTL network before being used in Cran and Tepper's documentary.

[23]*Nightline* 15–16.

[24]The image of the outdoor bathroom, whose connection to Koppel's question seems tenuous, is nevertheless a favorite of Tammy's, and it has occurred with some frequency during Tammy's media appearances after the PTL scandal broke. As late as December, 1988, Tammy was still resurrecting the outdoor bathroom, this time in reply to talk show host Sally Jesse Raphael:

> *Raphael:* How does somebody—how does the normal American family get caught up
> in all of this? Did you ever dream—If some, could somebody have come to
> this little girl from Minnesota . . . could somebody have said to her, "One day
> they're going to have you on the cover of a magazine. One day you're going
> to be caricatured on 'Saturday Night Live'?"

☐ **Criticism Is Written to and for an Audience**

> *Tammy:* I would have said there was no possible way. We had an outdoor bathroom. I was the oldest of eight children. . . .

(*Sally Jesse Raphael,* 12 December 1988. Transcription by the author.) Here the relevance of the image to the question asked is more obvious, yet not so obvious that the reader may not find its appearance somewhat indecorous.

[25] Jean Seligmann, "The Inimitable Tammy Faye," *Newsweek* 8 June 1987: 69.

[26] *Nightline* 3.

[27] *Nightline* 3.

[28] *Nightline* 3.

[29] Koppel's predicament also highlights an ironic consequence of the dislocation of public and private. Even though they were engaged in conversation together on the same live broadcast, the Bakkers and Koppel were not present within the same communicative mode: Tammy Bakker's presence was pseudo-private, while Koppel's was public. Hence their displays were accountable to different standards of conduct, to Koppel's dismay.

[30] Reported on Cable News Network, 18 June 1987. Transcription by the author.

[31] Arendt 52.

[32] More evidence of how frequently and easily the Bakkers can blur this line: both Ted Koppel's May 1987 *Nightline* interviews with the Bakkers and Sally Jesse Raphael's December 1988 interview with Tammy Bakker took place in the Bakker's home (or, in Koppel's case, with the Bakkers at home and Koppel in the studio). In the midst of the Raphael interview, Tammy fretted that her house needed dusting.

[33] A comparison with the case of Jimmy Carter suggests that this preparation of the audience, by repeated and incremental exposure to pseudo-private display, may be necessary to prevent the effect from backfiring. Compared to his recent predecessors, Jimmy Carter's "backstage" life frequently crossed over into his "onstage" performance as president. Yet for Carter, pseudo-private display (including framing cues spanning the range from his appearance for a nationally televised address in a cardigan sweater to the antics of his eccentric relatives, most prominently his brother Billy) seemed to produce a less-positive reaction, even if that reaction was not always well-voiced. Billy Carter, in particular, was at best a diverting sideshow to the Carter presidency; at worst he was an embarrassment and a liability. The analysis of pseudo-privacy so far suggests two possible explanations for this: First, the office of the presidency may be especially resistant to the transition to pseudo-privacy. Second, and more directly relevant to the present discussion, Jim and Tammy Bakker had a much longer time over which to accustom their audience to experiencing them in the pseudo-private mode, whereas Carter moved in a short time from relative anonymity to the presidency, leaving comparatively little time to accustom us to viewing him through the lens of pseudo-private display.

[34] *Nightline* 5–6.

[35] Sources already mentioned provide numerous examples of this attention to be found during the scandal's height. For example, "The Inimitable Tammy Faye" catalogues Tammy's attraction to "shoes and cubic zirconiums," and describes in some detail her passion for shopping binges. Often this attention, in matters that might otherwise seem undeserving, approached the level of farce. Koppel's *Nightline* interview dwelled at some length on the rumor of an "air-conditioned dog house" for the Bakker's dog, Max (16). This was later picked up by *Newsweek* ("Heaven Can Wait," 8 June 1987: 62) and was also featured in the infamous music video. The same *Newsweek* article featured a photo montage of a ceramic dachshund and other statuary from the Bakker's home, cited as examples of "excess" (61). This trend reached its apparent zenith on 22 November 1987 when the syndicated comic strip "Bloom County" mentioned the air-conditioned dog house in a strip caricaturing the Bakkers.

[36] Elizabeth Leland, "PTL: A Year Later," *The Muncie Star,* 20 March 1988: B8.

[37]As an illustration of this point, none of the news items, retrieved on-line through the Newsgrid information service under the keyword "PTL," during the week following the April 1988 announcement that the Internal Revenue Service had revoked the tax-exempt status of the PTL Ministries, gives more than passing mention to charges of blackmail, or mail or wire fraud, then associated with the demise of the ministry. The first item, "PTL Leaders Vow to Fight the IRS Ruling Stripping . . ." (25 April 1988, item 1844), mentions only "the high salaries of the Bakkers," and that PTL officials "blamed big salaries paid to Jim and Tammy Bakker for PTL's troubles." A second item from the same search, "IRS Revokes Tax-Exempt Status of U.S. Television . . ." (22 April 1988, item 1551), mentions the Bakkers' "extravagant" lifestyle and the sex scandal involving Jessica Hahn, but lapses significantly into passive voice at the mention of "thousands of dollars from a trust fund set up to assure her silence about her celebrated sexual encounter with Bakker," passing over the question of agency and responsibility. The remaining Newsgrid item, "TV Evangelist Jim Bakker Asks to Return to . . ." (22 April 1988, item 1506), does use the word "sins" in connection with Bakker's actions, but only in reporting Bakker's characterization of his own behavior. Even these references to possible public wrongdoing by the Bakkers are uniformly brief and ambiguous, as the influence of the shift from public experience to pseudo-private would lead us to expect.

[38]Indeed, although a full investigation of the question would be beyond the scope of this essay, the apparent rhetorical invulnerability of Ronald Reagan's so-called "Teflon Presidency," in which scandals and reversals never seemed to "stick" to the Chief Executive himself or affect his credibility with Americans, may well stem from exactly the phenomenon being considered here.

[39]Syndicated columnist David Broder's description of a glaring example from the summer of 1989 is worth quoting at length:

> One of the perverse rules of behavior of the Washington press corps is our tendency to savor being told secrets while ignoring what is on the public record. Eight years ago, there was a huge furor when William Greider published the previously private views of budget director David Stockman on the perils of the fiscal policy he had helped create and move through Congress.
>
> Stockman's phrases—his observation, for example, that "the hogs were really feeding" when the special interest lobbies finished with the tax bill—created a sensation. Stockman had made the comments in what were originally off-the-record, one-on-one conversations with Greider.
>
> The man who now holds Stockman's job as director of the Office of Management and Budget, Richard G. Darman, late last month sounded an equally urgent note of alarm about the selfishness of fiscal policy. But in contrast, he scarcely caused a ripple.
>
> Darman's mistake was that he didn't leak his views to a single reporter but stood up and delivered them, of all places, at the National Press Club.

See: "Budget Troubles No Less than under Past Administration," *Chicago Tribune*, Sunday 6 August 1989; Section 5:11. Broder's point is well-taken: the on-the-record public speech, which we still imagine to be the best way to place an issue on the public agenda, pales in its rhetorical force compared to pseudo-private display.

MAXIM 3

CRITICISM IS BOTH SERVED AND CONFINED BY THEORY AND METHOD

CHAPTER 11 [⎯⎯⎯⎯⎯⎯⎯]

THE METAPHOR OF FORCE
IN PROWAR DISCOURSE

Robert L. Ivie

In this commentary, Robert L. Ivie recounts how the rigor of theory and method helped him gain distance on his topic of research, American war rhetoric. He describes his study of the case of the War of 1812 as part of a larger critical project stemming from his ambivalence about his own military service during the Vietnam era. To give himself the distance he felt he needed to undertake a project so close to his own intense experiences, Ivie . began his study not with the war most close to him, but to one separated in time and cultural space: the War of 1812. Ivie also sought perspective on his subject in part by embracing a theoretical approach that would allow him distance from his texts.

COMMENTARY

Reflecting ten years later upon the process of writing "The Metaphor of Force in Prowar Discourse: The Case of 1812" reminds me that the essay was ten years in the making, the product of a larger project on the rhetoric of war that began in graduate school upon my return from two troubling years of active duty in the United States Navy during the Vietnam era. Throughout those two years, the longest of my life, I confronted the moral dilemma of obliging a patriotic duty at the expense of contributing to a wrongful cause. Stymied by my circumstances as a military instructor stationed at a naval air training facility in Millington, Tennessee—thus protected from combat as well as prevented from protesting the war—the dilemma eventually transformed itself into a quest for understanding and, perhaps, absolution from the purgatory of inaction and indecision over questions of moral purpose, specifically those surrounding the justification of war. Thus, I renewed my graduate studies with a desire to discern how we talk ourselves into war and quickly discovered an affinity between my burning question and Kenneth Burke's probing investigation of rhetorical motives.

Realizing that I was too close to the immediate experience of the Vietnam war, that I needed distance and breadth of perspective to initiate my study of American justifications of war, I began planning a dissertation that would employ Burke's conceptual machinery in an analysis of presidential war messages from 1812 forward. Following James Andrews's lead, I set out "to discover any consistent appeals which contribute toward a pattern of pro-war oratory." Burke's ideas seemed especially amenable to providing a method of intrinsic criticism, or systematic study of rhetorical strategies as symbolic action. The War of 1812 provided an intriguing starting point because not only was it the young republic's first declared war but also it had been labeled by historian Samuel Eliot Morison as "the most unpopular war that this country has ever waged, not even excepting the Vietnam conflict."

The first result was a term paper in 1972 that investigated what C. Wright Mills called "vocabularies of motive" by drawing upon Burke's notions of hierarchy and victimage, his dramatistic pentad and ratios, and various strategies of identification to analyze James Madison's war message of June 1, 1812, and the antiwar arguments of three of Madison's most prominent Congressional critics—Daniel Sheffey, Richard Stanford, and John Randolph. In addition to yielding a method of analysis, which I employed soon thereafter in a doctoral dissertation comparing seven presidential justifications for war, this initial study of war rhetoric in 1812 suggested essential differences between the symbolic orientations of prowar and antiwar speakers—a lead I did not investigate further until several years later when Ronald Hatzenbuehler and I undertook a joint project on Congressional decision-making in the early republic.

Upon further examination, the rhetorical struggle between proponents and opponents of war in 1812 underscored the importance of understanding war as a matter of choice grounded in symbolic action. Thus, I set about writing a paper that rejected deterministic images of war and advocated instead, by way of example, a comparative analysis of opposing strategies employed by prowar and antiwar speakers to dramatize an essentially ambiguous situation. This paper, presented in 1976 at the annual meeting of the Western Speech Communication Association, metamorphosed over the next five years into a reconceptualization of war rhetoric. As the initial draft submitted to *The Quarterly Journal of Speech*, it contained the seed of an idea that developed through two revisions into its final published form.

The 1976 draft appears in retrospect more prescient than perhaps it actually was. Nevertheless, I remember shipping it off to the editor of *QJS* with the uneasy sense that it contained an important notion not yet fully grasped. I had ventured as far as I could without benefit of the kind of dialectic that comes from serious editorial review. I hoped I had produced something sufficiently substantive to prompt the kind of critique that helps perplexed writers find their bearings. Indeed, the response confirmed the unrealized potential of the piece, encouraging me to keep searching for an elusive gestalt and providing Delphic guidance toward that end.

What I had achieved by this point was a rudimentary sense of the importance of integrative images to the rhetorical process, including the rhetorical process of scholars theorizing about war and involving mechanistic metaphors that cast human nature and the causes of war into a deterministic mold; rhetoric, ironically, was employed by scholars no less than by proponents of war to occlude choice. Thus, the extended debate in 1812 provided a valuable case study in how the option of peace was transformed rhetorically over a period of months (and, as I later discovered, years) into a perception of war's necessity.

My analysis of this debate was guided by a dramatistic orientation and thus untethered by mechanistic tenets to a content-analytic listing of recurring themes, or so I thought. I adopted (mostly implicitly) an organic metaphor to capture the integrative function of rhetorical action between and among what, for the most part, were Republican advocates and Federalist opponents of war with Great Britain. What emerged most clearly was the existence of competing perspectives, two relatively integrated symbol systems diverging along party lines, each grounded on different premises, with one more capable of enveloping the other in its legitimizing rhetoric. I had discovered that a different image guided each side's definition of the situation and that various reinforcing rhetorical strategies of argument, arrangement, and style had been concocted on their behalf. The outcome of the debate was a result of one image outmaneuvering the other.

Nevertheless, a tension between mechanistic and organic accounts of rhetoric's justificatory form and function continued to confound my search for an explanatory gestalt. The mechanistic inclination guided me toward a systemization of three sets of themes (intrinsicality of harms, intentionality of hostilities, and feasibility of redress), each with its subthemes (for example, intrinsicality of harms was characterized as itself a function of three additional "operations": one to specify the adversary's noxious behaviors and establish a concretization of damages, another to identify a universality of effects, and a third to substantiate the lawlessness of the adversary's conduct). This systemizing of themes, abstracted from the constituting language of the debate, served as a convenient template for comparing Republican and Federalist cases as they "evolved" in stages from prewar through transitional to prowar rhetoric. I set out to find the intrinsic coherence of belligerence, a coherence that had been constructed within an inherently ambiguous situation, by charting the evolution of recurring themes and presentational tactics in a justificatory structure that functioned as a "catalyst" for war. Presentational tactics were conceptualized as language devices for communicating the substance and salience of themes (themes that served as decision criteria) when evidence available to rhetors remained otherwise inconclusive.

This peculiar mixture of organic and mechanical thinking led to a linear search for an integrative structure, yielding among other things the observation that Republican rhetors had woven the image of the enemy's hostile intentions into the very fabric of their prowar discourse. One presentational tactic Republicans employed, I noted among a list of others, was to characterize the British enemy through decivilizing metaphors that were consistent with an ascribed motive of recolonizing the United States and inconsistent with England's professed goal of defending itself against the French. As something of an afterthought, I noted that the significance of such a tactic transcended its role as a catalyst for war in 1812 because it illustrated a way of engaging an underlying image of savagery that aroused the nation's fear and provoked its anger. In this way, I began tentatively to merge previously independent lines of critical inquiry, one of which had just culminated in a forthcoming essay on images of savagery while the other was still being revised to resubmit for editorial review. Again, my *QJS* readers displayed remarkable patience, advising me to drop the catalyst and feature the metaphor. But just how to feature the metaphor continued to baffle me until I began thinking of it less as a presentational mechanism and more as the seed of a motivating idea, the source of a guiding image.

Understanding metaphor as the linguistic source of rhetorical invention was the insight that finally brought the project to fruition, its gestalt derived from the metaphor of force. Force could now be understood as the principal war-legitimizing figure manifested, extended, and literalized through decivilizing vehicles, structures of argument, and various other rhetorical forms. This was the insight that guided both my analysis and my evaluation of Republican prowar rhetoric and its motivating perspective. It was the insight that transformed a structuralist analysis of savagery's three dimensions into a holistic understanding of its unity as an image.

Metaphor became the unifying principle and rhetorical dynamic that has animated my investigation of war-justifying discourse for a decade since. It has led me to explore the typology of decivilizing vehicles revealed in Ronald Reagan's rhetorical construction of the Soviet threat; to examine Harry Truman's strategic appropriation of the plain style as a literalizing medium of the image of Soviet savagery; to investigate the metaphorical construction of freedom's feminine fragility as the threatening reciprocal of savagery's masculine force; to devise a procedure for locating metaphorical concepts constraining the rhetorical invention of Cold War critics; and to examine the self-neutralizing cluster of motivating metaphors in the Johnson administration's Vietnam war rhetoric. Thus, a rhetorical theory of war has begun to emerge within a unified line of investigation, the key characteristics of which first became synthesized within a framework of critical inquiry into Cold War motives.

The rhetorical perfection of the metaphor of force into an attitude of belligerence raises the related question of what self-defining metaphor could inspire the construction of such a threatening image of the enemy. Accordingly, the critical quest that a decade ago yielded the gestalt of force turns now down the dark path of fear into the metaphorical depths of a nation's rhetorically constituted sense of insecurity.

CHAPTER 12 ⬚

PREMILLENNIAL APOCALYPTIC

Barry Brummett

In this commentary, Barry Brummett stresses the importance of theory in his own criticism. Yet Brummett is by no means a slave to method. His commentary uses words like "faith" and "hunch" to describe the attitude with which he approaches texts and begins the tentative process of selecting a theoretical approach to his text. Brummett's study of premillennialist rhetoric exemplifies his faith in action—the theoretical approach settled on in that study is reached only after some experimentation with ways of reading the text suggested by other theories.

COMMENTARY

My interest in apocalyptic rhetoric spans a number of published articles and convention papers. The essay in this book was my first article on the subject. My latest effort is a book. In negotiating with various publishers over bringing that book out, I was asked by one editor why I became interested in apocalyptic discourse in the first place. It was a loaded question, because the *subject matter* of apocalyptic, especially *contemporary* apocalyptic rhetoric, is not what one might call "respectable" in the academic tradition. People who truly believe that the world is about to end are considered on the cultural and intellectual fringe by many people, *especially* by mainstream academics. Indeed, when I first submitted the essay in this book to an academic journal, one reviewer sent back a downright abusive tirade questioning why anyone would want to study the discourse of (in his or her words) crazy people.

Because the editor's query was a loaded question, it put me on the spot. And perhaps for the same reason, I had not given much conscious thought to the question before. I was being asked why I became interested in the subject matter, but because of the sensitive nature of that subject matter, I was being asked to explain *myself*. In that moment, the relationship between the critic as a professional analyst and the critic as a person was brought to the foreground. That is the relationship that I think is or should be central to the critical process, and a relationship that I would like to feature in these remarks.

For me, criticism has always been the product of personal involvement and theoretical inspiration. Good criticism, I believe, requires both. The criticisms I have published have always concerned subject matters that I cared about strongly: political rhetors or groups or movements that I admired or despised; rhetorical situations that I found fascinating or intriguing; forms of literature, movies, or television that I personally enjoy. The same was true of apocalyptic discourse. Because of my religious upbringing and beliefs, I have always been aware of apocalyptic themes, although not as a *primary* concern. I understood that these ideas were the preoccupations of certain subgroups, if not my own, within the larger Church. I have always been fascinated by people who express their personal fears and obsessions by cloaking them in terms and symbols belonging to another order of discourse. I believe that this is what opponents of gay rights do in appropriating religious discourse to express their aesthetic preferences, for instance, and of course I argue that apocalyptic discourse does the same. Not being a very risky person myself, I am both awed and appalled by those who risk their rhetorical "all," as so many apocalyptics do in committing themselves to specific dates for the end of the world.

But there have been many subject matters that I have not addressed in criticism even though I found them personally fascinating. In the early 1980s, several African American children in Atlanta were killed by an unknown assailant. The circumstances resembled the earlier "Zebra" killings in San Francisco, a subject that I *had* studied, and so several people suggested to me that I write about Atlanta. I found the *subject* horribly fascinating, but I was and I remain *theoretically* uninspired. That is to say, I could think of no systematic explanation or way of thinking about the Atlanta murders that would generate insights about that experience. I could find no methodical way (or method, if you like) of saying something beyond the obvious about those murders. And so I left them alone.

By *theory* here I mean a system for understanding experience, usually involved in a set of questions or issues to consider that a person can apply to some subject matter so as to gain a better understanding of the subject matter. There are theories for everything: I have a theory for how to start my old blue clunker of a car and for why it does *not* start sometimes; I have a theory about what is eating the bean plants in my garden and for how to stop it; and there are many theories of how discourse works in life. Those last theories are what I use to say something about my experience of communication.

I do criticism when I experience the conjunction of both a real personal involvement in a subject matter *and* a realization that some theoretical explanation fits that subject matter and can be used (by me) to say something interesting and insightful about it. Typically, the beginning of the critical process involves a dialectic between those two prerequisites. I am unable to say which of the two comes first. Usually, I will read some interesting news item, and I will think about what it means, what the implications are, what is going on in the deeper levels of discourse about the item. And then it will come to me that a theory that I have read recently, or about which I have *also* been thinking, has some relevance to that news item. It seems to me that I could fit the two together and, in the process, say something new and interesting about the subject. But was it my ongoing thinking about the theory that directed my attention to that news item in the first place? I don't know.

I don't know the answer to that question because I think that a lot of criticism is saved by *faith* alone, in advance of works. In the early stages of many studies, I have simply had a hunch that I would be able to say something non-obvious or interesting about what was going on in some kinds of discourse. I had faith that the theory I was using would help me to notice things that others had not. I had faith that the subject matter was sufficiently deep and complex to allow new insights to be brought out of it. But I have never been able to see my way clearly to the end of any study when I was just beginning it, and the apocalyptic essay is no exception.

In the present essay, I began with a fascination for several apocalyptic texts that were currently popular, such as *The Late Great Planet Earth* or several pamphleteers who were setting specific dates for the apocalypse. I wanted to understand that discourse better, but I was unaware of a theoretical framework that would help me to do so. So I turned to other scholars of apocalyptic, and read widely in their commentaries. It seemed to me as if writers such as McGinn, Tuveson, and Barkun were discussing issues directly related to rhetoric without making that link clear. At the same time, I had been thinking about Karlyn Kohrs Campbell and Kathleen Jamieson's theory of rhetorical genres. Gradually, it became clear that Campbell and Jamieson could be used to make nonrhetorical theory serve rhetorical ends, to make the apocalyptic scholars I had been reading "talk" about apocalyptic as a rhetorical genre. With that realization came Campbell and Jamieson's *structure* of situational, substantive, and stylistic hallmarks of a genre. And that structure then provided an organized way to look at apocalyptic. I could then return to the subject matter and reconfigure/reconceptualize it following the structure provided by the categories of the theory.

The structure that theory provides constitutes the set of questions that the critic asks about the subject matter so as to generate insights about it. Useful criticism is, for me, not simply a wallow in a text. It is guided by an order inherent in a theory. The resulting act of criticism, whether it emerges in a paper or simply in an insight held by the critic, is a rewriting and reordering of the subject matter so as to see it more clearly. The naive observer experiences life, but the critic lays the template of a theory over life and says, "If you see it *this* way, additional levels of meaning and significance emerge."

The essays you read in this book are by academics, all of us professional rhetorical critics. We publish the results of our studies in scholarly journals and books, which are largely read by other academics. What's the point? The question is crucial to how criticism is done. Many of us begin our careers being motivated to publish criticism so as to get tenure, to be blunt about it. But that motivation cannot sustain the critical enterprise, personally or even institutionally. I think that considering what value lies within the whole enterprise of rhetorical criticism helps us to understand how the process itself works.

The value in rhetorical criticism lies in returning to that conjunction of the personal and professional with which I began these remarks. Rhetorical criticism should help people to understand their experience more richly, to see levels of meaning and significance that they would not have seen before, and to instill in people habits or techniques of "reading" discourse. Several implications follow from that claim.

Criticism must be *generalizable*. The reader must be enabled to use the criticism so as to understand other experiences better. For that to happen, the way or pattern of understanding that is embodied in the theory must be generalizable. If the reader is enabled only to understand the particular apocalyptic texts studied in my essay, then I think it has failed. If the reader can better understand a new set of texts she encounters next week, so much the better. And if the reader acquires an expanded repertoire of ways to understand all sorts of texts, apocalyptic or not, that would be best of all. Generalizability comes from theory, not subject matter.

Criticism is not necessarily concerned with *accuracy*. I have made several assertions about what is going on in apocalyptic discourse. This will sound strange, but whether those things are "really" going on is beside the point, it seems to me. The reason is that, as noted in the paragraph just above, I don't really care whether you understand Tim LaHaye's book better now. What I want my essay to do is to give you "practice" using a conceptual structure (the theory) to help you to see meanings in experience more richly. As long as that structure helps you to see meanings in experience *generally*, I don't care whether it is entirely accurate about the meanings in the focal experience that the criticism is "about."

Criticism must be *disseminated*. I am personally unhappy with the prospect of the critical essays I have written moldering away in journals, because to the extent that they do, then my criticism cannot help people to experience life more fully and richly. Academics ought not to be content with mere academic publication. Criticism should be passed on to as many people as possible. The best route that academics have for reaching the public is, obviously, students. I have used the apocalyptic essay, and every other criticism I have ever published, in my classes: I have taught my students using the criticisms of others. I have used techniques and insights of criticism to write opinion pieces for local papers, thus passing on ways of understanding experience through that avenue.

The personal and the professional can be paired, respectively, with subject matter and theory, or with real life involvement and the ability to say interesting things about that involvement. So I will end on the theme with which I began. Good criticism talks to you about what you have experienced, but it tells you that there is more to see than you have suspected. It shows you something more, and sends you out to live with ears and eyes that are more widely opened.

CHAPTER 13 $\boxed{}$

THE RHETORIC OF DEHUMANIZATION

Martha Solomon

In this commentary, Martha Solomon characterizes her own approach to criticism somewhat differently from the accounts of Brummett and Ivie, earlier in this section, by downplaying the role of theory in her early critical choices. Solomon gravitated toward the study of the infamous Tuskegee syphilis medical reports because of more general interests, but as her background reading increased her understanding of the consequences of those reports, she discovered a fit between certain theoretical writings and her emerging interpretations of the texts. Yet Solomon also notes that a critic's theoretical point-of-view may well change over time, suggesting very different ways she might approach the text were she to return to it today.

COMMENTARY

I have always relied on the kindness of strangers.
—BLANCHE DuBois, *A Streetcar Named Desire*

For me, inspiration for critical projects has often come, if not from strangers, at least from strange places. When I wrote "The Rhetoric of Dehumanization: An Analysis of Medical Reports of the Tuskegee Syphilis Project," I was at Auburn University, some twenty miles from Tuskegee, Alabama. James H. Jones, the author of *Bad Blood: The Tuskegee Syphilis Experiment*, which exposed the racism in the study, had recently spoken at Auburn University. But neither of those facts directly influenced my interest in this project. Indeed, I did not hear Jones's lecture nor know of the Tuskegee syphilis project until a colleague, who found little to like in living in a small Southern college town, expressed unusual enthusiasm (for her) for the lecture. It was in reporting her untypical enthusiasm for the lecture that I mentioned the topic to my husband. After a few minutes of animated discussion, he speculated: "There's an important article for you in that study."

The idea intrigued me enough that I began to explore the possibilities. Reading Jones's book, I found to my disappointment that his analysis that racism facilitated the study's continuance was convincing. He had, in a sense, preempted one avenue I as a rhetorical critic might pursue. However, I had a strong intuition that my husband's prediction of an article lurking here was accurate. My contribution was to be the rhetorical critic's inherent interest in how texts work. Then, I began to consider looking at the medical reports of the Tuskegee project themselves, since those were the texts that initially made the information about the study public. At first, I was stymied because Auburn had no medical school with an attendant library that would have the necessary journals; and getting materials xeroxed through interlibrary loan can be a tiresome, time-consuming, and sometimes frustrating task. But one of the unfailingly helpful librarians at Auburn's Ralph Brown Draughon Library suggested that our veterinary medicine school had an excellent collection of medical journals and might prove helpful. In fact, I was able to obtain copies of almost all the medical reports in one visit there. Thus, with little effort on my own part, I had a full set of texts discussing what had become a highly criticized study that had prompted the development of federal standards for the use of human subjects.

Although the details of how these reports came to my attention make this case different from other critical projects I have undertaken, my experience in this instance resembles almost all of the studies I have done in two respects. First, I am always primarily interested in *how* and *why* texts work for particular audiences. Believing that audiences construct meanings on and around works, I am fascinated by what in a work excites or irritates an audience member. Thus, rather than trying to determine what a rhetor "means" in a text or attempting to reconstruct the rhetorical situation surrounding the text, my focus is always on that complex, subtle, and elusive connection between a work and the audience it influences.

Second, I prefer to study texts that I know have worked or failed to work for a particular audience. Popularity is one signal of a text's influence. For example, I was drawn to *The Total Woman* because it was a best-seller, to *Chariots of Fire* because it was a popular and Academy Award–winning movie, and to Robert Schuller because he has survived and prospered as a televangelist. Political success, as in the case of the STOP ERA movement, is another indicator of a text's "working" for some audience. I am particularly intrigued by texts that work for an audience of which I do not consider myself to be a member. Thus, the medical reports of the Tuskegee syphilis study were precisely the kinds of texts I find myself drawn to explore because they had obviously been very successful in obscuring the ethical issues inherent in the project for the medical community.

Thus, unlike many critics I do not engage texts with a theoretical question or project in mind. Until recently, I have not had theoretical issues that direct my critical efforts. Nor did I, as some critics do, choose these texts because they were a type of discourse—scientific writing—that I have decided to explore. In short, this essay grew out of a concatenation of a general question that concerns most critics and the happy chance of locating a set of texts that played an important role in what became a national scandal.

As the project unfolded, what attracted my attention as a rhetorical critic was a small point in Jones's book. He reported that until the study was brought to public attention in the early 1970s by a Public Health Service official only one letter from the medical community had objected to the project although it had been reported in thirteen progress reports published in medical journals over almost forty years. The seemingly inexplicable silence of the medical community was in striking contrast to the widespread public outrage it produced in 1972. Why in forty years had only a single physician objected to what public opinion regarded as an atrocity? Racism was too simple an answer. Certainly, the United States had had and retains elements of a racist ideology. But it was not credible to me that all but one of the estimated 100,000 physicians who read those reports were blinded by their racism to the human consequences of the disease. Moreover, many physicians who read the studies were themselves African Americans. From my rhetorician's perspective, it seemed that the answer must lie in the nature of the discourse itself and how it functioned to produce their shared insensitivity.

The studies themselves were dry reading. Perusing them, I was impressed anew with the clinical sterility of scientific reporting. That reading experience led me to my first glimmer of insight: These were doctors and health officials writing to and for other doctors and health officials. They used all the techniques of scientific writing to wipe clean any "subjective" human elements from their reports in order to present their findings "objectively." Thus, I envisioned this project in part as a study of how the generic parameters of scientific reporting influence perceptions and systematically obscure some crucial elements of the reality they are recording.

Specifically, I wondered what particular factors in the reports had obscured the ethical issues that so upset persons outside the medical profession when they learned of the nature of the study from the media. I soon realized that those outside the medical profession, regardless of their ethnic background, identified, in the Burkean sense, with the men in the study, while the physicians who wrote and read the reports did not. This suggested the appropriateness of Kenneth Burke's idea of consubstantiality; this connection, in turn, prompted me to consider the depictions within the reports and suggested the pentad as a method that might be generative.

Although the details of this project differ from other work I have done, I frequently begin with Burke and his notion of identification. Starting there, of course, reflects my primary interest in why and how texts work for particular audiences; or to put it in Burkean terms, why audiences identify with the rhetor and his/her perspective. But I must also admit that although I begin with Burke, I almost never end up with him. While I gain insights and understanding from asking questions drawn from the pentad, the resultant analysis has a cookie-cutter predictability that does not satisfy me. This problem, I believe, inheres in most pentadic analyses. Burke's pentad is difficult to use effectively with subtlety, and Burkean analyses seldom tell me things I did not see for myself.

For this essay, however, I never got beyond Burke or pursued other approaches. At that time, Burke seemed the natural avenue for answering the questions I wanted to explore. If I were doing the essay today, I might draw on what I have learned about Foucault's ideas on the rules governing discourse, or pursue notions from cultural studies about hegemony, or consider the spheres of argument concept that Thomas Goodnight has proposed. But even a decade later, I remain convinced that in light of my interests, the texts, and the overtly political content, Burke offered a compelling heuristic. I should note that I find doing more than one "pass" with Burke's pentad and considering alternate depictions to be a very fruitful exercise regardless of whether I pursue that method in an essay. Indeed, I enjoy "playing" with the pentad as a means of exploring how texts can be parsed and how different construals suggest disparate interpretations.

One problem in working with Burke's pentad is that I see layers or series of depictions and often have difficulty sorting out what elements belong in which depiction. That was certainly true in this case. Initially, I tried to make all the pieces fit into a single pentadic analysis; despite my efforts, that approach did not work. Finally, two interpenetrated strands seemed to emerge from the medical reports. First, the bulk of the material in the reports was clinical observation of the impact of the disease. What loomed large in those details was the subjects of the study as the place where the disease was taking its toll. This realization led me to my first successful pentadic pass through the material: the patient as scene with syphilis as the actor. This depiction dehumanized the men being studied and accounted for why concern for them was eclipsed. Then, I revisited my observation that these were medical professionals writing for doctors. What, I wondered, made that bond so strong? The answer seemed to lie in the role or persona that the authors assumed in the texts. I began to tease out a second depiction: the depiction of the study. In that case, the men being studied became the agency through and by which the medical community was studying a phenomenon and contributing to human knowledge.

Two things united these depictions. In each case, a group of humans was moved from their usual status as agents to fulfill other roles in the depictions, scene in one case and agency in the other. Both depictions obscured their humanity. Additionally, on another level, viewing subjects (whether human or animal) as scene and agency seemed characteristic of scientific writing generally. These two observations became the core of my critical argument.

Discussing how these two features worked for the audience and drawing the implications of my analysis provided the final part of the essay. In the discussions of function and implications, I moved from describing the texts to evaluating and assessing them. For me, these sections are the easiest and most enjoyable part of writing essays because here I can attempt to answer the central question of how texts work and speculate about why audiences connect with some texts so forcefully.

This essay was an unusually easy one to write. From the beginning the materials themselves seemed to suggest the approaches to take. However, the process was not without its problems. On the one hand, teasing out the two depictions took some time because the strands were so interrelated and subtle. On the other hand, I found myself leaving out so much of the texts as I developed my pentads that I felt uncomfortable. Frequently, when writing criticism, I am troubled by how much of the material remains untouched and undiscussed in the analysis. Whenever I finish a project, I am keenly aware that I have, to borrow the terminology of Roland Barthes, created my own texts on and around the work I am studying. In this case, however, by far the largest portion of the medical reports consisted of clinical details and statistical data that did not seem to play a direct rhetorical role, except in establishing the tone of the reports as "objective" and "scientific."

As I wrote, I also felt myself constrained by Jones's analysis. His conclusions about the implicit racism in the Tuskegee study are compelling. My problem was, in a sense, to move beyond that important dimension of the study and explore a different, and in a sense, broader rhetorical problem. This need to negotiate a space for my ideas is common in doing criticism. Because I like to work on popular cultural texts, I am often writing analyses after other authors have commented on the works. Thus, I am always in danger of simply reiterating their observations or offering a fuller account than they have to support similar conclusions.

Finally, I should note that writing is for me a slow creative process. I labor over the language in some sections, particularly the justification and rationale for the study. It is not unusual for me to struggle with one or two paragraphs for several hours, while other portions flow rather quickly. Because I try to be precise, I find myself consulting a dictionary frequently. Moreover, I change directions and revise my arguments as I work with the texts themselves, trying to articulate my thoughts carefully and coherently. In this case, as in virtually every essay I have done, the introductory paragraphs, particularly those previewing the argument, are the last I write. I find myself sharpening and altering my focus in the process of writing as I realize what I want to say.

Finishing a project is both gratifying and frustrating. While I like the sense of developing and articulating an argument and I feel good about having "proved" my case, I am always a bit disappointed at the finished product. This sense of the inadequacy of an essay to one's initial conceptualization of it is, to my mind, inherent in the process of developing a critical argument. Requirements of length and focus make full articulation of one's ideas impossible.

The reviewers' comments on this essay suggested few substantive revisions, but they did press me to organize the argument more clearly and to focus it more sharply. Usually I have been fortunate, as in this case, in getting practical, constructive guidance from reviewers.

I followed the reviewers' suggestions about the essay rather closely. Although I am familiar with authors' horror stories about how reviewers want to control the essay, few editors or reviewers have tried to write an essay for me. In this case, they simply helped me argue what I wanted to say more effectively. The only comment I resisted was one reviewer's suggestion that I be more "outraged" about the studies. Because I tend to write on texts of which most persons in our profession (myself among them) disapprove, I am frequently urged to be more disparaging or condemnatory in my analysis. My goal has always been to explain rhetorical processes, not make social judgments. I recognize that all criticism is inevitably political and ideological to some extent, but I make an earnest effort to show how texts work rather than judge whether it is just that they should have worked at all.

Rereading this essay seven years after its publication was pleasurable. I like what I wrote, and I remain convinced that my assessment is accurate and fair. I would do it differently—not necessarily better—if I were doing it today. This essay has always been one of which I am fond; it was easy to write and I said something I wanted to say about the lures and dangers of scientific allegiance to "objectivity." I hope the essay is accessible enough for students and lay persons to make them alert to the terrible and wonder-working power lurking in language.

CHAPTER 14

CICERO'S REDEMPTIVE IDENTIFICATION

Michael C. Leff

In this commentary, Michael C. Leff takes a somewhat ironic look at the writing of one of his early essays on Cicero's Catilinarian orations. Leff dryly describes the spirit of his search for a method with which to approach Cicero's texts as bordering on the opportunistic. When one theoretical approach seemed unable to draw much of interest from his text, Leff describes himself as casting about from one theory to another without asking whether it was his own assumptions that might have needed reexamination. Leff is ambivalent in retrospect about the outcome, suggesting that while the finished essay was not without its insights, his fixed attention to a narrowly drawn method ultimately restricted his ability to draw conclusions about Cicero's texts.

COMMENTARY

I no longer remember precisely when I wrote the first version of this essay. It was a long time ago—Lyndon Johnson was president and I was a graduate student. Somewhat later, with help from my friend Jerry Mohrmann, I revised the essay for publication in *Explorations in Rhetorical Criticism,* a book (edited by Mohrmann, Charles Stewart, and Donovan Ochs) that was designed to open new approaches to criticism. Like the book in general, the essay did not command a wide audience, and as the years passed, I more or less forgot about it. Consequently, I was surprised and a bit dismayed when the editors of this volume indicated that they wanted to reprint the essay along with some of my reflections about it. At this distance, my own essay seemed alien, and in rereading it, I had the eerie sense that it not only belonged to a different time and place but to a different person altogether.

Distance is a technical term that refers to the stance a critic takes in relation to the object of study. The young man who wrote the essay that follows, like most of his contemporaries, believed that critical distance was a good thing; it preserved objectivity and allowed space for the application or construction of theory. More recently, fashions have changed, and critics often emphasize the value of "engagement." Objectivity is no longer assumed to be either possible or desirable, and with increasing frequency and vehemence, critics are asked to abandon the role of disinterested spectators and to recognize their function as rhetorical advocates.

My current view falls somewhere between these two positions, since I try to practice a kind of interpretative criticism that simultaneously involves distance and engagement. From this perspective, the end of criticism is not to build or test "theory" but to understand the utterance of another person. Such understanding is never "objective," since it depends upon an interaction between the discourse of the interpreter and the discourse of the other, and this interaction occurs between two positioned subjects and not in some zone of impersonal, objective neutrality. The interpreter attempts to assimilate a text that is distant or alien into his or her understanding, but the discourse the critic produces is always other than the discourse that is being studied, and the critic's understanding can never replicate another person's understanding of the world. Interpretative criticism, then, is a never-ending oscillation between distance and engagement, between identifying with the other and maintaining distance from the other.

Since self-understanding is incomplete and mutable, the critic's position is not entirely stable. Time passes, fashions change, and the accumulated weight of the interpretative discipline, which opens the critic to different rhetorical voices, gradually begins to change the critic's own view of rhetoric. Little wonder, then, that, after more than two decades, my essay seems so distant that commentary on it requires an act of critical self-reflection almost as complex as the interpretation of some other person's text.

On first reflection, the essay seemed to originate by accident. It just happened that my reading of Burke's *Rhetoric of Motives* coincided with a frustrating effort to engage the rhetoric of Cicero's Catilinarian Orations. In studying the Ciceronian texts, I had followed the then conventional method that began with an argumentative analysis. The objective was to lay bare the logical structure of the texts—to identify the key premises, show their relationship to one another, and locate the evidence supporting the premises. The more I tried to groom the text into this tidy form, however, the more clearly I realized that the endeavor was futile. Cicero's speeches just did not behave like the speeches of intercollegiate debaters. They did not march from premise to premise in an even stride, but they ambled through images, innuendoes, and emotional outbursts whose power I could sense but could not explain. At this point, Burke came to the rescue. He offered a way to encounter the symbolic dimension of rhetorical discourse, and an approach that could give a rational account for things that did not seem rational on the surface. In particular, his "theory" of redemptive identification allowed for an explanation of Cicero's apparently irrational tendency to exaggerate.

The details of this story do indeed refer to matters of coincidence, but, on further reflection, the plot line has a familiar ring. It embodies a general pattern that entered into the consciousness of rhetorical critics at the time and exerted a powerful influence on the orientation they adopted toward their work. The key element in this pattern is a fixation on theory—or more specifically on theory, conceived after the social scientific model, as a coherently organized body of principles distanced from and superior to any particular instance of practice. Operating on this basic premise, the critic is positioned to move in a vertical direction. That is, critical explanations proceed either downward from abstract, theoretical principles to specific practices or upward from practices to principles. In either case, explanation rests upon principles distant from and more abstract than anything manifest in rhetorical practice. To put this point negatively, the critic is discouraged from attending to rhetorical developments within specific cases or moving laterally across cases, except insofar as comparative study becomes grist for a theoretical mill that refines the raw material of practice into abstract regularities.

My own essay was grounded firmly, though unconsciously, in the vertical, theoretical orientation. Having found the existing "theory" inadequate for my purposes, I did not pause to consider whether the resistance of the texts suggested a flawed conception of the nature of theory and its relationship to critical practice. Instead, I hastened to find another "theory" as a replacement. This reaction was hardly accidental; it reflected the temper of the time. The essay rested comfortably within *Explorations in Rhetorical Criticism,* since the book as a whole represented an effort to multiply theoretical perspectives. The editors had instructed each contributor "to sketch a theoretical position and apply it," but in my case, the instructions were unnecessary. Already infected by the same pseudo-pluralistic virus, I had performed the required steps in the earlier version of the paper.

This bias distorted both my use of Burke and my reading of the speeches. Instead of attempting to understand and assimilate Burke's complex critical position, I tore a section of the *Rhetoric of Motives* loose from its context and rearranged it into a tidy methodological grid. Had I studied Burke more attentively, I would have discovered an alternative conception of theory per se, rather than an alternative theory in the conventional sense. By adopting a wider Burkean perspective, I might have seen the theorist as a positioned subject engaged in a kind of rhetorical practice, and I might have recognized the possibility of grounding interpretative work in cases rather than in disembodied abstractions. This same narrowing of vision also limited my approach to Cicero's texts. Unaware of other possibilities, I had assimilated the technical lore of classical rhetoric into a modern frame of reference. I did not view the standard classical system as a loose inventory of strategies grouped for convenience under a limited number of headings. I merely assumed that the system constituted a "theory" and that it ought to provide a method for critical inquiry. As a result, the conventional categories, which I, along with many others, still retained even as we appropriated new "theories," appeared as separate and distinct modules to be invoked in methodical order. The critic first read down through the text to analyze its argumentative appeals, and then invoked the same procedure to analyze its style. This fragmented approach, which runs contrary to the spirit of both Burke and Cicero, left me in a position where I could not read across a text so as to understand the interactions among argument, style, and context. Consequently, I floundered until I could borrow a "theory" that accounted for one of the prominent features in Cicero's speeches (that is, the extensive use of hyperbole), and I then fixed attention on that feature. This exercise was not without some value, but for reasons I did not then understand, it blocked a more fully realized interpretive effort. As Robert Cape has demonstrated recently (in his 1991 dissertation, "On Reading Cicero's Catilinarian Orations"), a more fluid use of the standard categories yields a much more sensitive reading of the *Catilinarians*.

Despite these misgivings, I still retain a certain fondness for the young man who wrote the following essay. He makes a noteworthy attempt to produce some sparks by striking a set of venerable texts against the thought of an important contemporary rhetorician. At times the interaction really seems to work, especially in the analysis of the metaphors of disease, parentage, death, and rebirth. In general, his problem is that he does not understand his own position as a critic. Note that when he comes to state his purposes in the last paragraph, he resorts to an almost meaningless jumble of phrases—something about living texts, historical documents, the grand possibilities of theory, and split-level realities. He does not realize that if he wants to understand other people's utterances, he must first make a serious effort to understand his own purposes. Given the blindness and confusion of this essay, I doubt that he will ever sort things out adequately, but he really seems committed to the task of opening old texts to contemporary understanding, and if he persists in this endeavor, he might improve his own self-understanding.

MAXIM 4 █████████████████████████

CRITICISM RARELY TRAVELS A STRAIGHT LINE TO ITS END

CHAPTER 15 ⸻

PUBLIC MEMORIALIZING
IN POSTMODERNITY

Carole Blair

*In this commentary, Carole Blair describes how her study of the Vietnam
Veterans Memorial, in collaboration with Marsha Jeppeson and Rick Pucci,
nearly "imploded" at an early stage, when the coauthors were unable to
come to agreement on what kind of response the Memorial seemed to evoke.
Only after some struggle did they conclude that this problem was in fact the
key to a new argument; that is, that a vital part of the Memorial's
rhetorical character was its radical multivocality, its capacity to speak in
many voices and evoke many responses simultaneously. Blair's essay
recounts how the three critics transformed what had been a blind spot into a
suggestive and original point of view on memorializing.*

COMMENTARY

This account of the accompanying essay must begin by recognizing two
potential problems. First, my account is mine, not Marsha Jeppeson's or
Rick Pucci's. My coauthors' accounts of inventing this essay would be very
different from this. The problem should not be dismissed; this is a very
partial sketch. Second, I was concerned that I might be so contaminated by
my participation in the larger project of this book that my story would fail
to account for what "really happened," as Marsha, Rick, and I constructed
our essay on the Vietnam Veterans Memorial. I was wrong about that; I don't
think I understood what happened until contemplating the larger project.
Just as this book attempts a first step toward exposing the professionalization of rhetorical criticism in general, I've moved closer to recognizing how
implicated my own practices have been in that professionalization. So, while
this is principally a story about how the accompanying essay came to be, it's
also a story about what I didn't know or at least didn't acknowledge during
the process.

I had occasion to visit the Vietnam Veterans Memorial many times; I lived in the Washington area for awhile, and during that time I visited the site frequently. I actually don't know how many times I went there, but I would guess about thirty. In my first visit, I knew I would someday write about the Memorial. I was profoundly moved by it. And I knew even then that my response was more than the sum of its parts. Yes, I knew people whose names were inscribed on the wall; finding each of them was a wrenching ordeal, but I felt compelled to do it. And yes, I was drawn to the unusual, genre-busting design of the wall. I remember thinking how appropriate it was that the Memorial honored the dead and missing but still managed to parody the body counts that were trotted out as signs of "victory" or "progress" during the Vietnam conflict. But even those components of my reaction weren't the sum of my feelings or a measure of the depth of my response. Why did I feel compelled to go back to the Memorial over and over? Why was it such a draw for me? What made it different for me than the other noteworthy sites in Washington, to which I paid a second or third visit only if friends visited and we went out to "see the sights" of Washington? How could this granite marker, and later its additive statue and flag, evoke such emotion? I knew that, if I ever found the answers to those questions, I would be able, in fact compelled, to write about the Memorial.

In the five years between my departure from the Washington area and my arrival at University of California, Davis, I would read others' commentaries on the Vietnam Veterans Memorial. There were six critical essays written in our field alone. While I learned a great deal from my occasional reading, there was little in it that helped me to understand my own response. That made it even more clear to me that I *had* to write about this thing, that I had to figure out what about the Memorial was so utterly engaging. But I still waited, because I was completely frustrated by my attempts to understand its power.

At UC, Davis, Marsha and Rick, who were then students, asked me (separately) to read and comment on an essay each had written in prior criticism courses. Both essays had to do, in varying degrees, with the similarities and differences between the Vietnam Veterans Memorial and the NAMES Project International AIDS Memorial Quilt. Though the papers were very different in orientation, both were quite insightful. Both lacked what I believed was probably necessary to turn them into publications or conference papers—a clear theoretical base and/or generalized implications for rhetorical theory or criticism.

The time had come for me; my interest was piqued again. Both Rick and Marsha were serious about pursuing their projects. Both were so sensitive to the nuances of the two memorials that I thought we might, together, figure out the power of the Vietnam Veterans Memorial. So I suggested that the three of us work together on an essay. Their compromises were to let me and each other in on their projects; mine was to deal with the AIDS Quilt, which I had not yet seen.

☐ Criticism Rarely Travels a Straight Line to Its End

Marsha, Rick, and I met time and again to discuss our essay. We would discuss the similarities and differences between the two memorials, our own reactions to them, and possible theoretical bases or implications that would make our essay "fit" for publication in a scholarly journal. We had no difficulty with the first task. Our discussions about the similarities and differences were lively, productive, and nuanced. More than once, those conversations were engaging enough to attract strangers to join them. In fact, we probably owe some of our insight to those who added to our discussions.

When it came to discussing our own reactions to the memorials, it appeared that our project might implode. We simply could not agree on what responses the memorials evoked. Our temporary blunder was to not see the productive value of our seemingly irresolvable conflict. We were all trying to turn the memorials into univocal artifacts and our essay into one that provided *the right answer*. The point, of course, was that the memorials are both radically multivocal in their rhetoric. Still, it took us a while to realize that our disagreements were precisely the point of, not an impediment to, our essay.

Our realization about the multivocality of the memorials helped us toward our theoretical position. So did our observation that rhetorical critics who had written about the Vietnam Veterans Memorial had not treated the specificity of its language—that of memorial architecture. Writings about "postmodernity" should have occurred to me immediately as the key, for they would have allowed us to deal with these issues directly. But it wasn't until we began to think about the implications of something we already knew—that there was a groundswell of national-scope memorial activity in the United States—that we reached for our theoretical stance. Since the Vietnam Veterans Memorial's dedication, the AIDS Quilt, Civil Rights Memorial, Free Speech monument, Korean War Memorial, Kent State memorial, and the Astronauts Memorial had all at least been proposed; some of them had been constructed. Could our era—arguably a postmodern one—harbor a penchant for a new memorializing rhetoric? If so, what were its characteristics and conditions? What about the specific cultural language of architecture could help to account for it? Would all of these new memorials rearticulate the tensions of postmodernity? Our theoretical position resulted from all of these considerations.

But we had to be careful with our theoretical stance. We could not argue that there was a new, objectively observable "genre" of postmodern architecture. For one thing, postmodern criticism is suspicious of such claims. For another, we weren't working with enough "instances" of such memorials to make a genre claim, even had we wanted to (which we didn't). So what we had to do very carefully was to write *suggestively toward* the idea or hypothesis of an emerging memorial discourse, and to argue that new memorials might be read productively *as if* they were part of this new discourse.

We hypothesized that a new memorial architecture might reflect some, but not all, the characteristics of postmodern architecture. Furthermore, we suspected, given our research of later memorials, that the Vietnam Veterans Memorial probably was the first "voice" in this new discourse and that it set out the possibilities for further memorializing. Finally, we decided that the AIDS Quilt appropriated that same discourse and further radicalized it.

I volunteered to draft the essay, because I was more familiar with the literature of postmodernity and postmodern criticism than either Rick or Marsha. In fact, because of our different levels of understanding, we probably made a better team than if we had all been equally knowledgeable. Postmodern criticism is notoriously difficult, and those who engage in it tend to fall into using its dense, forbidding prose as a consequence of using its ideas. But since we were committed to this project as a threesome, it was vital that we all understand and agree on *all* of its contents. Because Marsha and Rick were less likely to be trapped in the linguistic thicket of postmodern critique, they were the perfect initial referees for the early drafts of the paper. If one of them didn't understand or accept the legitimacy of a sentence, it didn't make it into the final draft.

The early drafts of the essay actually were quite similar to the "finished" product; we never made it as far as the AIDS Quilt. We didn't give up on it; the three of us are working on a separate paper about it now, and Rick has written his master's thesis on it. The accompanying essay does not address the AIDS Quilt for a very simple reason: No journal editor would have dreamed of accepting an essay that threatened to be fifty pages long. We pushed the patience of *Quarterly Journal of Speech*'s then editor Martha Solomon with the length of the essay as it now stands. We had no choice but to reorient the project toward just one of the memorials and to promise each other we would write the second essay.

That made an enormous change in what we argued in the essay. Much of what we had seen and discussed in the Vietnam Veterans Memorial was the result of having considered it in relation to the AIDS Quilt, and vice versa. Some of the issues we wished to explore had to be dropped, because they wouldn't have made sense in the absence of our comparative-contrastive case. For example, we might have argued that the Vietnam Veterans Memorial wall is in some important senses multiply metaphorical—it can be seen as a book, as the outstretched arms of a human embrace, as the rise and fall of a lifecycle, as a sequential representation of the domestic experience of the war, and as a composite of the notorious body counts. By contrast, the AIDS Quilt literalizes the memorial function by incorporating into itself valued possessions of the persons who have died. Its symbolism is, as a result, arguably more direct, more concrete (no pun or irony intended), and more oppositional than that of the Vietnam Veterans Memorial. Such arguments must wait, however, for a separate essay.

Our essay also does not address the fact that its character grew out of our disagreements. It's not that we wished to hide our conflict. We simply believed that any such "personal" revelations would have been excised in the journal review process. Although our disagreements shaped the essence of our paper, they needed to be recast so as to provide the requisite sense of "distance." And so we smuggled our disagreements in under the guise of other critics' conflicting assessments and reactions. Of course, that seems ridiculous. But our own disagreements had occurred in conversations over lunches and drinks, not in the privileged arena of published writing.

Our essay does not speak to our inclination to write about the Vietnam Veterans Memorial, for much the same reason. Critical scholarship gives no apparent credence to a critic's personal reactions or to the depth of those reactions. A critical essay's merit is judged, in part, by its ability to justify the historical/political significance of the rhetorical event it criticizes or to argue that an analysis of that event helps us to understand rhetoric more generally. So, our responses to the Memorial could not have served as justification for a scholarly essay. Instead, to justify yet another essay on the Vietnam Veterans Memorial, we quoted other people's reactions, essentially conceding that the Memorial's ability to affect them was more important than its capacity to affect us.

Perhaps there is one positive aspect of not having revealed our personal reactions in the essay. I'm still not certain that I can comprehend fully the intensity of my own response to the Vietnam Veterans Memorial. It wasn't until I faced writing this essay on invention that I began to grasp one of the factors that must have made my response to the Memorial so pronounced. I had intended to suggest here that the Memorial had evoked a deeply personal response and that was why I wanted to write about it. Somehow I believed that would adequately answer the question of why I wrote about the Memorial rather than remaining content with a passing interest in it. But of course, my intended response begged the question. I, like other critics, am interested in a great many things that I have not been even tempted to write about. And I'm sure any critic would answer the question of why s/he wrote about a rhetorical event by saying that s/he had a strong personal reaction to it. The question still remained, as I realized only when concentrating on this book. I was still divesting the critical process of my own personal engagement with the Memorial.

As I thought about the question further, I realized that at least one of the answers had to do with how my personal history was tangled up in the history of the Vietnam conflict. I was four years old when the first American was killed in Vietnam and twenty when the last was killed. Every night during those years, I ate dinner while watching the "war" on TV news. I remember being sickened by the sights I saw. I remember the terror that I would actually *see* my cousin, the guy down the street, or one of my friends blown up by a mortar shell or picked off by a sniper. And every few months, I would listen to the president of the United States—Lyndon Johnson and later Richard Nixon—say why the United States had to be involved *in spite of* the views of American citizens, even in spite of a *majority* of that group.

It was not just that watching real suffering and death while I ate my peas became so "natural," a frightening enough consequence. It was also that I, and no doubt other children my age, had no hope of holding on to the innocence and idealism of youth. Nothing I saw on television squared with the principles or "truths" about American virtue that I learned about in school. The Vietnam Veterans Memorial honors those Americans who fought and died in Vietnam. For me, it marks one other thing: my childhood prematurely turned adult and sharply skeptical because of the Vietnam conflict.

CHAPTER 16 [ ]

THE RHETORIC OF AMERICAN FOREIGN POLICY

Philip Wander

In this commentary, Philip Wander describes how a politicized and polemical manuscript about the American government's Vietnam war rhetoric—he calls it "an antiwar speech with footnotes"—collided unsuccessfully with journal editors and reviewers for years. Then after shelving the project for a decade, Wander discovered that it might be "safely" reintroduced as "historical scholarship," rather than as a politicized and polemical statement. Wander's commentary traces the fate of this "reborn" essay.

COMMENTARY

In her poem "My Guilt," Maya Angelou talks about the guilt she feels, as a poet, when writing about injustice—slavery, heroes dead and gone, and lynchings. Her guilt lies in the pride she takes from not screaming about what she sees and feels. On the scaffold, the page before her, she takes to dying like a man. She does it to impress the crowd. Her sin, she says, lies in not screaming loud.[1]

Whatever the "Vietnam war" has come to mean, the war was horrifying in 1967. I woke up every morning feeling or knowing that I would feel angry. I took the war personally. My mind was being filled with carnage. Riding my bicycle to work one day, I saw a poster of a small child crying, suffering from burns caused by napalm. It had been pasted on an olive drab U.S. mail box. The color recalled America's glorious past (the Second World War) as well as an over-investment in camouflage paint.

I went to rallies, marches, joined a speaker's bureau at San Jose State where I met "old" and "new leftists" like Robin Brooks (once identified by *Look Magazine* in the late 1950s as one of the most "dangerous" professors in the United States) and David Eakins from history (a well-known and widely respected "new Left" theorist), Bob Gliner from sociology (who has produced several documentaries shown on public television), and Jack Kurzweil from electrical engineering (a leading political organizer in the Bay Area), and a number of students who taught me about the place of passion and organizational skills in politics.

What I learned was that the only way I could continue being a "professor" (that is, teaching) and working toward tenure (that is, becoming a "lifer," a goal I would have scoffed at at the time) was by integrating moral and political commitment into my work. This was not a matter of principle, it was a matter of survival, and it had to do not only with a professional life, but with people fed into a slaughterhouse to slaughter others. These "others" included mothers and babies, grandfathers and aunts who lived thousands of feet below young, high-tech American missionaries who, in a modern, electronic work-a-day-world, flew their "missions" over primitive, non-Christian, underdeveloped peoples.

I decided to go through the *Department of State Bulletin* to determine how this horror had been justified. A few hours every other day, often between classes, I read every speech, letter, toast (I remember John Foster Dulles invoking Buddha), etc., made by government officials about Vietnam or Indochina, from the 1950s up to 1972. What I discovered was that official statements, abstract, ritualized, melted away. What remained was a small child crying. I felt angry, betrayed. I had heard my father's war stories a hundred times (he had served in Germany with the "Black Cat Division," the Thirteenth Armored, during WWII), when Hitler existed and there were camps to liberate.

It was tough to write under these conditions, especially to do scholarly writing about Vietnam. After a presentation at a Western Speech Association meeting during this period, Lloyd Bitzer asked me in all seriousness: "How do you know that the war is wrong?" I answered, "When I was a boy and visited my grandfather on his farm in Iowa, I would have known, looking up in the air, that having bombs dropped on us was wrong." But I remember thinking at the time, "Jesus, what *is* wrong, if dropping bombs on small children, mothers, and grandfathers is not wrong?"

I kept my thoughts to myself. Along with Bitzer and others of our generation, I participated in a system that avoided controversy (or housed it in the "past"), recoiled from feeling, and equated moral and political commitment with a lack of scholarly restraint. Detaching feeling from thought and writing was part of what it meant to be a professional. This calamity was not caused by Bitzer or Wander, but we participated in, reproduced, and were (and are) to some extent defined through it.

During the Vietnam war, we could scream our protest and not be disappeared. To some extent this reminded us that the United States was and is a great place to live. But the same could not be said for the Vietnamese or, for that matter, American soldiers who were fighting and dying in a war in which many of them did not believe. The war, recalling Pericles' Plague Speech, was not about democracy. We were not bringing democracy to Vietnam, any more than the French tried to bring it to Indochina. It was about tyranny (or fascism as we called it), about the domination of another weaker people. Whatever the terms *fascism, Stalinism,* or the *Holocaust* now mean, it was occurring then, but it was proceeding under terms like *duty, patriotism, foreign policy. It had to be stopped!*

The first incarnation of "The Rhetoric of American Foreign Policy" was as an antiwar speech with footnotes. In the same year, Steve Jenkins and I published an essay advocating "worthwhile" scholarship. Encouraged by the response, I sent off a manuscript about the official justification of the war in Vietnam to the *American Quarterly* (replete with quotations from R. G. Collingwood). It was politely rejected. I turned it around, and sent it to *Philosophy and Rhetoric.* Two referees and the editor concurred in their rejection. One of the rejection letters included the following rhetorical question: "What if one stuffed Richard Nixon's speech of 1969 in Wander's face?" The letter was unsigned.

Rejections hurt. My first rejections took a week to shake off. They still take a couple of hours. They hurt, because they open up, if only for a moment, little fissures of self-loathing, fear, feelings of inadequacy as a scholar, a human being, a lover, a son, etc. In such moments, the appeal of Kafka's story about a man slowly becoming a cockroach becomes real. Bluntly stated: Having Nixon's speech stuffed in my face pissed me off.

In relation to "The Rhetoric of American Foreign Policy," however, my metamorphosis had only just begun. I revised and sent the manuscript to the *Quarterly Journal of Speech,* where the editor was my dissertation advisor and friend, Edwin Black. I admired him and his work. Imagine my childish delight then when his referees recommended publishing the manuscript with "minor revisions." Edwin, however, with whom I have had and continue to have many arguments over politics, crossed out the more political/ polemical sentences and paragraphs. He told me to read George Orwell's "The Politics of the English Language" and respond to the comments sent by the referees. I revised, placing the good (that is, the political-polemical) stuff into footnotes. It came back again. Again, without explanation, controversial passages were crossed out. Again I revised, stuffing the "offensive" passages into footnotes. It came back a third time. This time when I sent it back I could not reread the piece. It was rejected.

Wanting father's approval, or mother's love, wanting to be a famous author in "the field," wanting to write about Vietnam (notice the slippage here from the ideals "professed" above) added up. In writing and revising and having my manuscript rejected, I discovered how easy it was to sell out. I had, in fact, tried to sell out. Fortunately for me, no one was buying. I have always been grateful to Edwin for letting me off the hook. He has been kind enough over the years not to remind me of it, though my reputation as a "radical," "Marxist," "ideology critic" (names I have found odd and limiting, though not objectionable) invites a retrospective.

About the essay: I jammed the revisions into a folder, filed it under "foreign policy," and left the field. I started writing media criticism. I took a vow to write what I truly believed in the way that I wanted to say it. The war was over. Ten years later, fumbling through my files for another paper, I unearthed the folder, read the manuscript, and realized that it had now become "historical scholarship." The difference between polemic and history has to do not only with tone ("emotional," "polemical," "un-well-rounded"), but also with timing and, in the case of scholarship, primary research. Words that evoked outrage during the war had cooled. I thought, "Maybe I could rewrite the piece." This was followed by another thought, "But what for? Vietnam is over. Let it rest." Exhuming Vietnam, confronting my manuscript—my "revisions"—was damned painful.

Then, one day in a used book store, I ran across Jean Paul Sartre's indictment of American actions in Vietnam drawn up for the war crimes tribunal set up by Bertrand Russell. What Sartre said and the way he said it surprised me. He opposed the war and wrote the indictment while it was still going on, but there was no stirring moral indictment accompanied by photographs of napalm victims. The United States, Sartre argued, was continuing a policy pursued by France, Belgium, and Great Britain in the nineteenth century, a policy of domination. If a country or a nation wants to dominate a people who do not want to be dominated, it must be prepared to use terror and, if necessary, to kill every man, woman, and child (in effect, to commit genocide), if it is to retain control when collectively challenged.

Thucydides warned against a policy of empire. The Mytilinian debate and the Melian dialogue have to do with "disciplining" a colony and a neutral city-state in the interests of empire. Thucydides made a distinction between a war and an act of domination that I found helpful. War has to do with a violent conflict between two city- or nation-states when the outcome is in doubt; domination has to do with a violent conflict where there is no doubt about the outcome. Slowly it became obvious to me that Vietnam was not unrelated to other historical events. It was no longer history imprisoned in memory or the past.

There was work to do, but I ran into an academic prejudice. It held that events talked about in official statements about foreign policy and how officials in this or other countries responded to them was the stuff to be analyzed. Obvious now, but a breakthrough for me at the time—foreign policy rhetoric is aimed not only at elites, but also at domestic audiences. It certainly affects domestic audiences. President Reagan, during this period, was arguing that a revolution in Nicaragua could spill over into Mexico leading to massive immigration into the United States. Listening to him, I recalled all those thick, red arrows that for thirty years had been curving and hooking into the United States. Each arrow carried in its wake Soviet (and/ or Chinese) armies, or millions of refugees into Galveston, New York, Los Angeles, sometimes Seattle, or nuclear missiles.

Nicaragua had no air force or missiles or navy. The Sandinistas were not poisoning coffee. But America paid for "freedom fighters," gave them "humanitarian aid" (to stem the tide of communism), slipped money under the table it turned out, after Congress had drawn a line. America was not fighting a war, it was engaging in domination, but it was domination explained to an audience fearful of a vast, surging "it." This "it" included anything and everything that was "un-American."

At a Speech Communication Association convention in Washington, D.C., I was a critic respondent on a panel organized by and including several people who had been or were speech writers and organizers in significant political campaigns. After listening to their comments, I noted that the word "imperialism" had not been uttered, and furthermore that, regardless of the facts, I did not think they would recommend that any candidate use that word. Afterwards, Bob Shrum, who had been Teddy Kennedy's and George McGovern's speech writer (and who had been an outstanding debater at Georgetown), muttered that the American people were not ready to hear it.

Shrum was correct—that is, correct within a two-party, mass media democracy operating under the shadow of a "Soviet Union." This is part of the joy and the responsibility of "scholarship": saying what ought to be and needs to be said, even when no one is ready to hear it. There is no guarantee that such speech will get into print, but if scholarly discourse can sustain the harsher truths, a small, public platform remains.

There is something else which must be said. "The Rhetoric of American Foreign Policy," with its Aristotelian bent and scholarly flare, reeks of compromise. Strategic, necessary, useful compromise, but in relation to the Philippines, Guatemala, Brazil, Iran, Vietnam, Chile, Nicaragua, Angola, Indonesia, and the millions of men, women, and children of color who have been sacrificed to our "national interest"—I take the history of invasions and the ongoing CIA machinations as the warrant for such morbid conclusions—writing in English may be understood as an offense. On Monday, October 26, 1992, a *New York Times* editorial appeared entitled, "The Mozote Horror, Confirmed." In 1981 American-trained Salvadorian soldiers murdered a thousand men, women, and children in the remote village of Mozote. At the time, just after the story broke, the Reagan administration certified that the Salvadorian government was "making a concerted and significant effort" to promote human rights and end "the indiscriminate torture and murder of its citizens." The finding was necessary for releasing U.S. military aid to El Salvador. Ten years later, the remains of scores of children are being exhumed there.

The unspeakable truths of American foreign policy, the millions of souls sacrificed to make and keep our "sphere of influence," mock the rhetoric of American foreign policy. They also mock "The Rhetoric of American Foreign Policy." The immensity of the horror and the style and tone of the saying of it create an unresolvable tension. W. E. B. Du Bois once commented on this problem. He addressed the problem of race during a period in which lynchings were widespread. His own wife and child had been terrorized during a pogrom in Atlanta. "I realize that the truth of history lies not in the mouths of partisans," he wrote, even as he was pulled toward partisanship, "but rather in the calm Science that sits between. Her cause I seek to serve, and where-ever I fail, I am at least paying Truth the respect of earnest effort." In the conflict between partisan and historian/critic/scientist, between professing and professionalism which occurs in the face of horror, there are moments when scholarship muffles what ought to be screamed.

▓ Note

[1]Angelou, Maya. "My Guilt." *Just Give Me a Cool Drink of Water 'fore I Die.* New York: Bantam Books, 1971. 46.

CHAPTER 17 ⬜

REMINISCENCES OF LOS ALAMOS

Bryan C. Taylor

In this commentary, Bryan C. Taylor raises an important issue when he suggests that, as critics, we are never fully aware of or in control of our own inventional processes and practices. Hence, all reflections on our own invention as critics are going to be partial, including his own account of his research in nuclear history. Rather than being purely the inventors of *criticism, Taylor suggests, we as critics are also* invented by *it.*

COMMENTARY

I have the luxury of writing this essay while actually being *in* Los Alamos, where, in the late summer of 1992, I am studying the Laboratory's Bradbury Science Museum. As I begin, I am working in the museum director's cramped and spartan office. The office is located in a metal trailer wedged into the side of a hill between a metal foundry and a cryogenics lab. A dozen other "temporary structures" surround this one, sprawling testimony to the organization's chronic shortage of office space. The noise from the foundry's machinery is constant and distracting. Overhead, though, silver and purple rainclouds are silently regrouping after a storm. Their shadows fall across the Jemez Mountains that rise to the west, and the tall pines there shift in color from green to black, black to green.

This is my luxury: I can reflect on "inventing" the essay, *"Reminiscences of Los Alamos,"* smack in the middle of its apparent referent. Daily, I travel the same ground where John Manley, Joseph Hirschfelder, and Norris Bradbury talked and worked while *they* invented the atomic bomb between 1943 and 1945. My sense of nuclear history and how I came to it are continually sharpened as a result.

But I am also challenged by writing this here. The wartime Los Alamos of those scientists is gone forever. Both the Laboratory and the surrounding town have since grown dramatically, and few of their original structures remain. The community energetically recovers and promotes that history, however, through a variety of images, artifacts, and stories (for example, at the Bradbury Science Museum). This promotion depicts the wartime Los Alamos as if it were a "factual" event whose meaning is self-evident. This unreflective realism is directly opposed to the post-structuralist orientation of the *"Reminiscences"* essay, which asserts that discourse does not refer to a preexisting, "objective" reality. Instead, discourse reflects in its images, metaphors, and silences the cultural construction of humans, their world, and their history *as* meaningful.

In the essay, I examined how the discourse of Los Alamos scientists could, then and now, define the Bomb as a "real," "useful," and consequential object. My commitment to that critical orientation now creates a dilemma. I am surrounded here by representations of wartime Los Alamos. With varying explicitness, they all insist that "something happened," and that I accept its facticity. These forms can be compellingly "real," as when I encountered the office chair belonging to wartime laboratory director Robert Oppenheimer in a warehouse. One arm was slightly more worn than the other, and the hair stood up on the back of my neck. At such times, I lose my detachment about *how* the meaning of such objects is created, and to what ends. They seem naturally *to exist,* and I surrender to them.

Then, at other times, when the employees of the museum argue passionately about the "right" way to present Los Alamos history to visitors, I recover my critical bearings. Yes, something happened at Los Alamos, but the meaning of that event is created through discourse, and is subject to dispute and revision. That dispute is particularly acute in the current post–Cold War climate in which the narratives of Soviet threat and nuclear deterrence that traditionally defined Los Alamos are no longer legitimate, and its scientists must reestablish their worth to the nation.

I outline my current situation to indicate where the *"Reminiscences"* essay has led me. This is the place from which I now try to reconstruct its invention. I believe, in fact, that this is the *only* way that the process of invention can be fully analyzed. I am strongly influenced by critical and "counter-rational" theory that depicts social action as overdetermined (influenced by multiple and conflicting forces), and as "pre-sensical" (with intention and meaning attributed by actors retrospectively). The social act of criticism is no exception. I certainly had *some* preexisting goals and techniques in 1987 for analyzing these three narratives. Convention, in fact, dictated that I articulate them: here, the "theoretical issues" section of the essay functions as a reassurance to the reader that I am in fact a "rational" critic who first derived, and then systematically applied, various "methods" to the selected texts.

This section is partially a fiction, however, fabricated as a concession to the "methodism" that pervades contemporary critical inquiry. That methodism positions the critic as the generative site of invention (he or she "did" it), asserts that such activity is primarily cognitive, and implies that it occurs immediately *prior* to the critical act. Methodism also implies that critic is both relatively conscious and in control of all the forces activated in that practice. In recounting my analysis of the three assumptions, I take issue with these assumptions.

Writing, and thus criticism, I argue, are "embodied" practices. They are always connected to the writer's unique history of pleasure and pain, and are grounded in the psychic traces of bodily experience within institutions (for example, the family, school, church). We write about what we love and what we fear, and although we may efface the fact with our "academic" voice, we invent—and are invented—*from* other places, times, and voices. Not all are cited.

The *"Reminiscences"* essay came from many places. Its immediate context involved my Ph.D. coursework at the University of Utah in critical theory and cultural studies. There, I read and talked and wrote about the relationships between culture, communication, power, and subjectivity. I was strongly affected by discussions that challenged me to see common forms and practices (e.g., conversation) as instrumental to the reproduction of social structure and ideology. I struggled to pay attention to (and sometimes deny) the ways in which I was implicated in that reproduction (e.g., as a university instructor). I was supported and challenged in this process by friends and professors who sought to embody critical theory in their practices (e.g., in promoting diversity and dialogue in the classroom). This education was both painful and exhilarating. The pain came from learning new ways to see and speak about social life as a site of power relations. The exhilaration came from hard-won understanding of those relations. One theme that consistently emerged in these discussions was that criticism should "matter," that it should "make a difference" to a community larger than our academic discipline.

Before I was a graduate student, though, before I moved to Utah, before all this, I was a child. I was a child in a suburban home in Western Massachusetts. I was the child of a mechanical engineer and a homemaker who moved East from Kansas because my father found work in New England's large industrial plants. I have many bodily memories of being that child: the smell of burning leaves in the fall, the taste of chocolate birthday cake, the blur of vacation scenery through the back window of a Dodge van. These were some of my recurring pleasures. But I also endured, as do many children, recurring violence: violence that fell on my body from hands, fists, belts, and, above all, from angry and frightening voices. These were not the only things I knew, but they were important. That violence hurt me and it silenced me. I could not understand it, and it marked me anyway.

One afternoon in 1986 I was browsing in a bookstore by the university

188

and was struck by the pale and melancholy face staring out from the cover of a volume entitled *J. Robert Oppenheimer: Letters and Recollections.* I was vaguely aware that Oppenheimer was a physicist who had worked on the Manhattan Project during World War II and that his reputation was later ruined during the McCarthy era. I bought the book and entered into the world of nuclear weapons (or, to be more precise, formally acknowledged its presence). Oppenheimer's poignant letters to his family and friends between 1918 and 1945 charted the fate of an intellectual within the developing "organization" of nuclear weapons: the amoral and patriotic embrace of "service," the delight in technique, the repression of moral dilemmas.

Since I was taking a seminar on autobiography, I wrote an essay exploring those themes. The seminar professor criticized the essay as commonsensical, and challenged me to see it as the beginning of a long-term study, one that would require extensive research and revision of my ideas. While I was angered by his criticism, it spurred me on. I rewrote the essay again and again, reading extensively about the rich and secret world of wartime Los Alamos. I wanted to understand the environment in which a man of Oppenheimer's poetry and intelligence would come to make nuclear weapons his life's work. It was not that I thought it was somehow inconceivable, but the irony hooked me. It is probably no accident, further, that I pursued the project while living in Utah, where I encountered the lingering anger and bewilderment of "downwinders," residents who had been affected by radioactive fallout from nuclear tests conducted at the Nevada Test Site during the 1950s and 1960s. One statistic summarized their suffering, and I will never forget it: during that period the rate of *childhood* leukemia in Southern Utah doubled.

During this time, I began to work on the project in my dreams. In one, the western horizon of Salt Lake City erupted in blinding nuclear fire. I woke up sweating and shaking, having accessed the nuclear terror that psychologists such as Robert Jay Lifton believe lies buried in the cultural unconscious. In another, Oppenheimer's aging face shimmered before me and spoke: "Leave me alone." In a final dream, I believe we reconciled. We approached each other on a deserted downtown street, and he seemed urgent to speak with me. When we were close, he pulled on my sleeve. He opened his mouth, and a swarm of Monarch butterflies flew out.

In the fall of 1987 I enrolled in a seminar on "counter-rational" organizational theory taught by a visiting professor. This material set me to thinking about Los Alamos—with which I was now fascinated—as an organizational phenomenon: a distinct historical life-world in which speech and writing were used to conceptualize and coordinate human labor, materials and technology. I also was involved at that time in a small study group reading critical theory. I had stumbled across *Reminiscences of Los Alamos* while "shopping" for background material in the university library. As I read, however, it moved on my conceptual grid from "context" to "text." I knew that I wanted to try again to write about nuclear autobiographies, and the critical theory I was reading helped me to see the relationship between personal narrative and social structure anew.

The text held ten separate reminiscences. Three were from women, and I set those apart for a future project that would study the "difference" in gendered Los Alamos voices. Of the other seven, I was drawn to the three selected because they most clearly recalled the "organization" of Los Alamos. I remember the act of writing the essay vividly: my list of "questions" laid beside the text like scalpels; my ambition to "see" patterns beyond what was immediately apparent, and "hear" voices that had been excluded; my involuntary shudder as the "fission" metaphor took shape and clarified the organizational operations of ideology; an accidental encounter with *Nazi Doctors* that made me take a deep breath and up the stakes of the analysis; the silent companionship of a Burmese cat named Grace Jones; endless pots of coffee.

I let that first draft sit for several months while I worked on different projects. I felt that it was good work, however, and presented it a year later at a national conference. The panel members and the audience at my presentation were supportive, and I began to consider submitting the essay for publication. Conventional wisdom in my graduate program held that "having something in print" when I started my job search would improve my chances. That time was approaching, and so—ambitiously—I sent the essay to *the* leading journal in our field. I trembled a bit opening the envelope containing the acknowledgment of its receipt, and then again five weeks later, opening the fatter envelope that I knew contained *the verdict*. I was stunned: the three reviewers of the essay were extremely positive and had strongly recommended its publication. The editor, however, had committed the pages remaining under his editorship, and recommended that I resubmit it to the journal's *new* editor. Verdict deferred, but I was giddy with the near-miss.

The next miss was not near, and it established my belief in the arbitrariness of the journal review process, and the polysemy of texts. As advised, I resubmitted the unchanged essay to the same journal under its new editor. This time, the three reviewers savaged it: I had neither justified the theoretical perspective nor validated it; there were excessive typographical and grammatical "errors" (one reviewer devoted a half-page to correcting my use of the verb "gloss"); and—most egregiously—there was an "offensive" and "excessively political" tone in the analysis. That tone was most evident for the reviewers in a concluding sentence that originally followed a Richard Feynman quote: "It remains for us to think and speak about *it*: this organized violence, both banal and extraordinary, which is imminent—poised to strike at us—and immanent—poised to strike *as* us." One of the previous reviewers had described this passage as "superb."

I take rejection no better than the next author, and I vented anger and indignation, but I also believed that the reviewers had misunderstood the analysis. Their caricatures of the theoretical perspective led me to believe that they were not familiar with it. They simply denied its validity and demanded "more": "Simply to point to the existence of some words or ideas in a discourse does not constitute anything near evidence that other words or ideas are constrained." This comment clarifies two principal burdens of deconstruction: providing an overview of the text for the reader which clarifies its patterned elements so that claims about its absences have foundation, and continually arguing "first principles" of critical theory with more conventional readers.

Undeterred, I sent the article—again *with no changes*—to a regional journal with a reputation for publishing innovative work. This time, I worked with two supportive reviewers who suggested including the paragraph on narrative theory, and who sharpened my use of organizational communications concepts. After the revisions were complete, the journal editor noted that "even ten years ago I do not think you could have drawn the Nazi–Los Alamos parallel without crossing the line between scholarship and journalism." He deleted the essay's final sentence quoted above: "I think it does cross the line."

Let me now summarize two themes in this minor odyssey pertaining to invention. I return in the process to my earlier challenge to conventional understandings of invention: that it is a relatively original and conscious act, performed immediately prior to criticism.

Simply put, my invention of the essay came—at least in part—from a collaborative, irrational, unconscious, historical, and embodied place: from my own "invention" within my family, and then more directly from the discursive milieu of my graduate education. I have come to see more clearly since I wrote the essay that I study nuclear weapons because I am trying to understand the relationships between violence, fear, silence, and discourse. I am drawn to those relationships because they formed an important part of my early world. I believe that in my volcanic unconscious, where repressed experiences are continually converted to metaphors and metonyms, falling blows have reappeared as falling missiles. What I wish to emphasize is that *I did not fully know this when I wrote the essay.* Invention, it would seem, has its own secrets: this one has emerged only recently.

Finally, my experience with the essay's three submissions was sobering, but valuable. It clarified the "open secret" of the review process: Its stunning arbitrariness. I believe that the essay generated wildly divergent reactions because it is "undisciplined": It merges two previously distinct zones of study (nuclear criticism and organizational communication), and it is explicitly political. I learned, however, that I did *not* have to compromise those features to secure the essay's publication. I continue to invent and be invented.

CONTRIBUTORS

Thomas W. Benson is Edwin Erle Sparks Professor of Rhetoric at the Pennsylvania State University.

Carole Blair is Professor of American Studies at the University of California, Davis, Washington Center.

Barry Brummett is Professor of Speech Communication at the University of Texas.

Maurice Charland is Associate Professor of Communication Studies at Concordia University.

Gary A. Copeland is Professor of Communication and Film at the University of Alabama.

Bonnie J. Dow is Associate Professor of Speech Communication at the University of Georgia.

Thomas J. Frentz is Professor of Communication at the University of Arkansas.

Roderick P. Hart is F. A. Liddel Professor of Communication at the University of Texas.

Robert L. Ivie is Professor and Chair of Speech Communication at Indiana University.

Michael C. Leff is Professor of Communication Studies at Northwestern University.

Elizabeth W. Mechling is Professor of Speech Communication at California State University, Fullerton.

Jay Mechling is Professor of American Studies at the University of California, Davis.

William L. Nothstine is a writer and editor in Portland, Oregon.

Michael M. Osborn is Professor Emeritus of Theatre and Communication at the University of Memphis.

Janice H. Rushing is Professor of Communication at the University of Arkansas.

Bryan C. Taylor is Associate Professor of Communication at the University of Colorado.

Philip C. Wander is Professor of Communication Studies at San Diego State University.

Martha Solomon Watson is Sanford Berman Professor and Dean of The Greenspun College of Urban Affairs at the University of Nevada, Las Vegas.